LOST IN SPACE

BOOK YOUR PLACE ON OUR WEBSITE AND MAKE THE READING CONNECTION!

We've created a customized website just for our very special readers, where you can get the inside scoop on everything that's going on with Zebra, Pinnacle and Kensington books.

When you come online, you'll have the exciting opportunity to:

- View covers of upcoming books

- Read sample chapters

- Learn about our future publishing schedule (listed by publication month *and author*)

- Find out when your favorite authors will be visiting a city near you

- Search for and order backlist books from our online catalog

- Check out author bios and background information

- Send e-mail to your favorite authors

- Meet the Kensington staff online

- Join us in weekly chats with authors, readers and other guests

- Get writing guidelines

- AND MUCH MORE!

**Visit our website at
http://www.pinnaclebooks.com**

LOST IN SPACE

THE ULTIMATE UNAUTHORIZED TRIVIA CHALLENGE FOR THE CLASSIC TV SERIES

James Hatfield
and George "Doc" Burt

Pinnacle Books
Kensington Publishing Corp.
http://www.pinnaclebooks.com

PINNACLE BOOKS are published by

Kensington Publishing Corp.
850 Third Avenue
New York, NY 10022

First Kensington Trade Printing: March, 1998
First Pinnacle Printing: April, 1998
10 9 8 7 6 5 4 3 2 1

ISBN 0-7860-0550-5

Printed in the United States of America

This book is dedicated to:

Tony d'Amico, the co-administrator of the Internet *Lost in Space* Mailing List; and Flint Mitchell, editor of LISFAN, the foremost fanzine devoted to the TV series. Without sounding too melodramatic, this book might never have come into existence without their combined efforts on such short notice. They provided videotapes of all the episodes, invaluable resource material, double-checked our facts, and always came forward with enthusiasm to lend a hand. Thanks, Tony and Flint—we made it! (And, by the way, Tony . . . I'm still going to drink Fosters, even if it is a "tourist" beer!)

My wife, Nancy, the most important person in my life, who is always in my corner (and still makes the best sandwiches when I can't get up from the computer). I am a very privileged man to have such a best friend, companion, lover, and partner in life; and, of course, author and dear friend, Ruby Jean Jensen, who took the time seemingly a century ago to humor a little boy who wanted to write about aliens and monsters. I *love* you, R.J.

—*J.H.*

My grandchildren, Travis Lloyd Davis ("Little T") and the newest edition to the family, Chelsey Lynn Davis. Hopefully, this whole new generation will enjoy the universe of *Lost in Space* as much as I did when I was a boy; and Max Kamie, an absolute prince of a man, who unselfishly gave up his valuable time to train me in the new computer world of SAP. I will *always* be indebted to him. Thank you, Max.

—*"Doc"*

CONTENTS

ACKNOWLEDGMENTS

(Also Known as "We Couldn't Have Done It Without You")

This book could never have been written without the assistance of *Lost in Space*'s loyal and dedicated fans. Our gratitude goes to: Flint Mitchell, Tony d'Amico, Scott Beiner, Gerald Lee Seward, Jeffrey R. Batten, Jeff Story, Paul Monroe, William E. Anchors, Gary "Frances," Vince Brown, Ed Shifres, Frederick Barr, Ken Sharp, Ken Holland, Jeff Blair, Tom Blake, Dan Karpf, Shea Justice, Kathryn Goelzer, Richard Pastore, Debra Matofsky, Robert C. Coyle, Jr., Brian Boskind, Gary Frascarelli, David Leary, Marsheela Kulchar, John F. Kaiser, Jr., David L. Beland, Lee Sobel, Brad Knight, John Eshlenen, Adelyn Rothstein, Glen Marc Trotiner, William F. Sopha, Bob Burd, John M. Azarian, Raymond Macon, Richard Rholt, Gen Aris, Dana Freeman, Steven P. Bloom, Tom M. General, Kim Brokaw, Mark Fingerman, Roger Williams, April Wilson, Phil Lublin, Kat Stein, Frank Di Marzio, Gil J. DeSilva, Rob Kondoff, Dave Perkins, Carlos Martinez, Erik Entwistle, David Lanteigne, Kirk Roderick, Tom Calhoun, Michael Gates, Darryl Foster, Dwight Kemper, Eric Caruso, Joseph Alston, Sabrina H. Williams, Thomas Evatt, Rodney Hammack, Joe Benkle, Gary Rudyk, Ollie Savander, Randal T. Nyerges, Doug Patrick, John Shutt, Malcolm Davis, Ted J. Klosowksi, Frank Sturniolo, Larry Deluca, Michael Mitlitsky, Jeff Brown, Dai Buckley, Randy Robb, John S. Horvath, Greg Johnson, Jerry Woolley, Lex Kennedy, Alan Andrews, Greg Lemieux, Russ Wishman, Paul Buscemi, Mike Clark, Dennis Alexander, David Ross, William

Stumpf, Charles Mento, Ian Lejuez, Larry Commons, William Pappas, William T. Hine, Kraig Rogers, Perry Corvese, Chris Resor, Darrell Hovious, Mary Hoffman, Jack Townsend, Scott Randall Dickerson, John Joyce, Michael Jaquays, Lars Liljeblad, and Chuck Edwards. Our apologies, of course, to anyone we may have neglected to mention. We'd also like to thank the fans on the Internet *Lost in Space* Mailing List forum—we got some great ideas as we lurked and read your discussions. We appreciate it, gang. Really.

We owe a special debt of gratitude to a true artist and friend, Edwin E. Echols, a senior designer for a marine engineer and naval architectural firm in Houston, Texas. His artwork for the TECH SPECS pages of this book were an important contribution and, as usual, he came through for us when we were behind on the scoreboard, backed into our own end zone, and going fourth and long with only a few seconds left on the clock.

Most importantly, we'd like to thank Tracy Bernstein, our editor at Kensington Books, who recognized potential on this project and had enough faith in our wordsmith skills to recruit us to write the ultimate *Lost in Space* trivia challenge. We'd also like to take this opportunity to express our appreciation to some other exceptional folks on Third Avenue in New York: Barbara Bennett (who keeps us out of trouble and always puts the check in the mail), Amy Morgenstern and Amy Stecher, production editors, who deserve a medal for all the damn alien books with the crazy spellings we keep writing), and, of course, Adam Levison (a determined man on a mission to have us read around the world). And, while we're in the neighborhood, we'd certainly be amiss if we didn't thank our agent, Marcia Amsterdam (whose enthusiasm is contagious), and the promotion triplets we love to work with because we're such publicity hounds: Laura Shatzkin, Debra Broide, and Sue Razaire.

Special acknowledgments from J.H.: I owe a debt of gratitude to a fun group of people who always seem to lighten things up with good food and spirits and even better companionship when I'm struggling to meet a deadline: Colon and Dana Washburn, Mark Levine, Daymon and Betty Taylor; Bob and Karla Elliott, and Dusty White. Also, I want to thank Bruce Gabbard for repairing my computer when I was only three shakes of an ant's ass from chucking it out the window; and Dr. Jeffrey L. Tate, M.D., for making sure I don't have "miles to go before I sleep" anymore.

Special acknowledgments from "Doc": I want to offer my heartfelt thanks to two fine people who are not only fans of our books, but also keep an eye on the money tree—Bill Garst and Christy Atkins. On a more personal note, I would also like to express my gratitude to: Elizabeth Vail, Jim Johnson, Sarah Williams, Al Jaschke, Ed Lum, John Dozier, and Marty Hess.

It's a long list, but you can bet the farm that we overlooked someone and we'll hear about it!

INTRODUCTION:

Still Lost in Space

"America had become very space-minded and CBS was interested in a family show. We took the space and family and combined them. That and a conglomeration of other things defined Lost in Space.*"*

—Irwin Allen, series creator and producer,
in a 1985 *Starlog* interview

Even before the debut of *Lost in Space* on Wednesday night, September 15, 1965, we became enthralled with the CBS promotional spots for this exciting new series. The idea of a space family departing an overcrowded Earth for colonization in another star system appealed to us, especially in light of America's troubles at the time. President Kennedy had been assassinated only twenty-two months earlier, our fathers, brothers and friends were dying by the thousands in the rice patties of some little Asian country we had never heard of before, while violent crime and racial hatred in our own chaotic streets back home were pushing us closer to the edge of civil war. We so desperately wanted pure escapist fare on television and we certainly got it with the first episode of *Lost in Space*.

Over the next three years we were captivated by the adventures of the intrepid space family Robinson, their pilot Maj. Don West, the trouble-making stowaway Dr. Smith, and, of course, the Robot, a loyal and protective mechanical man every boy in America wanted to have for his best friend. Although a popular show with a unique blend of family values, love, and struggles to survive in hostile worlds, the series was abruptly canceled after its third season and went into worldwide syndication in 1969, where it entrenched itself as part of our cultural mythology (who's never heard the phrase "Danger, Will Robinson! Danger!").

During the past thirty plus years, the *Jupiter 2* spaceship has enjoyed a popular and successful voyage not only through international syndication, but also daily on the USA cable network and later the Sci-Fi Channel. Fans' devoted ardor has built upon the foundation of those classic, eighty-three cherished episodes, spawning a diverse array of products, ranging from fanzines (fan created magazines) and homemade apparel to collectibles of the REMCO Robot and plastic assembly model kits that now sell for several hundreds of dollars. Finally, in April 1998, *Lost in Space*, the show that became a worldwide phenomenon, blasted off to the big screen as an $80 million sci-fi epic starring William Hurt, Gary Oldman, Mimi Rogers and Matt LeBlanc, featuring enormously impressive sets utilizing over 650 visual effects, a record high for the move-making industry.

Who is truly a devoted *Lost in Space* fan? Is it someone who attends a sci-fi convention to catch a glimpse of June Lockhart or Billy Mumy or Jonathan Harris? Is it someone who is delighted to possess the complete collection of episodes on videotape (including the originally unaired "No Place to Hide" and the animated series pilot)? Is it someone who trades Dr. Smith/Robot insults with friends on a cyberspace chat group, spends the money to design and operate a *Lost in Space* site on the World Wide Web, or someone who knows every episode's title, storyline, guest star, director, writer, and specific dialogue?

Of course, the answer is "all of the above" and it is for those loyal fans that we compiled the book that you now hold in your hands. In the spirit of any worthwhile trivia challenge of this magnitude and scope, there are a variety of different quizzes on the following pages. Questions on the original pilot and the eighty-three classic episodes are included in chronological order. Also included in the episode-by-episode sections are short synopses (*Ship's Log*), insightful behind-the-scenes information (*Space Age* **Fast Fact**), and a **THAT DOES NOT COMPUTE** nitpicking discussion detailing bloopers, scientific snafus, inconsistencies, impossibilities and just plain screw-ups. Before you fire off those nasty letters to us, please remember that *Lost in Space* was, and remains to this day, one of our favorite shows. We were kids when it originally aired and space travel was enough to keep us glued to our TVs every week. As creator and producer, Irwin Allen's objective was not to over-analyze or intellectualize the storylines, nor scientifically educate the viewing audience. More often than not, continuity was an afterthought. The show was purely and simply intended to be family entertainment, so Allen decided that no one would notice if he made outlandish changes such as adding a Space Pod and its launch bay in the third season. Did any of those plot incongruities bother us back then? No, of course not. But as we look back years later, we realize that it's those little bloopers that give *Lost in Space* its flavor and distinction and now it's fun to point them out in each episode. We may be fans, but we're not unobservant.

Strategically placed throughout this ultimate trivia challenge are a variety of different thematic categories that will test your knowledge of episode dialogue (**COMMUNICATION CHANNELS**), guest stars (**GUESTS OF HONOR**), major character profiles (**ALPHA CONTROL INTELLIGENCE DOSSIERS**), technical specifications of the *Jupiter 2*, the Robot, and other equipment (**TECH SPECS**), Dr. Smith's classic alliteratives for the Robot (**NEVER FEAR, SMITH IS HERE**), behind-the-scenes (**THE GALACTIC *CASTAWAYS*, DIRECTOR'S CUT, OUT OF THIS WORLD FX**, etc.) and fandom episode rankings.

All correct answers count as 1-point, except the specifically designed **MEMORY BANKS OVERLOAD** questions, which count as 5-point bonus points because they are intended to seriously challenge the die-hard *Lost in Space* fan.

In the back of this book you will find the Answer Key, plus a specific line to calculate and enter your score as you play along per category. On the very last page you will compute your total score for this Ultimate *Lost in*

Space Trivia Challenge and determine your United States Space Corps rank.

You can start at the beginning and work your way through to the end, or flip around and pick out random questions that test your knowledge of particular episodes or categories. Whatever course you choose to take, you are sure to know more about *Lost in Space* when you've finished this trivia challenge than you did when you started.

In the immortal words of the alien hunter, Megazor: "Onward!"

—*James Hatfield & George "Doc" Burt*

P.O. Box 5453
Bella Vista, AR 72714
or e-mail: scifi.trivia@usa.net
Also visit our website: www.omegapublishing.com

A FEW NOTES ABOUT SOURCE MATERIAL

Although the adventures of the *Jupiter 2* expedition have continued with a long line of hugely successful comic books in print (several penned by former series star Billy Mumy), we have only used sources associated with the *Lost in Space* television series (i.e. the episodes themselves and reference sources such as *The Alpha Control Reference Manual*, archival material from the U.C.L.A. Theater Arts Library, studio episode guides and press kits, etc.). A comprehensive bibliography can be found in the final pages of this book.

Die-hard fans will immediately recognize that there are some nagging inconsistencies in much of this source material. For example, the 20th Century Fox press kit/ episode guide and William E. Anchors' in-depth book *The Irwin Allen Scrapbook, Vol. II* both state that Sue England was the voice of Gundemar in "The Questing Beast" episode. But several primary sources such as the U.C.L.A. Theater Arts Library and former cast and crew members state that Ms. England was *scheduled* to supply the audio tracks for the creature but was unable to arrive at the studio on that particular day and her replacement, June Foray, actually provided the voice. Or, take the name of the warrior spirit in "Follow the Leader": it is spelled "Kanto" in some material, but "Canto" in the 20th Century press kits, U.C.L.A. Theater Arts Library archives, and several other primary sources. When there wasn't a clearly more authoritative source, we opted to go with a simple "majority wins" approach.

OCTOBER 16, 1997

"This is the day . . . This is the beginning . . ."

NO PLACE TO HIDE
The Original Unaired Pilot Episode

Ship's Log: *The Robinson family and their assistant, Dr. Don West, depart an overpopulated Earth aboard the Gemini 12 on a mission of colonization to a planet orbiting Alpha Centauri, but when their colossal spacecraft is knocked off course by a meteor storm, the expedition crashes on an unknown alien world.*

That Does Not Compute

Why is it postulated that the *Gemini 12*'s voyage will take ninety-eight years, traveling at the speed of light, to reach Alpha Centauri? The star system, as any average student of high school astronomy knows, is approximately 4.5 light years from Earth.

The *Gemini 12*'s launch date is October 16, 1997, but after the spaceship's crash landing, John dates his logbook as March 2001, claiming that the crew didn't know exactly how long they traveled in hyper-sleep (although the ship's atomic clock indicates three-and-a-half years). He also notes that the lost expedition had just completed six months stranded on the unknown alien world, which leads us to conclude that the correct date should be mid-October, 2001.

Trivia Challenge

1. (Fill in the Blank) The Robinsons were chosen as the first space colonization family because of their "unique balance of scientific achievement, emotional stability, and _____ resourcefulness."

2. (True or False) The *Gemini 12* encountered an unpredicted rain of meteors traveling at speeds up to 30,000 mph.

3. Who repaired the spaceship's radio telescope?

4. (Fill in the Blank) With temperatures on the planet dropping to one-hundred-and-fifty degrees below zero in forty-eight hours, John believed that the *Gemini 12*'s _____ batteries would not be able to withstand the drain even if the crew was able to insulate the galactic vehicle against the extreme cold.

5. What type of pill did John ask Penny for while they were crossing the vast inland sea in the Chariot?
   A. Caffeine
   B. Protein
   C. Mineral

6. (Fill in the blank with the correct number) After examining the tracks of the Cyclopian giant, John estimated that the creature was _____ times as large as anything they thought of as human.

MEMORY BANKS OVERLOAD

(All three questions must be answered correctly to obtain the 5-point bonus)

1. Identify the school of higher learning where Dr. John Robinson was employed as a professor.
2. (Fill in the Blank) Dr. Maureen Robinson was the first woman to pass the _____ Space Administration's grueling physical and emotional screening for intergalactic flight.
3. (Fill in the Blank) Dr. Donald West was a graduate student at the Center of _____.

SPACE AGE FAST FACT

Although originally scripted to be a ninety-minute pilot episode, budgetary restrictions cut "No Place to Hide" down to an hour. In addition, writer Shimon Wincelberg persuaded Irwin Allen to film the pilot in color, but 20th Century Fox balked at paying the extra $30,000 to $40,000 and demanded that the producer personally pay the difference if he wanted to shoot in color. The notoriously frugal Allen objected to fronting the additional funds and "No Place to Hide" was filmed in black and white.

Soon after the pilot was sold to the CBS network and just prior to actual filming of the *Lost in Space* series, NASA retired the *Gemini* space exploration program in favor of the Apollo lunar missions, forcing Allen to rename his spacecraft after the *Jupiter* airship he used in his early 1960s feature film, *Five Weeks in a Balloon*, thus the ship designation of *Jupiter 2*.

"No Place to Hide," which cost between $600,000 to $700,000, was at that time the most expensive television pilot ever filmed.

1.1
THE RELUCTANT STOWAWAY

Original Airdate: 09.15.65
Earth Year

Ship's Log: *During America's first colonization mission to other worlds, the Space Family Robinson and their pilot, Major Don West, become hopelessly lost in space after Dr. Zachary Smith, an agent for an enemy power, sabotages their Jupiter 2 spacecraft.*

That Does Not Compute

After Don falls from his freezing tube, Dr. Smith removes the major's right glove from his flight suit in order to administer medical attention. After Don walks over to the astrogator, a close-up of his hands show him to be wearing both gloves.

Although the matriarch of the space family is introduced in this episode as Dr. Maureen Robinson, she is never again referred to by her scientific title. Instead, she spends the next three years acting as the expedition's Chief Cook and Bottle Washer while her husband performs all the science experiments.

When the ship's environmental control robot takes the elevator to the upper level to sabotage several of the *Jupiter 2*'s key life support systems, he can be heard saying "destroy" but the lights are not engaged on the mechanical man's chest plate.

During John's spacewalk scene in the closing minutes

of the episode, Don communicates with him via the transmitter. In actuality, Guy Williams stood off stage and fed lines to Mark Goddard and then during postproduction Williams' lines were mixed to sound as if they were being emitted from the communication device. However, one line in particular, "I sure can try," still sounds as if Williams is just out of camera range.

While John dangles out in space with a broken tetherline and Maureen attempts to shoot him a new one, the metallic suspension unit holding Guy Williams up is briefly noticeable (it can be seen more clearly in the introduction to the next episode).

Trivia Challenge

1. (Fill in the blank with the correct number) The Robinson family was selected from more than _____ million volunteers eager to be sent on the first colonization spaceflight.

2. (True or False) The *Jupiter 2* "super spaceship" stood nearly three stories high.

3. Difficulty with which type of loading valve caused a delay in the launch of the spacecraft?
    A. Helium-nitrogen
    B. Liquid oxygen
    C. Hytritium-nitrate

4. How many years were the Robinsons and Maj. West supposed to remain frozen in suspended animation during their voyage to the Alpha Centauri star system?

5. Which level of the *Jupiter 2* housed the sophisticated guidance control system?

6. What type of motors powered the intergalactic vehicle?
    A. Antimatter
    B. Subatomic
    C. Atomic

7. (True or False) Nearly two decades of "intensive

research and preparation" preceded the historic launch of the *Jupiter 2*.

8. What did Dr. Smith supposedly find on Will Robinson's tongue?
   A. "a touch of virus"
   B. "an unsightly and contagious viral organism"
   C. "the origin of a contagion"

9. Why did John venture outside the ship into space?

MEMORY BANKS OVERLOAD

How much did the *Jupiter 2* colonization mission cost?

SPACE AGE FAST FACT

In episode writer Shimon Wincelberg's earlier drafts of the script, Dr. Smith was parked in a car outside the *Jupiter 2*'s invisible force field. Desperately seeking a way to get aboard the spacecraft in order to sabotage it, he conned a young woman into picking a flower for him who, of course, walked directly into the ship's imperceptible protective shield and was instantly incinerated. Wincelberg also noted in the script that the villainous doctor wore a poison-tipped ring with a big heart on it that read: "MOTHER." Series creator and producer Irwin Allen ordered both scenes deleted from the final script.

1.2
THE DERELICT

Original Airdate: 09.22.65
Earth Year

Ship's Log: *After John and Maureen are pulled to safety from outside the Jupiter 2, the crippled ship is engulfed by a massive spacecraft inhabited by large, bubble-shaped aliens who communicate in an advanced, electronic language.*

That Does Not Compute

While John is helplessly adrift outside the *Jupiter 2*, the spaceship's scanner alarm warns Don of the danger of an approaching comet and its potentially destructive heat. Comets are small, frozen balls of dust and gas with long, luminous tails, *not* blazing infernos.

During the scene in which the wounded alien is joined by others in chasing after Dr. Smith and Will, a stage crew member in sneakers and jeans is clearly visible behind the second alien pushing it along.

In this episode the nefarious Smith reprograms the Robot to obey only his voice commands. Although he is never seen erasing these orders, the other members of the expedition receive responses from the Robot in subsequent episodes beginning with "There Were Giants in the Earth."

Trivia Challenge

1. What did Don use to cool the jammed hatch, which had expanded due to the heat from an approaching comet?

2. Identify the character who thought that the galaxy directly ahead of *Jupiter 2* was "possibly Andromeda."

3. (Fill in the Blank) Judy described the mammoth alien spacecraft as "a _____ ship."

4. What was the source of the alien ship's power?

5. Who referred to the bubble-shaped alien life-forms as "non-human colonists"?
   A. Dr. Smith
   B. John
   C. Don

6. (True or False) John and Maj. West discovered a control console aboard the alien vessel that displayed sections of the galaxy with planets classified according to their relative mass.

7. What type of weapon did John use to blast open the alien spacecraft, releasing the *Jupiter 2?*

MEMORY BANKS OVERLOAD

Which character made the comment, "We're settlers, not explorers"?

SPACE AGE FAST FACT

For years, fans of the series have debated the identity of Dr. Smith's employers. The script was deliberately vague and hinted only at "countries that would go to any lengths of sabotage." The series was filmed in the mid-1960s, at the height of the Cold War, but the timeline of the show was set in the late 1990s and the writers and producers didn't want to "go out on a limb" and predict that the Soviets or the Chinese would still be our enemies in thirty years.

NEVER FEAR, SMITH IS HERE

(With Stellar Insults)

PART I

"The alliteratives I used with the Robot have always been a source of great pleasure to me.
I used to sit up all night just dreaming them up!"

—Jonathan Harris during an interview

In "Forbidden World," Dr. Smith told the Robot, "You are a machine. You do not have the mental and physical attributes of a mortal. You cannot be insulted." But as any true *Lost in Space* fan knows, hardly an episode passed in which the scheming stowaway didn't attempt to verbally abuse the beloved mechanical man. Match the following classic insults to the episode in which they were vocalized.

1. _____ Primitive pile of pistons
2. _____ Animated weather station
3. _____ Roly-poly rowdy
4. _____ Neanderthal ninny
5. _____ Plasticized parrot
6. _____ Clumsy has-been
7. _____ Steely-eyed sorcerer
8. _____ Treasonous tyrant
9. _____ Cybernetic skeptic

A. "War of the Robots"
B. "Return from Outer Space"
C. "The Deadly Games of Gamma 6"
D. "The Time Merchant"
E. "The Hungry Sea"
F. "The Cave of the Wizards"
G. "The Ghost Planet"
H. "Deadliest of the Species"

10.	_____ Mealy-mouthed rogue	I.	"The Galaxy Gift"
11.	_____ Lead-lined lothario	J.	"Trip Through the Robot"
12.	_____ Pusillanimous pip-squeak	K.	"Flight into the Future"
		L.	"The Space Vikings"

NEVER FEAR, SMITH IS HERE

(With Stellar Insults)

PART II

1. _____ Arrogant automaton
2. _____ Cackling canister
3. _____ Digitized dunce
4. _____ Garrulous gargoyle
5. _____ Tyrannical tin-plate
6. _____ Deplorable dunderhead
7. _____ Tin-plated tattletale
8. _____ Mumbling mass of metal
9. _____ Quivering quintessence of fear
10. _____ Addlepated amateur
11. _____ Ramshackled Romeo
12. _____ Demented diode
13. _____ Monstrous, metal-lurgical meddler
14. _____ Lily-livered, lead-lined lummox

A. "Flight into the Future"
B. "The Girl from the Green Dimension"
C. "Wild Adventure"
D. "Castles in Space"
E. "Ghost in Space"
F. "Forbidden World"
G. "The Lost Civilization"
H. "Deadliest of the Species"
I. "Treasure of the Lost Planet"
J. "Prisoners of Space"
K. "The Thief from Outer Space"
L. "The Space Croppers"
M. "Visit to a Hostile Planet"
N. "Wreck of the Robot"

MEMORY BANKS OVERLOAD #1

(Fill in the Blank)

In the episode "My Friend, Mr. Nobody," Dr. Smith called the Robot a "_____ bag of bolts."

MEMORY BANKS OVERLOAD #2

Identify the episode in which Smith referred to the mechanical man as a "book-making booby"?

MEMORY BANKS OVERLOAD #3

(Fill in the Blank)

In "The Mechanical Men" Dr. Smith insulted the *Jupiter 2* automaton when he called him a "frightful _____ frump."

MEMORY BANKS OVERLOAD #4

Name the episode in which the Robot was verbally branded by Smith as a "traitorous transistorized fugitive from a junkyard."

1.3
ISLAND IN THE SKY

Original Airdate: 09.29.65
Earth Year

Ship's Log: *John's Parajets misfire and he plummets to the surface of an unknown and possibly hostile planet, but when the Jupiter 2 attempts to follow, the sabotaged spacecraft crash lands in a barren desert area.*

That Does Not Compute

After the *Jupiter 2* makes a forced landing on the planet, Will orders the Robot to test the outside environmental conditions to determine whether the alien world can sustain human life. Look closely and you can see a note paper inside the mechanical man's bubble head.

Dr. Smith touches the Robot's electrically hot claw without any ill effect only seconds after the automaton discharges his mechanical hands to demonstrate that his defense systems are active.

In the scene where the huge alien mass depletes the space Chariot's power, an electrical cable is clearly visible at the bottom of the television screen.

Trivia Challenge

1. What did Dr. Smith utilize as a simple way to allegedly check all of the Robot's circuits?

2. Why did John believe the Robot was still malfunctioning?

3. Which two classic literary authors did the Robot quote during a conversation with Dr. Smith?
   A. Yeats and Kipling
   B. Shakespeare and Butler
   C. Tennyson and Wordsworth

4. Who believed that Dr. Smith should be sent on a survey mission to the planet's surface because he was an "environmental control expert"?

5. What caused John's Parajets to misfire when he descended from the *Jupiter 2*?

6. During the search for John on the planet's surface, who kept their "eyes glued" to the Chariot's infrared scanner?

7. How often was the Robot ordered to check on Dr. Smith's safety?

8. Which "tidier" term did the villainous doctor prefer instead of the word "destroy" in relation to his order to the Robot to murder all *Jupiter 2* "unessential personnel"?
   A. "liquidate"
   B. "eliminate"
   C. "remove"

9. Identify the character who called the Robot "my good man."

MEMORY BANKS OVERLOAD

According to the Robot, what was the atmospheric pressure of the planet?

SPACE AGE FAST FACT

Shimon Wincelberg, who penned the storylines for the series' first six shows, originally proposed having the *Jupiter 2* travel to different planets every week, in the process discovering new environments and societies, and encountering alien spacecraft. Realizing that his grand plans greatly exceeded Irwin Allen's budget, the *Jupiter 2* was essentially grounded on one planet for the first season. Interestingly, Wincelberg also wrote the classic *Star Trek* episode, "Dagger of the Mind," another sci-fi series which was forced to invent the transporter because the cost of landing the *Enterprise* on a different alien world week after week would have been too expensive.

1.4
THERE WERE GIANTS IN THE EARTH

Original Airdate: 10.6.65 Earth Year

Ship's Log: *At their remote weather station site, John and Maj. West discover that the unknown planet's temperature will soon drop far below zero, making it necessary to abandon the Jupiter 2 spaceship and travel south to the planet's warmer regions.*

That Does Not Compute

After Dr. Smith removes the Robot's power pack to save Will's life, you can still hear the automaton's head mechanism grinding away.

While Will is attempting to repair the Chariot, the cameraman's reflection is clearly visible in the exploratory vehicle's Plexiglas windows.

In the scene where the giant Cyclops forces John and Maj. West into a mountain cave, the creature reaches in to grab them with its right hand. A close-up shot, however, shows the mammoth monster's left hand.

Trivia Challenge

1. Who accused Dr. Smith of programming the Robot to obey only his voice commands?
   A. Will
   B. Don
   C. John

2. Will successfully stalled the Robot from killing him with laser bolts by testing the mechanical being's circuits with imaginary chess moves. What was the mechanical man's response to Will's "King's pawn to king's five"?
   A. "Queen's knight to king's bishop two"
   B. "King's knight to king's bishop one"
   C. "Queen's bishop two to king's knight"

3. Who referred to the Robot as a "tin monster"?

4. (Fill in the Blank) Dr. Smith remarked to Judy and Penny that the planet's soil had "all the _____ of the Mississippi Delta."

5. Which vegetable did Smith request to be grown in the hydroponic garden?
   A. "iron-enriched potatoes"
   B. "little green onions"
   C. "culinary delight carrots"

6. To what classic literary character did Will compare himself while attempting to reprogram the Robot?

7. According to the Robot, how many meters tall was the gigantic Cyclops?
   A. Twelve
   B. Fourteen
   C. Sixteen

8. What did John discover in a microscopic sample of the planet's native soil?

MEMORY BANKS OVERLOAD

Identify the six vegetables that Judy told Dr. Smith she was planting in the hydroponic garden.

SPACE AGE FAST FACT

The role of Dr. Smith was written specifically for actor Carroll O'Connor, who eventually turned it down. Roger C. Carmel also declined the part, explaining that he didn't want to do weekly episodic television at that point in his career. Finally, the role of the evil saboteur was offered to Jonathan Harris, who personally transformed the evil villain into a comedic character over the course of the series.

1.5
THE HUNGRY SEA

Original Airdate: 10.13.65
Earth Year

Ship's Log: *After John discovers that the planet's elliptical orbit will soon bring the unknown world dangerously close to its sun, the Robinsons and Maj. West endure intense heat, quakes, and storms in an attempt to return to the Jupiter 2.*

That Does Not Compute

In one scene aboard the *Jupiter 2*, the Robot's head sensors cease from rotating. However, by the following scene, they are in operation once again.

When the Robot attempts to warm up a pot of coffee for Dr. Smith, the sound effects of the mechanical man's electrical charges do not correspond with the animated bolts.

As the Robot traverses the frozen inland sea to warn the Robinsons of the fast approaching heat from the planet's sun, his power temporarily flicks off.

Trivia Challenge

1. What was the command that Dr. Smith once gave the Robot (stored in his "busy little memory cells") and then canceled in this episode?

2. (Fill in the Blank) Dr. Smith complained to the Robot that he "could get more _____ from a cuckoo clock."

3. In how many moves could the Robot typically beat Dr. Smith in a game of chess?
   A. Three
   B. Five
   C. Ten

4. What caused transmission static in communications between the Chariot and the *Jupiter 2*?
   A. Solar flares
   B. Cosmic interference
   C. Heat acceleration

5. Who did Don sarcastically call "the ultimate computer"?

6. What was on the Robot's tape readout when it arrived at the Robinsons' and Maj. West's campsite?

7. Identify the "supreme question," as asked by John in his ship's log.
   A. Could they learn to trust Dr. Smith?
   B. Would they ever find their way to Alpha Centauri?
   C. Could they survive?

8. According to Dr. Smith, what was the only home the Robinsons had ever known?

9. Who called the Robot an "animated hunk of machinery"?

MEMORY BANKS OVERLOAD

What were the six words that the Robot repeated when he approached the campsite?

SPACE AGE FAST FACT

Convoluted plots and complex special effects created delays in filming the series each week, resulting in a typical episode's completion only *seven days* ahead of its scheduled airtime. Threatened with a fine of $50,000 if the show was delivered late, Irwin Allen kept the cast and crew on the sets for extended periods, sometimes as much as twenty-four hours at a time.

GUESTS OF HONOR

PART I

Test your knowledge of Lost in Space's *memorable guest stars.*

1. He played Quano's father, the Ruler, in the first season episode "The Challenge," and a Klingon on the original *Star Trek* series (reprising the role almost thirty years later on *Deep Space Nine*). Who is he?
   A. William Campbell
   B. Michael Ansara
   C. John Colicos

2. "Let's be careful out there" was the late Michael Conrad's trademark dismissal every week as Sgt. Esterhaus during *Hill Street Blues'* opening roll call. What was his character's name in the episode "Fugitives in Space"?

3. Lyle Waggoner co-starred as Col. Steve Trevor in the *Wonder Woman* series. In which episode of *Lost in Space* did he make a guest appearance as Mechanical Man #1?

4. She appeared as Verda in both "The Android Machine" and "Revolt of the Androids," as well as an agent who literally sold her client's soul in "Space Beauty." Who is this actress?

5. Which actor played the wooden soldier in "The Toy-

maker" and the mummy creature in "The Cave of the Wizards"?

   A. Hoke Lowell
   B. Larry Dean
   C. Jim Boles

6. Who appeared as the talking carrot Tybo in "The Great Vegetable Rebellion" and as an equally vocal entrepreneur on the original *Star Trek* series whose tribbles caused a great deal of trouble?

   A. Alan Hewitt
   B. Jim Mills
   C. Stanley Adams

7. (True or False) Hans Conreid, who guest starred as the dragon-hunting Sir Sagramonte in the episode "The Questing Beast," is better known as the voice of Snidely Whiplash in the *Dudley Do Right* cartoons.

8. In addition to portraying the hermit Tiabo in "Forbidden World," this late actor starred as TV's Mr. Peepers and lent his vocal chords to the cartoon Underdog superhero. Who was he?

9. Lou Wagner's film credits include three of the *Planet of the Apes* movies (as Zira's nephew, Lucius). What role did he play in the *Lost in Space* episode "The Haunted Lighthouse"?

10. He played an alien boy in "The Challenge" and years later battled a monstrous extraterrestrial that crashed to Earth in *The Thing*. Name this actor.

MEMORY BANKS OVERLOAD #1

Edy Williams was a major sex symbol of the 1960s and 70s. Identify the *Lost in Space* episode in which she played an alien.

---

11. Daniel J. Travanti is best known for his portrayal of Capt. Frank Furillo on television's *Hill Street Blues*.

Identify the alien demolition leader he portrayed in the *Lost in Space* episode "Collision of Planets."
   A. Ekan
   B. Ilan
   C. Sekah

12. Ford Rainey appeared briefly as the President of the United States in "The Reluctant Stowaway." In which other Irwin Allen series did he assume the same role?
   A. *Voyage to the Bottom of the Sea*
   B. *Time Tunnel*
   C. *Land of the Giants*

13. Identify the actor who assumed the role of Gen. Squires.

14. Which actor played Gromack in "The Deadly Games of Gamma 6" and Mort in "A Day at the Zoo"?
   A. Liam Sullivan
   B. Gregory Morton
   C. Ronald Weber

15. He was an intergalactic buccaneer in "The Sky Pirate" and "Treasure of the Lost Planet" before killing himself and his wife in 1990. Who was this tragic actor?

16. This Academy Award-winning performer appeared in the first season episode, "The Space Croppers" and years later provided the voice for the possessed Linda Blair in *The Exorcist*. Name this actress.

17. Which actor appeared as Enforcer Claudius in "West of Mars"?
   A. Lamar Lundy
   B. Allan Melvin
   C. Fritz Feld

18. He was an intergalactic police officer seeking an escaped prisoner in the *Lost in Space* episode "All That Glitters," but is best remembered for his portrayal as Col. Klink, the POW camp commandant in *Hogan's Heroes*. Who is this actor?

19. Al Lewis played Zalto the Magician in "Rocket to Earth." In which television series did he regularly portray a vampire?

20. Who played both Phanzig in "Condemned of Space" and the intergalactic Junkman in the series' final episode, "Junkyard in Space"?

MEMORY BANKS OVERLOAD #2

One of Hollywood's busiest actors, he played an alien ruler in one of *Lost in Space*'s first season episodes and was later approached to play Megazor in "Hunter's Moon," a role Vincent Beck eventually accepted. Name this actor.

---

21. Melinda Fee was a regular in *The Invisible Man* television series and appeared in the theatrical films *The Aliens are Coming* and *Nightmare on Elm Street, Part Two: Freddy's Revenge*. Identify the *Lost in Space* episode in which she played Madame Fenestra.

22. Who played the frog-like life-form in "The Golden Man" and the alien leader in "Deadliest of the Species"?
    A. Lew Gallo
    B. Robert Easton
    C. Ronald Gans

23. Sherry Jackson was Angela Cartwright's co-star in the *Make Room for Daddy* series. What role did she play in the *Lost in Space* episode "The Space Croppers"?

24. He was *"verrry* interesting" as a comedian on *Laugh-In* and as Fedor, the revolt-leading machine disguised as a human in the episode "Princess of Space." Who is he?

25. Kym Karath played the youngest von Trapp child, Gretl, in *The Sound of Music* (alongside Angela Cart-

wright). In which episode of *Lost in Space* did she guest-star?
  A. "Return from Outer Space"
  B. "The Lost Civilization"
  C. "Visit to a Hostile Planet"

26. Identify the two episodes in which dwarf actor Harry Monty appeared?

27. (True or False) Dawson Palmer, a semi-regular on the series under the heavy makeup of various alien creatures, appeared as the Moss Monster in "The Android Machine."

28. Sheila Mathews guest-starred as Ruth Templeton in "Return from Outer Space," Brynhilda in "The Space Vikings," and Aunt Gamma in "Princess of Space," but what became her most significant role in the *Lost in Space* universe?

29. Michael J. Pollard received an Oscar nomination for his supporting role in 1967's *Bonnie and Clyde*. In which episode did he appear as an alien boy?
  A. "The Challenge"
  B. "The Haunted Lighthouse"
  C. "The Magic Mirror"

30. Robert Pine starred as the captain in the television series *CHiPs* for six years. What was the name of his character in "Visit to a Hostile Planet," the episode in which the Robinsons returned to 1940s Earth?
  A. Craig
  B. Bryan
  C. James

31. (True or False) Edy Williams played the female warrior Noble Niolani in "The Colonists."

32. He played Bartholomew, the youthful alien who wanted to grow up, in "The Promised Planet" and a sheriff in the 1980 horror film *The Children*. Who is this actor?
  A. Larry Ward

B. Keith Taylor
C. Gil Rogers

MEMORY BANKS OVERLOAD #3

(Fill in the Blank)

Before guest-starring as the ice princess, Reyka, in "Castles in Space," actress Corinna Tsopei had worn the crown of Miss _____.

---

33. Identify the famous horror film actor who portrayed the amulet-wearing Mr. Arcon in "The Galaxy Gift."

34. Besides playing Miss Teutonium in "Space Beauty," this actress appeared in several films in the 1960s, including *My Fair Lady*. Who is she?
    A. Miriam Schiller
    B. Linda Gaye Scott
    C. Tracy Bernstein

35. The late Reta Shaw appeared regularly as Martha Grant, the housekeeper in *The Ghost and Mrs. Muir* series. What role did she play in the *Lost in Space* episode "Return from Outer Space"?

36. Torin Thatcher portrayed the evil wizard Sokurah in *The 7th Voyage of Sinbad*. In which series installment of *Lost in Space* did he guest star?
    A. "The Space Trader"
    B. "A Day at the Zoo"
    C. "The Haunted Lighthouse"

MEMORY BANKS OVERLOAD #4

This young actor appeared with Elvis Presley in the movie *Harum Scarum* and played Zachary Smith as a boy in "Kidnapped in Space." What's his name?

37. In addition to his best-known role of Lurch on *The Addams Family*, actor Ted Cassidy played the legendary Bigfoot monster on *The Six Million Dollar Man*, and appeared in episodes of the original *Star Trek*. Identify the *Lost in Space* episode in which he guest-starred as an alien slave.

38. Who was the green-skinned beauty who portrayed Athena in "Wild Adventure" and then reprised the role in "The Girl from the Green Dimension"?

39. Malachi Throne guest-starred as "The Thief from Outer Space," but in which episode of *Star Trek* did he portray Commodore Jose Mendez, commanding officer of Starbase 11?
    A. "The Menagerie"
    B. "Mirror, Mirror"
    C. "The Ultimate Computer"

40. Identify the actor who appeared twice as the leader of the Derby-wearing, black-clad Saticons.

41. British actor Michael Rennie is best remembered for the lead role in the science fiction classic, *The Day the Earth Stood Still*. In which two *Lost in Space* episodes did he appear?

42. This former guest star once hosted *Saturday Night Live*. Who is he?

43. Robby the Robot, introduced in the 1956 sci-fi movie *Forbidden World*, also appeared in which two *Lost in Space* installments?

44. Tol Avery guest-starred as the Warden in the third season's "Fugitives in Space." Identify the long-running comedy series in which he voiced the narration during the opening credits.

45. In addition to portraying Sesmar in the *Lost in Space*'s "The Dream Monster," this actor also played the legendary Organian council leader, Ayelborne, in the

classic *Star Trek* episode "Errand of Mercy." Who is he?

46. This veteran character actor played an intergalactic miner in "Blast Off into Space," the premiere episode of the second season. Who was he?

47. Liam Sullivan played an android in "His Majesty Smith." What was his character's name in the original *Star Trek* segment "Plato's Stepchildren"?

MEMORY BANKS OVERLOAD #5

Who was the actor who guest-starred as Farnum B in the episodes "A Day at the Zoo" and "Space Beauty"?

MEMORY BANKS OVERLOAD #6

Name the three episodes in which Fritz Feld portrayed Mr. Zumdish.

GUESTS OF HONOR

PART II

Match the guest-stars to the Lost in Space *characters and episodes in which they appeared.*

1. _____ Warren Oates
2. _____ Grant Sullivan
3. _____ Claire Wilcox
4. _____ Gary Tigerman
5. _____ Woodrow Parfrey
6. _____ Harry Raybould
7. _____ Henry Jones
8. _____ Gerald Mohr
9. _____ James Westerfield
10. _____ Dennis Patrick
11. _____ Francoise Ruggieri
12. _____ Abraham Sofaer

A. Mr. Keema "The Golden Man"
B. Stacy "Visit to a Hostile Planet"
C. Marvello "Space Circus"
D. Urso "The Girl from the Green Dimension"
E. Sobram "The Flaming Planet"
F. Moela "The Sky is Falling"
G. Morbus "A Visit to Hades"
H. Jeremiah Smith "Curse of Cousin Smith"
I. Jimmy Hapgood "Welcome Stranger"
J. Alien 764 "Kidnapped in Space"
K. Oggo "A Day at the Zoo"
L. Col. Fogey "The Haunted Lighthouse"

MEMORY BANKS OVERLOAD

Identify the actor whose roles included a Tauron in "The Sky is Falling" and IDAK in "Revolt of the Androids."

1.6
WELCOME
STRANGER

Original Airdate: 10.20.65
Earth Year

Ship's Log: *While searching for a missile-like object that was sighted on radar, the intrepid space colonists encounter Jimmy Hapgood, a United States astronaut who became lost while heading to the far reaches of Earth's solar system several years earlier.*

That Does Not Compute

During the scene in which John, Maj. West, Will, Dr. Smith, and the Robot first encounter Hapgood, you can see the mechanical man's power pack in place in the first close-up shot, clearly missing in the next, and back in position in the third camera angle.

Trivia Challenge

1. (Fill in the Blank) Dr. Smith referred to the spacecraft sighted on the radar screen as a "_____ devil."

2. What was Hapgood's nickname for his galactic vehicle?

3. The astronaut was on a mission to which planet in Earth's solar system when he became lost in the void of space?

4. What did Will charge Hapgood for helping the astronaut decontaminate his spaceship?

5. What kind of soup did Maureen serve Hapgood after he hurt his back?
   A. Chicken and noodle
   B. Space chowder
   C. Vegetable (made from their hydroponic garden)

6. Identify the character who commented that Will and Penny were not "average children."

7. What three words did Hapgood laser into the rock to signify that he had visited the planet?

MEMORY BANKS OVERLOAD

What was the month, day, and year of Jimmy Hapgood's mission launch date from Earth?

SPACE AGE FAST FACT

Jonathan Harris (who was paid $1,750 per week during the series' first season) has stated repeatedly in interviews that he patterned the Dr. Smith character on every kid he has ever known in life.

1.7
MY FRIEND, MR. NOBODY

Original Airdate: 10.27.65
Earth Year

Ship's Log: *Feeling lonely and rejected, Penny wanders into a large cave where she encounters an "imaginary" friend, in reality a disembodied life force that has existed below the surface since the planet's birth.*

That Does Not Compute

The *Jupiter 2*'s astrogator is mysteriously missing in this episode and is neither seen nor mentioned again until the second season premiere, "Blast Off Into Space."

Trivia Challenge

1. What was Penny returning to the drill site when she unknowingly walked into the area just as Don detonated explosives?

2. (True or False) John and Don were test drilling for radioactive materials to refine into enough atomic fuel to lift the disabled *Jupiter 2* off the planet.

3. Penny called her "imaginary" friend, "Mr. Nobody," but who originally referred to him as "nobody"?

4. (Fill in the Blank) Dr. Smith accused the Robot of not having any "Indian _____ blood."

5. According to Dr. Smith, the Robot was programmed to withstand how many tons of pressure?

6. Identify the classic children's book Penny took into the cave to read?

7. Who described the life force's beautiful metamorphosis into pure cosmic energy as "a new Milky Way"?

MEMORY BANKS OVERLOAD

How did Penny describe her concept of death to Mr. Nobody?

SPACE AGE FAST FACTS

The first season's silver spacesuits were made of heavy, non-pliable, fire-fighting material, which caused the actors to lose two to three pounds every time they wore the costumes for scenes. In addition, the suits were so tight and restrictive of movement that cast members were forced to lie on special slantboards if they wanted to rest between shots.

1.8
INVADERS FROM THE FIFTH DIMENSION

Original Airdate: 11.03.65
Earth Year

Ship's Log: *Due to a malfunctioning guidance system, an alien craft carrying two luminous "anti-human" beings from the fifth dimension lands on the Robinsons' planet to effect repairs.*

That Does Not Compute

Don makes a comment about Will being sore at him for not going rock hunting, but the scene he's referring to was cut from the final version of the script and never filmed.

In the episode's climactic scene, Bob May's legs and a power cable are clearly visible at the bottom of the Robot suit.

Trivia Challenge

1. Who originally spotted the aliens' spacecraft on the scanner?

2. Why did the aliens need a humanoid brain?

3. Who called Dr. Smith "a scoundrel, a thoroughly bad sort, hopelessly unreliable"?

4. (Fill in the Blank) The aliens called Earth "a minor planetoid still in a near _____ state of development."

5. In reality what was the hand-held device that Dr. Smith claimed to Will was an ion generator?

6. How long had the aliens been traveling?
   A. From the commencement of time and space
   B. Since long before the earliest moments of Earth's history
   C. Before humanoids came into existence

MEMORY BANKS OVERLOAD

(Fill in the blank with the correct number)

The Robot stated that it could blast the pain ring from Dr. Smith's neck with a _____-volt charge.

SPACE AGE FAST FACT

Series story editor Tony Wilson based the trouble-making Dr. Smith character on the colorful, but irritating, Long John Silver in the Robert Louis Stevenson literary classic, *Treasure Island*.

1.9
THE OASIS

Original Airdate: 11.10.65
Earth Year

Ship's Log: *During a severe drought, Dr. Smith impulsively eats some luscious, tropical fruit and grows into a towering, paranoid giant convinced that the Robinsons are plotting his death.*

That Does Not Compute

We can accept without protest the fact that the fruit wildly and rapidly affected Dr. Smith's internal organs and transformed him into the Earthling equivalent of the Cyclops monster, but it's a real stretch of the imagination to believe that his uniform and shoes were similarly influenced. A quasi-Incredible Hulk look with a ripped tunic and bare feet would have added some needed credibility to the episode.

Trivia Challenge

1. During John's log entry, what did he describe as the colonists' "greatest problem"?

2. Who called Dr. Smith an "injustice collector"?

3. Believing that the Robinsons and Maj. West deliberately planned to kill him with the possibly poisonous

native fruit, Dr. Smith fled the camp to die in the wilderness. What did he steal as an act of revenge?

4. What did Dr. Smith write on his mound-plated white "flag"?

5. (Fill in the blank with the correct number) John estimated that Smith had grown "as tall as _____ men and just about as strong."

6. Which gland in Dr. Smith's body did John theorize had gone "out of control" due to the effects of the fruit?

MEMORY BANKS OVERLOAD

How did Dr. Smith extract the water from the storage tank for his shower?

SPACE AGE FAST FACT

Bob May, the stuntman inside the functional Robot costume, assumed he would also provide the voice of the mechanical man. He was deeply offended and embarrassed when he watched film footage from one of the series' first episodes and discovered Dick Tufeld's voice had been dubbed over his own.

ALPHA CONTROL INTELLIGENCE DOSSIER

#1-57566-063-6
Professor John Robinson

1. What was John Robinson's middle name?
   A. Stewart
   B. Edward
   C. Sims

2. (True or False) He was born the fifth child of a lower income family in Lowell, Massachusetts USA on January 7, 1958.

3. What rank did Robinson hold in the United States Space Corps?

4. (Fill in the Blank) Always at the head of his class academically, Robinson also excelled in sports. During his sophomore year at East Side High School, he became the youngest student to ever have played the position of _____ on the football team.

5. (True or False) Robinson declined several college football scholarships and chose instead to enroll at the Massachusetts Institute of Technology in 1976 in his home state.

6. (Fill in the Blank) Robinson sought a degree in Planetary _____ Sciences.

7. After meeting the beautiful and brilliant student,

Maureen Tomlinson, the two became inseparable as a couple. What was the date of their wedding?

    A. December 15, 1976

    B. June 10, 1977

    C. October 26, 1978

8. (Fill in the Blank) Robinson graduated with honors in 1981 after earning his master's degree in _____ and Applied Planetary Geology.

9. His first job was as an instructor of geophysics at the University of California at Los Angeles, where he continued his education and received a doctorate in 1985. Which prestigious honor did he win for outstanding teaching ability and leadership while at the school?

    A. Zane Morris Award

    B. Flint Mitchell Exceptional Achievement Merit

    C. Tony d'Amico Grant

10. (Fill in the blank with the correct number) After _____ years of teaching, Robinson and his family (his wife and three children) moved in the spring of 1988 to Houston, Texas, where he accepted Alpha Control's offer to work on a new program to study the adaptability of humans to life on alien planets.

11. (Fill in the Blank) While working at Alpha Control's enormous scientific and training facility, Prof. Robinson was deeply involved in the program to develop the Deep _____ Telescopic Probe series of interstellar spacecraft, which were launched in December 1988.

12. (True or False) After the probes provided definite proof that the Alpha Centauri star system contained two planets (Delta and Gamma) capable of supporting life, Prof. Robinson was awarded a position with Alpha Control's Colonization Studies Division.

13. On which date did Alpha Control announce that it

would begin taking applications from families for the *Jupiter 2* colonization mission?

A. April 1989
B. August 1991
C. February 1993

MEMORY BANKS OVERLOAD

Despite genuine concerns regarding the hazards of space flight, Maureen eventually agreed with her husband to volunteer the family for the *Jupiter 2* mission to Alpha Centauri. How many years did the Robinsons spend in intense training before they left Earth on October 16, 1997?

TECH SPECS #1

Match the letter to the correct parts and equipment on the Jet Pack.

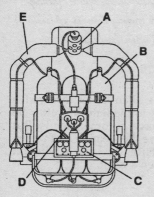 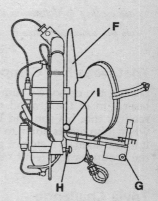

Technical drawing by Edwin E. Echols.

1. _____ Fuel supply
2. _____ Power converter
3. _____ Harness module
4. _____ Primary propulsion regulator
5. _____ Calibration
6. _____ Harness module release
7. _____ Propulsion unit
8. _____ Flight control
9. _____ Fuel intake valve

1.10
THE SKY IS FALLING

Original Airdate: 11.17.65
Earth Year

Ship's Log: *A breakdown in communication between the Jupiter 2 crew and a telepathic alien space family attempting to determine whether colonization is possible on the unknown planet leads to open hostilities.*

That Does Not Compute

During the episode's climax, the alien father throws his laser gun to the ground on his immediate left after he realizes that his son and Will have become friends. But when John bends down to retrieve the weapon and return it to the alien as a sign of good faith, the laser is lying on the ground a few feet to the alien's right.

Trivia Challenge

1. Which female member of the Robinson family did the hysterical and frightened Dr. Smith grab by the arm and push inside the *Jupiter 2* to save her from being "disintegrated" by "a horde of mechanical monsters"?

2. Who referred to the crustacean-shaped alien probe as "nothing more than a harmless data computer"?

3. Who was the source of the comment, "How gratifying

it is to work for the betterment of mankind, to strive for the unattainable"?

4. What did Will inadvertently do that contaminated the air with terrestrial germs, making the alien boy sick?

5. What did the aliens use to transport their equipment to the surface of the planet?
   A. A molecular displacement device
   B. A matter transfer beam
   C. A matter-energy converter

MEMORY BANKS OVERLOAD

Identify the aliens' homeworld.

SPACE AGE FAST FACT

The first season laser pistol was not an original design, but was based instead on a toy made by REMCO called the "Okinawa Gun." Initially manufactured in the early to mid-1960s, the gun was part of an entire line of toy weapons for the "Monkey Division," which loosely copied the Mattel G.I. Joe series.

1.11
WISH UPON A STAR

Original Airdate: 11.24.65
Earth Year

Ship's Log: *Banished from the Jupiter 2 campsite, Dr. Smith takes refuge in the wreckage of an ancient, alien spacecraft, where he discovers a wishing hat that creates reality out of thoughts.*

That Does Not Compute

When John, Maj. West, and Will escort Dr. Smith back to the derelict spaceship to return the wishing machine, Maureen immediately reactivates the *Jupiter 2*'s force field before the male members of the expedition are outside of the invisible shield's range.

Trivia Challenge

1. Why did the hydroponic garden die?

2. What was the maximum number of times the "thought machine" could function in a single day?

3. Who called the device a "wishing machine" similar to Aladdin's lamp?

4. Identify the character John accused of sacrificing "moral principles for something material."

5. What did Dr. Smith ask his "servant" to bring him?
   A. "Hot, invigorating tea" with one lump of sugar
   B. Coffee with two lumps of sugar and "a bit of cream"
   C. "Nectar of the gods"

6. Who referred to the wishing hat as a "thought translator"?

7. Which character called it a "machine that makes dreams come true"?

8. (Fill in the blank with the correct number) Will made _____ attempts to send small rockets with SOS messages on them up into space in the hope that someone would find them and send a rescue ship.

MEMORY BANKS OVERLOAD

What two items did Will debate requesting before he finally decided to wish for apples?

SPACE AGE FAST FACT

Always a lover of comic books, young Billy Mumy drew and wrote one about Guy Williams and June Lockhart, called "The Comb and His Crime-Busting Beauty, Cara Mia." Williams, who was always combing his thick hair on the set, was nicknamed "The Comb" by his fellow cast members.

1.12
THE RAFT

Original Airdate: 12.01.65
Earth Year

Ship's Log: *John and Maj. West construct a small spacecraft capable of carrying two of the stranded colonists back to Earth, but Smith accidentally traps young Will and himself in the ship, which takes off and eventually lands on a planet that the doctor believes is "home, sweet home."*

That Does Not Compute

When the Robot releases the small spacecraft's balloon tie-downs, Will and Dr. Smith peer out one of the portholes to determine whether they have actually taken off from the planet. However, the camera view from the small side window is as if the two castaways are looking through a porthole in the bottom of the spacecraft. The viewing audience sees the top of Robot's head bubble as the ship ascends into the night sky.

Trivia Challenge

1. Which of the following was the subject of the book Dr. Smith was writing?
    A. "The collective failure of intergalactic colonists"
    B. "The social psychology of galactic castaways"

    C. "Studies in futility by castaways in a group experiment setting"

2. Who described Will's unsuccessful attempts at sending SOS messages on small rockets into space as his "ship-wrecked sailor experiments"?

3. Who called Dr. Smith "a bag of wind"?

4. What piece of equipment did John and Maj. West remove from the *Jupiter 2*'s engine room and convert into the small, two-person space vehicle?

5. Who christened the diminutive ship the S.S. *Space Raft?*

6. What was the one-word command Dr. Smith used to order the Robot to release the spacecraft's balloon tie-downs?
    A. "Castoff"
    B. "Homeward"
    C. "Launch"

7. Erroneously believing that he and Will had returned to Earth, in what desolate, barren region of the planet did the scientist assume the galactic vehicle had landed?
    A. The Mojave Desert
    B. The Badlands
    C. The Texas Panhandle

8. Doubting that they were on Earth, what did Will activate as a tracking signal on the small spacecraft?

MEMORY BANKS OVERLOAD

Identify the piece of equipment the Robinsons and Maj. West utilized to secure a direction signal on Will's homing device.

SPACE AGE FAST FACT

Looks can certainly be deceiving as demonstrated by the conservative-appearing June Lockhart. In reality, she was known by the cast and crew as a "rock and roll goddess" who hosted parties at her house and on the studio lot with the Hour Glass band (later known as the Allman Brothers). She also escorted Billy Mumy and Angela Cartwright to the Whiskey-a-Go-Go to hear other rock and roll groups.

1.13
ONE OF OUR DOGS IS MISSING

Original Airdate: 12.08.65
Earth Year

Ship's Log: *After a fierce meteor storm, the Robinson women and Dr. Smith search a nearby valley and discover the wreckage of a small spacecraft, a puppy, and a patch of alien fur.*

That Does Not Compute

During the attack by the large, hairy mutant, John falls and hits his head on a rock. A short time later, he regains consciousness and shoots the creature with his laser gun. As he stands up, he places the weapon in his holster, but when he reaches out to comfort Judy after the mutant attack the gun is once again in his hand.

During the final confrontation with the creature, John fires his laser pistol at the beast as it slowly crawls back to the large, sandy crater. The last few shots result in the tip of the weapon flashing on and off, but no animated laser beam is emitted.

More importantly, what the hell ever happened to the dog? We can only assume that the next episode was subtitled: "One of Our Dogs is *Still* Missing."

Trivia Challenge

1. Which apocalyptic term did Dr. Smith use to describe

the heavy meteorite storm, believing that it was in actuality a "barrage" of firepower before an alien invasion?

    A. "Judgment day"
    B. "Doomsday"
    C. "Day of reckoning"

2. What did Maureen discover inside the wreckage of the small spaceship?

3. Who found a patch of alien fur in a tree?

4. Why had John, Maj. West, Will and the Robot left the *Jupiter 2* camp on an expedition in the Chariot?

5. What type of planetary "creatures with no exact counterparts in nature" did John consider in his handwritten notes to be his "greatest concern" for the safety of the *Jupiter 2* crew?

6. (Fill in the Blank) Dr. Smith informed the puppy that he had "penetrated" its disguise, erroneously believing that the small canine was actually a dangerous _____ from another planet.

7. Who asked Dr. Smith, "What's going on in that devious mind of yours?"

MEMORY BANKS OVERLOAD

According to John, the small dog had been the test subject for what type of experiment?

SPACE AGE FAST FACT

After a widely-distributed publicity photo of June Lockhart and the horned monster clearly displayed the creature suit's front zipper, the actress nicknamed the episode's alien "The Horny Mutant."

A FIRST TIME FOR EVERYTHING

It's been said many times and many ways that you always remember your "first." Access your memory banks to recall some of Lost in Space's *inaugural events.*

1. Where was Dr. Smith hiding when he made his first appearance in "The Reluctant Stowaway"?

2. In which episode did Smith insult the Robot for the first time, initiating one of the series' trademarks?
   - A. "The Derelict"
   - B. "Island in the Sky"
   - C. "The Hungry Sea"

3. Dr. Smith was exiled from the *Jupiter 2* campsite repeatedly throughout the series. Identify the episode in which he was first banished.

4. (True or False) The Robot first sings and delivers his trademark line, "That does not compute" in "Invaders from the Fifth Dimension."

5. In which series segment did John first begin logging the expedition's adventures?

6. Identify the episode in which Will first returned to Earth.

7. Starting with which installment of the series did the *Jupiter* 2 crew (except Penny and Smith) begin wearing the outfits that were seen throughout the second season?

8. (True or False) "My Friend, Mr. Nobody" was the first storyline in which Dr. Smith was tempted by riches, initiating a familiar character trait.

9. In which episode was the drilling rig and Maureen's dishwasher glimpsed for the first time?
   A. "The Oasis"
   B. "Welcome Stranger"
   C. "My Friend, Mr. Nobody"

10. Identify the series segment in which the Robot's tape readout was first seen.
    A. "The Hungry Sea"
    B. "The Raft"
    C. "Attack of the Monster Plants"

11. Which episode marked the first appearance of the full *Jupiter* 2 mock-up?

MEMORY BANKS OVERLOAD #1

Name the episode in which the *Jupiter* 2's main viewport blinders first appeared.

---

12. (True or False) The Space Pod wasn't seen until the third episode of the final season.

13. Which installment of the series marked the first and only time during the first season that the *Jupiter* 2's landing legs were shown?
    A. "The Reluctant Stowaway"
    B. "The Derelict"
    C. "There Were Giants in the Earth"

14. In which episode did the *Jupiter* 2 crash on an

unknown planet that would be the stranded colonists' home for the entire first season?

15. (True or False) The first appearance of the spaceship's seismograph and the second season laser pistol occurred in "Wild Adventure."

16. (Fill in the blank with the correct number) The episode "Wild Adventure" marked the first of _____ times during the series that the *Jupiter 2* flew near, or actually landed on, Earth.

17. Name the series segment in which Penny's love of classic literature and music was first introduced.

18. In which episode did the audience learn the Robot's model number?
    A. "War of the Robots"
    B. "Wreck of the Robot"
    C. "The Ghost Planet"

19. (True or False) In "Attack of the Monster Plants" the *Jupiter 2*'s search light was shown in use for the first time.

20. In which early installment of the series did the crew (except for Will and Smith) begin wearing their first season outfits?
    A. "Island in the Sky"
    B. "There Were Giants in the Earth"
    C. "The Hungry Sea"

MEMORY BANKS OVERLOAD #2

Name the episode in which the television audience heard the Robot's classic "Warning! Warning!" for the very first time.

---

21. Identify the first season segment in which the monkey-like alien creature, Debby the Bloop, made her inaugural appearance.

22. In which installment of the series was the *Jupiter 2* porthole window in the room next to the upper level crawl ladder seen for the first time?
    A. "The Magic Mirror"
    B. "The Space Croppers"
    C. "Forbidden World"

23. (True or False) In "The Android Machine," the expedition drilled for fuel for the first time since landing on the planet in the second season.

24. Identify the episode in which the Robot's soil digger made its first appearance.
    A. "Island in the Sky"
    B. "The Raft"
    C. "The Sky Pirate"

25. In which episode from the first season was the Robot's chess claw seen for the first time?
    A. "One of Our Dogs is Missing"
    B. "Welcome Stranger"
    C. "Island in the Sky"

26. (True or False) The Robot's chess claw was seen in the series' second season episode "West of Mars" for the first time since year one's "My Friend, Mr. Nobody."

27. The malevolent Saticon aliens made the first of two appearances in which series segment?

28. Identify the first season episode in which the Chariot all-terrain rover was first shown.

29. In which series installment did Maureen's sonic washer and automatic cooker make their premiere?
    A. "Invaders from the Fifth Dimension"
    B. "Welcome Stranger"
    C. "There Were Giants in the Earth"

MEMORY BANKS OVERLOAD #3

Name the episode in which the *Jupiter 2*'s crew first wore their light-colored parkas.

---

30. (True or False) The Jet Pack and the force field generator both made their first appearance in "Island in the Sky."

31. Which second season episode saw the first appearance of the air vent units outside of the galley and the upper level weapons storage closet?
    A. "The Dream Monster"
    B. "The Golden Man"
    C. "Curse of Cousin Smith"

32. Name the episode whose scene of a spacecraft lifting off would be used as stock footage virtually every time an alien ship was launched into space throughout the rest of the series.

33. Which episode's cliffhanger was the first to notify viewers that the following week's installment would be pre-empted with the words: "Sorry! To be continued 2 weeks from tonight. Same time! Same channel!"?
    A. "The Sky Pirate"
    B. "The Magic Mirror"
    C. "Return from Outer Space"

MEMORY BANKS OVERLOAD #4

Identify the series segment in which the Robot laughed for the first time.

---

34. Which episode was the first of two that included a shot of an ancient-looking *Jupiter 2* spaceship?

35. Identify the episode in which Dr. Smith first insulted the Robot with the classic alliterative "bubble-headed booby."
    A. "The Challenge"
    B. "His Majesty Smith"
    C. "My Friend, Mr. Nobody"

36. (True or False) The term "galactic castaways" was originally used by Dr. Smith in "The Raft."

37. In which series segment did the Robot first complain that his electro-force beam was "extremely low"?
    A. "Wreck of the Robot"
    B. "War of the Robots"
    C. "Treasure of the Lost Planet"

38. Name the episode in which the *Jupiter 2* crew (with the exception of Dr. Smith) began wearing their third-season outfits.

39. (True or False) The scene of the *Jupiter 2* landing in a white circle was first seen in "A Visit to a Hostile Planet."

40. (True or False) The atomic missile's inaugural appearance was in "The Ghost Planet."

41. Which episode marked the audience's first glimpse of the laser cannon?
    A. "The Haunted Lighthouse"
    B. "Space Destructors"
    C. "Deadliest of the Species"

MEMORY BANKS OVERLOAD #5

The Space Pod's bay door, located between the upper deck elevator and the freezing tubes, originally did not have a window. Identify the third season episode in which it first appeared.

1.14
ATTACK OF THE
MONSTER PLANTS

Original Airdate: 12.15.65
Earth Year

Ship's Log: *Duplicating cyclamen plants reproduce an evil replica of Judy, who conspires with the incorrigible Dr. Smith in an attempt to steal all of the Jupiter 2's newly refined and concentrated fuel source.*

That Does Not Compute

Initially John and Maj. West's bodies sink into the "treacherous, man-devouring" sand pit in a matter of seconds. Their descent abruptly ceases at the shoulder/neck area, however, and they remain in that position for a few minutes—long enough for Dr. Smith to return to the *Jupiter 2* for help and Will to saunter unhurriedly to the site.

The exiled Dr. Smith is only a few yards from the campsite when Maureen realizes that the fuel canisters are missing from the table. She immediately calls for John, who in turn, orders Don to go after the revenge-seeking stowaway. In the next scene, the major emerges from the other side of a large boulder, out of breath as if he has been running after Smith for a lengthy distance. Suddenly, the doctor is spotted with the Robot in tow carrying some of Smith's personal belongings. How did the slow-walking "oh, my aching back" Smith get so far ahead of Don in such a short period of time and when did the Robot appear on the scene and begin hauling some of the doctor's property?

Trivia Challenge

1. What did Will use to pull his father and Don from the quicksand?

2. What type of fuel was contained in the canisters that Dr. Smith stole after he was exiled from the *Jupiter 2* campsite?

3. (True or False) Dr. Smith discovered the replication abilities of the cyclamen plants after his watch was duplicated.

4. Identify the Chariot weapon that John and Maj. West used in an unsuccessful attempt to kill the monster plants when they grew into a jungle-like thickness surrounding the *Jupiter 2*.
   A. Laser canon
   B. Ion cluster grenades
   C. Neutron gun

5. According to Will, who had conducted experiments on the cyclamen earlier, what was the freezing temperature of the plants?
   A. Forty-six degrees
   B. Forty-four degrees
   C. Thirty-eight degrees

MEMORY BANKS OVERLOAD

(Fill in the Blank)

Dr. Smith lectured Don: "Try to remember that the _____ man deplores violence, Major."

SPACE AGE FAST FACT

"Attack of the Monster Plants" (co-written by the husband of Irwin Allen's secretary) was Marta Kristen's favorite *Lost in Space* episode.

1.15
RETURN FROM
OUTER SPACE

Original Airdate: 12.29.65
Earth Year

Ship's Log: *Will uses the Taurons' abandoned matter transfer unit to transport himself to Earth on a maser beam, but the townspeople in the small community where he materializes believe he is just a runaway boy with a wild imagination.*

That Does Not Compute

Will says that the Vermont town was "behind in the times," but caught in a time warp is a more fitting description, with nothing about it seeming any more modern than 1966 rural America. Although it is supposed to be a "desperately overcrowded" Earth in the late twentieth century, the community is anything but suggestive of overpopulation, there are no television sets in any of the homes, everyone drives early-model vehicles, and the town's telephone system still utilizes a Hooterville-like single operator who connects all calls. Are we to actually believe that no one recognized Will even though the Robinsons were probably featured on every television news program, magazine and newspaper in the country, perhaps the world? It is only a few months after the *Jupiter 2* has been lost in space, and unless the entire town is suffering from some sort of collective amnesia, *somebody* should have recognized the boy immediately. Perhaps this was an episode of Irwin Allen's *Time Tunnel* instead.

Trivia Challenge

1. What culinary delight did Dr. Smith prepare for himself from the egg he and Penny found nestled at the Taurons' deserted matter transfer unit?

2. What was the name of the small Vermont town where Will was transported?

3. (Fill in the Blank) After his father threatened to destroy the alien matter transfer device, Will posted a handwritten sign on it that read: *"WARNING!* This _____ is property of the Taurons! If you try to destroy it you will be *severely punished!*

4. Where did Davey Sims assume Will bought his handheld radio transmitter?
   A. At the general store
   B. A dime store
   C. From the back of a comic book

5. Where was Alpha Control located?

6. Which of the following was the name of the boys' home where Will was almost shipped?
   A. County House for Wayward Children
   B. St. Mary's Lighthouse for Runaways
   C. Hatfield County Home for Boys

7. Identify the one item Will brought back with him from his quick trip to Earth (Hint: it was needed for the *Jupiter 2*'s malfunctioning food storage purifier)?

MEMORY BANKS OVERLOAD

At what time did Will order the Robot to signal the alien device to transport him back from Earth?

SPACE AGE FAST FACT

Young actor Kurt Russell was originally cast in the role of Davey Simms, but for some unexplained reason was replaced by Donald Losby. A scene was also cut in which the boys at the county home were assembled in a large room watching television when Will entered.

1.16
THE KEEPER.

PART I

Original Airdate: 01.12.66
Earth Year

Ship's Log: *An intergalactic zookeeper who travels the universe collecting creatures from every planet, decides he wants to add Will and Penny to his menagerie.*

That Does Not Compute

When the Keeper first appears at the *Jupiter* 2 campsite, he puts aside his staff as a gesture of peace and approaches the marooned colonists to introduce himself. But when he turns around to walk back and retrieve it, the light adorning the top of the rod is clearly visible in his hand.

Trivia Challenge

1. What type of creature was contained in the small glass cage that the Robot brought back to the campsite?

2. Who compared the Keeper to a jack-in-the-box toy?

3. (Fill in the Blank) The Keeper informed Will that his lightweight staff was constructed of _____ matter.
   A. ultralight
   B. phased (or dematerialized)
   C. weightless

4. (Fill in the Blank) On the Keeper's homeworld, "the forces of _____ were the servants of the people, not the masters."

5. What type of communications device was aboard the alien's mammoth spaceship?
   A. Visual communications transmitter
   B. Audio-visual radio
   C. Microwave relay transponder

6. (True or False) The Keeper told Dr. Smith that he would possibly venture to Earth on his next expedition in about 300 to 400 years.

7. How many light years away was the Keeper's homeworld?
   A. Six
   B. Ten
   C. Twelve

8. What was the source of power for the alien's staff?
   A. Ionogenic particles
   B. An enclosed subspace field
   C. Cosmic energy

9. Which two examples of the "hundreds and hundreds" of creatures aboard his intergalactic vehicle did the Keeper cite to Will and Penny in an attempt to lure them aboard his ship?
   A. A bumblebee that talked like a parrot and a fish that danced on land
   B. A butterfly that sang like a bird and a frog that laughed
   C. A horse that spoke ten languages and a cow that could play classical music

10. What unusual and primitive weapon did Don use to shatter the light atop the Keeper's staff?

MEMORY BANKS OVERLOAD

(Fill in the Blank)

The Keeper complained to the alien leader, "Unfortunately, Earth people live by _____ as well as by instinct."

SPACE AGE FAST FACT

"The Keeper" (both parts) is Billy Mumy's personal choice for the best *Lost in Space* series segment. The sci-fi classic *The Day the Earth Stood Still*, in which episode guest star Michael Rennie played the lead, is also Mumy's favorite science fiction movie.

1.17
THE KEEPER,

PART II

Original Airdate: 01.19.66
Earth Year

Ship's Log: *After Dr. Smith sneaks aboard the Keeper's massive spaceship and accidentally releases all of the caged creatures, the alien issues the space family Robinson an ultimatum: deliver Will and Penny or he will allow the beasts to overrun the planet.*

That Does Not Compute

When the Robinsons and Maj. West venture forth to locate the creature the Keeper left behind as a reminder of his visit to the planet, Don almost slips and falls, but quickly regains his footing and keeps on walking with his laser gun drawn.

Watch closely towards the end of the episode as the camera moves in for a close-up of Dr. Smith locked away once again in a glass cage. In the reflection of the glass you can see the assistant camera operator push June Lockhart out of the way.

Trivia Challenge

1. According to Don, what were the only two things that Dr. Smith liked to do?
    A. Complain and sleep

B. Run from work and run even more from work
C. Sleep and eat

2. Whose hand did the Keeper grasp first and telepathically check for a "guilty conscience"?

3. Who point-blank warned the alien, "If you want to take Will and Penny, you've got to fight us for them"?

4. Who first offered themselves to the alien as Earth specimen substitutes for Will and Penny?

5. What type of creature pinned the Chariot to the ground?

6. Identify the "dangerous animal" that the Keeper left behind on the planet "as fitting punishment for the trouble" the Robinsons had allegedly caused him.

MEMORY BANKS OVERLOAD

(Fill in the Blank) As punishment for releasing his creatures, the Keeper threatened to place Dr. Smith in one of his cages with "information" posted on the door that read: "FOOLISH EARTHMAN. LOW INTELLIGENCE LEVEL. HAS LITTLE REGARD OR _____ TO HIS KIND. SPECIMEN MUST BE REGARDED AS THE WORST EXAMPLE OF ITS SPECIES."

SPACE AGE FAST FACT

Episode guest star Michael Rennie, who made a pact with his former acting partner, Jonathan Harris, to quit smoking years earlier, died of emphysema at the age of sixty-five.

ALPHA CONTROL INTELLIGENCE DOSSIER

#1-57566-096-2
Dr. Maureen Robinson

1. (True or False) Maureen Tomlinson was born in Los Angeles, California on June 25, 1958.

2. What were her parents' names?
   A. Edwin and Judith
   B. Robert and Karla
   C. James and Margaret

3. (Fill in the Blank) The aircraft navigation systems design firm founded and owned by her father was Tomlinson _____ Corporation.

4. (True or False) Maureen was educated at a private school for gifted children.

5. What was the cause of her parents' tragic death in 1966?
   A. A plane crash
   B. A chemical explosion at her father's company
   C. An automobile accident

6. Who became Maureen's legal guardian?

7. After her first year of college, she married fellow student John Robinson. With whom did the couple live in Los Angeles for the next four years while pursuing their educations?

8. In which year did Maureen earn her bachelor's degree in chemical engineering?
   A. 1977
   B. 1980
   C. 1982

9. Identify the company specializing in solid fuel propellants for the U.S. military and NASA which hired Maureen after she graduated from college.
   A. Alt-Fuels for Tomorrow, Inc.
   B. Providian Energy Sources
   C. Tetrodyne Chemicals

10. (True or False) After the birth of her third child, William, she left her job to pursue a career as a full-time mother and housewife.

MEMORY BANKS OVERLOAD

After her husband John took a job with Alpha Control, the family moved to Houston, Texas, where Maureen returned to school and subsequently obtained her master's degree in 1991. While undergoing four years of training at the United States Space Corps facility to become "the first family in space," she finished her doctorate studies. Identify the field in which Maureen earned her Ph.D.

TECH SPECS #2

Match the letter to the correct equipment aboard the Chariot all-terrain exploratory vehicle.

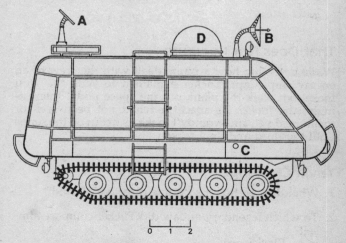

Technical drawing by Edwin E. Echols.

1. _____ Engine exhaust P/S
2. _____ Solar panel
3. _____ Gun hatch
4. _____ Scanner antenna

1.18
THE SKY PIRATE
Original Airdate: 01.26.66
Earth Year

Ship's Log: *The stranded colonists repair the ship of Capt. Alonzo P. Tucker, a roguish but likable space pirate who was abducted by aliens visiting Earth over a hundred years earlier.*

That Does Not Compute

While depicting how a pirate dealt with the crew of an enemy ship, Capt. Tucker explained to Will, "... you make 'em walk the plank out the space pod." Interestingly, the *Jupiter 2*'s space pod had not been seen or mentioned yet, and wouldn't make its debut on the series until the third and final season.

Trivia Challenge

1. What did the Robot's "prime directive" forbid?

2. To which legendary outlaw did Tucker compare himself?
   A. Blackbeard
   B. Robin Hood
   C. Jean Laffite

3. What did the space pirate use to destroy the first alien probe?

4. What was the name of Tucker's robotic parrot?

5. What did aliens use to "scoop" Tucker off of Earth in the late 1880s?
   A. "Tractor beam"
   B. "Transporter device"
   C. "Force ray"

6. According to Don, what type of galactic vehicle was Tucker's spacecraft?

7. Identify the shipboard device that the aliens kept Tucker and others in to prevent their aging.
   A. A time containment field
   B. Animated suspension tube
   C. A time freezer

8. From which planet did Tucker's alien pursuer originate?
   A. Beto II
   B. Cygnet IV
   C. Sygma III

9. In which year was Capt. Tucker born on Earth?
   A. 1858
   B. 1845
   C. 1861

MEMORY BANKS OVERLOAD

Identify the race of specimen-collecting aliens who abducted Tucker from Earth.

SPACE AGE FAST FACT

Child labor laws regulated the number of hours Billy Mumy and Angela Cartwright could work daily on the series and also required them to attend school on the show's set. Because Jonathan Harris and Billy Mumy had so many scenes together, the veteran actor had to resort to stealing the boy away from class for rehearsal by bribing the teacher with a bottle of perfume

1.19
GHOST IN SPACE

Original Airdate: 02.02.66
Earth Year

Ship's Log: *Smith detonates a blasting explosive in a gaseous bog and in the process creates an invisible, destructive force which the superstitious doctor is convinced is the spirit form of his late uncle Thaddeus.*

That Does Not Compute

During the pre-credits sequence, John is rendered unconscious after only two or three seconds' exposure to the ionized gas. Amazingly, Will and Don remain fully cognizant while attempting to revive John even though the dense fumes continue to pervade the area. The gas is noticeably absent during close-up shots of John's resuscitation, but long shots show a fog-like shroud of fumes encompassing the group.

If Dr. Smith was accidentally trapped aboard the *Jupiter 2* during lift-off, how is it possible for him to be in possession of a friar's robe, an exorcising weapon, and a book of mystic charms to ward off his family poltergeist?

Trivia Challenge

1. Which drill site did John and Maj. West assign Dr. Smith to blast?
   A. Alpha

B. 5
C. Niner

2. Why did Smith need scarlet paint?

3. How many toes did the invisible bog monster have on each of its oversized feet?

4. Identify the two spiritualistic mediums Dr. Smith used in attempt to communicate with the spirit of his uncle Thaddeus.

5. What did the invisible alien feed on?

6. (True or False) Dr. Smith used a dagger and garlic in his misguided effort to exorcise the demons from the spirit of his dead relative.

7. What did Will lose when he fell into the gaseous bog?

8. What destroyed the invisible alien creature after it materialized?

MEMORY BANKS OVERLOAD

What was the one word that the Robot used to describe the invisible force's genetic code?

SPACE AGE FAST FACT

After Don rescued John from the bog, it was originally scripted for the major to perform mouth-to-mouth resuscitation, but CBS censors ordered the scene cut, believing that the viewing audience (mostly children) would be disturbed to see two men's mouths touching.

1.20
WAR OF THE ROBOTS

Original Airdate: 02.09.66
Earth Year

Ship's Log: *Will repairs what appears to be a damaged, corroded Robotoid but is in actuality a highly advanced mechanized monster created by aliens who wish to capture the Earthlings for their experiments.*

That Does Not Compute

Penny is absent from the entire episode without explanation. Not only is she missing during meals, she is nowhere to be found when the menacing Robotoid assembles the *Jupiter 2* crew together and imprisons them in the spacecraft. Although Angela Cartwright may have had other professional obligations or scheduling problems, would it have been so hard to show Maureen sliding her daughter's cabin door shut, with an empty bowl of soup and a typically maternal expression of concern, along with a line or two of dialogue that explained that Penny was still in bed with a bad case of "space sickness"?

When the Robinson family are informed by the Robotoid that they are no longer in command, Will runs off to rendezvous with the *Jupiter 2* Robot. In a scene shortly afterward, Bob May's legs can clearly be seen while the mechanical man is walking.

The climactic fight scene between the Robot and the Robotoid has obviously been cut and pasted, demonstrated by its poor editing.

Trivia Challenge

1. What was the difference between a Robot and a Robotoid?

2. Who accused the Robot of possessing the "human emotion" of jealousy?

3. (True or False) The Robotoid had been "aware," or activated, ever since his primary electrostat matrix had been refined two days earlier.

4. What was the first command that Will gave to the newly restored mechanical creature?
   A. "Run a systems check"
   B. "Walk"
   C. "Explain where you came from"

5. According to John, what job was "too complex" for the Robot?

6. (Fill in the Blank) Dr. Smith threatened to reassemble the Robot into a _____ vehicle.

7. What did the Robotoid remove from the force field to render it inoperable?
   A. The battery cells
   B. The ionic calibrator
   C. The energy projector

8. What prevented the Robot from committing "suicide" while he was in the wilderness?

MEMORY BANKS OVERLOAD

How many properly functioning computer units were operational inside the Robot?

SPACE AGE FAST FACT

The cast and crew were sometimes concerned that Bob May truly believed that he was the Robot. He painted the interior of his dressing room silver and detailed his director's chair with the same color and the addition of small knobs. During rehearsals, when he wasn't in costume, he even walked around on the set with his arms in position like the Robot. More disturbingly, May would "get incredibly passionate" about being inside the Robot's outfit.

1.21
THE MAGIC MIRROR

Original Airdate: 02.16.66
Earth Year

Ship's Log: *In an intergalactic version of Alice's THROUGH THE LOOKING-GLASS, Penny falls through a large, alien mirror into another dimension and discovers a nameless boy who tells her that there is no way out.*

That Does Not Compute

As with Penny in the previous episode, "War of the Robots," two more major characters are noticeably missing in action in this installment of the series. Although Billy Mumy's guest appearance on another television show necessitated his character's absence, where was the Robot? Perhaps fishing or dismantling the Robotoid?

Although Debby the Bloop is obviously a female, John refers to the simian-like creature as a "he" when discussing her with Dr. Smith.

Trivia Challenge

1. What type of storm caused the alien mirror's interdimensional passage to open?

2. (True or False) The mirror's frame was made of pure

silver, a precious metallic element that appealed to Dr. Smith's greedy nature.

3. What did the Bloop bring back from her quick trip to the dimension on the other side of the mirror?

4. What type of small animal did the alien boy once keep as a pet before it ran away?

5. (Fill in the Blank) The nameless alien boy's shiny, gold "cannon" fired _____ particles.

6. What did the alien boy lack which prevented him from leaving the other dimension?

MEMORY BANKS OVERLOAD

How many dollars an ounce did Dr. Smith estimate he would be paid for the precious metal framing of the large alien mirror?

SPACE AGE FAST FACT

Jonathan Harris, who suffered from a severe case of claustrophobia, turned down a role in the sci-fi classic *Planet of the Apes* because he knew he wouldn't be able to sit through the long hours of makeup application.

COMMUNICATION CHANNELS

Season One

The planetary radio transmission relay stations are still not operating properly. It's now your responsibility to fill in the communication gaps created by space static.

1. Who commented in "Welcome Stranger," that "the quickness of the mind has deceived the eye"?

2. Identify the character in "The Reluctant Stowaway" who remarked that the military mind only understood "kill or be killed."

3. (Fill in the Blank) In "The Sky is Falling," Smith noted: "Where emotion is involved, _____ is not required."

4. In which episode did Dr. Smith boast, "I happen to have the gift of seeing myself as others see me and vice versa"?
    A. "The Keeper, Part I"
    B. "The Raft"
    C. "His Majesty Smith"

5. In "Invaders from the Fifth Dimension," who made the astute observation, "On this planet, we are the aliens"?

6. (Fill in the Blank) A frustrated John called Smith "our

increasingly _____ extra passenger" in "The Derelict."

7. (True or False) In the episode "Island in the Sky," Dr. Smith referred to John as "a true trailblazer on the frontiers of space."

8. Which member of the *Jupiter 2* expedition believed that the Robot had suffered a "nervous breakdown" in "There Were Giants in the Earth"?

9. Identify the episode in which the Robot kept repeating the phrase, "All systems pre-empted. Fixed position must be maintained."
    A. "Return from Outer Space"
    B. "Attack of the Monster Plants"
    C. "War of the Robots"

10. (Fill in the Blank) In "The Keeper, Part I," Dr. Smith warned, "Beware of _____ bearing gifts."

11. Who referred to the Robotoid as a "monster"?

12. Which alien commented that "forever's not such a long time"?
    A. Mr. Nobody ("My Friend, Mr. Nobody")
    B. The Keeper ("The Keeper, Part II")
    C. The Boy ("The Magic Mirror")

13. (Fill in the Blank) When Will asked the Trader where he was from, the space entrepreneur replied, "I'm from everywhere, a _____ of the galaxy."

14. In which series segment did the greedy Dr. Smith opine: "On Earth, being rich means being powerful"?
    A. "All That Glitters"
    B. "The Space Trader"
    C. "Wish Upon a Star"

MEMORY BANKS OVERLOAD #1

Which *Jupiter 2* crew member once remarked, "There wouldn't be enough room on one planet for two Dr. Smiths"?

15. (True or False) In "War of the Robots," Dr. Smith labeled the *Jupiter 2*'s automaton as simply a "piece of scientific equipment."

16. (Fill in the Blank) The announcer during pre-launch of the *Jupiter 2* considered "man's colonization of space beyond the stars" to be "one of _____ great adventures."

17. Name the episode in which John complained that he felt as if he "was hit by a truck."

18. Who commanded the Robot to keep his "pilot light burning" in "Island in the Sky"?

19. (Fill in the Blank) Also in the first season episode, the mechanical man noted that he was "not programmed for free _____."

20. Who made the assertion in "The Space Trader" that Dr. Smith couldn't sleep because he suffered from "a guilty conscience"?

21. (True or False) After gazing upon the *Jupiter 2*, astronaut Jimmy Hapgood dubbed the spaceship "a right pretty vehicle."

22. In which episode did Smith refer to the planet Priplanus as a "veil of tears"?
    A. "Welcome Stranger"
    B. "The Space Croppers"
    C. "Island in the Sky"

23. Identify the character who described the "unknown universe" as the "greatest of mysteries."

MEMORY BANKS OVERLOAD #2

Name the series segment in which Dr. Smith made the derogatory comment that Don was a "rather violent and stubborn type."

24. (Fill in the Blank) Maj. West warned John not to trust Smith, describing the scheming doctor "as slippery as a _____ of eels."

25. (True or False) In "There Were Giants in the Earth," Dr. Smith protested that Priplanus was "a most hostile planet."

26. In which episode did Smith make the observation that the *Jupiter 2* expedition had witnessed "Mother Nature at her mightiest"?

27. In "Change of Space" the Robot calculated that the extragalactic vehicle was capable of "unlimited thrust, _____, and speed."

28. Whose description of Priplanus was a "colorful island in space"?

29. Although Dr. Smith usually aimed his verbal warfare at Don, he collectively called the major and John "lame-brain, _____ skeptics" in "The Hungry Sea."

30. In which installment of the series did Smith complain to an alien, "The human body is not a grab bag"?
    A. "Invaders from the Fifth Dimension"
    B. "The Space Croppers"
    C. "The Magic Mirror"

31. (Fill in the Blank) Always eager to keep Smith in line, Don boasted in "The Oasis," that the incorrigible doctor wouldn't "have enough _____ to swat a fly when I get through with him."

32. In which episode did Smith make the comment, "I'm a scientist, not a fighting man"?
    A. "The Space Trader"
    B. "Invaders from the Fifth Dimension"
    C. "The Sky is Falling"

33. (Fill in the Blank) Smith dubbed the abandoned Tauron matter transfer unit "a _____ of molecular magic."

34. Who remarked in "The Keeper, Part I" that "sometimes violence is a necessity"?
    A. The Keeper
    B. Maj. West
    C. Dr. Smith

35. (True or False) Capt. Tucker characterized Smith as a "delicate kind of a cuss."

36. (Fill in the Blank) Cornered by an alien probe, Capt. Tucker described the device to Will as "the eyes and nose of a particular _____ that has tracked me clear across space."

MEMORY BANKS OVERLOAD #3

Identify the alien who berated Dr. Smith, "You not only act like a fool, you talk like one."

---

37. Who accurately characterized John as someone "who uses his mind instead of his fists"?

38. Effra in "The Space Croppers" called Will "a cute little fella," but who nicknamed the Robinson boy "the Little Dipper"?

39. (True or False) The Canto warrior spirit in the physical form of John told Dr. Smith, "You may hide the truth from everyone else . . . you cannot lie to yourself."

40. In which episode did Don perfectly sum up Smith's

character, "You're a self-centered, selfish individual whose primary concern is only one thing—himself!"?
- A. "The Derelict"
- B. "Wish Upon a Star"
- C. "The Sky is Falling"

41. What was the Robot's response in "Invaders from the Fifth Dimension" after Don ascertained that the *Jupiter 2* had been "attacked by an invisible alien who eats energy"?
- A. "That, of course, does not compute"
- B. "My memory banks cannot compute an alien with an appetite of this proportion"
- C. "The word 'consumes' would be more applicable"

42. In which episode did the confounded Robot moan, "Nothing computes anymore!"?
- A. "All That Glitters"
- B. "The Space Trader"
- C. "His Majesty Smith"

43. (True or False) In "A Change of Space," as Dr. Smith attempted to pry information about the alien ship from the Robot, the mechanical man snapped back, "What do you want from me, blood?"

44. (Fill in the Blank) The always greedy and materialistic Smith noted in "His Majesty Smith" that the rubies were "as large as _____ eggs."

45. Who uttered the pearl of wisdom, "A full stomach makes for a happy disposition"?

46. Identify the episode in which Dr. Smith asked, "Whatever happened to the Renaissance man?"

MEMORY BANKS OVERLOAD #4

Name the episode in which Don accurately told Dr. Smith, "You're not exactly George Washington when it comes to telling the truth."

1.22
THE CHALLENGE
Original Airdate: 03.02.66
Earth Year

Ship's Log: *An alien boy living on the planet to undergo survival and leadership tests, challenges Will to a series of contests to prove his superiority over the Earthling.*

That Does Not Compute

The *Jupiter 2* spaceship, and especially the control room's observation window, have repeatedly been subjected to all sorts of natural and unnatural phenomena, from meteor storms to alien attacks, but when Quano throws his spear at the ship's main window, the primitive weapon easily shatters the glass.

Although actor Michael Ansara frequently shaved his head for roles, he refused to oblige Irwin Allen's request for the part of the Ruler in this episode. In several scenes you can see the wrinkles in the rubber cap atop the actor's head.

Trivia Challenge

1. How many years old was Quano, the alien boy?
    A. Twelve
    B. Thirteen
    C. Fourteen

2. Who taught Quano the English language?

3. Which royal title did Dr. Smith consistently use to address the boy after learning that his father was the supreme ruler of their homeworld?
   A. "Majesty"
   B. "Highness"
   C. "Excellency"

4. In actuality, what was the ornament that hung around Quano's neck?

5. (Fill in the Blank) After driving the cave beast away, The Ruler commented to Will, "Even the _____ man experiences fear."

6. How did The Ruler signal the start of the boys' challenge?

7. What did the Robot deliberately burn out in his system to avoid answering Dr. Smith's questions?
   A. Primary fusion core
   B. Short-term memory circuits
   C. Voltage regulators

8. How was it possible for Dr. Smith to overhear The Ruler tell Quano that he had to win the challenge with Will or all the witnesses would be destroyed?

MEMORY BANKS OVERLOAD

(Fill in the blank with the correct number)

During the volta-blade duel between John and The Ruler, Maj. West estimated that there were "at least _____ volts" in each of the sword-like weapons.

SPACE AGE FAST FACT

Lost in Space fans who hadn't watched the series when it was originally aired on CBS, may not know that the first and second season episodes ended with "TO BE CONTINUED NEXT WEEK! SAME TIME, SAME CHANNEL." Independent television stations showing the series in syndication on a daily basis were concerned that viewers would tune in "next week." Irwin Allen was quoted in the June 1, 1965 edition of *Daily Variety* as saying that *Lost in Space*'s episodic cliffhanger endings were the first of their kind in the history of television.

1.23
THE SPACE TRADER

Original Airdate: 03.09.66
Earth Year

Ship's Log: *After a galactic merchant drums up business by destroying the stranded colonists' garden with a weather machine, a hungry Dr. Smith agrees to become the property of The Trader in decades in the future in exchange for food, not realizing that the contract's fine print allows the unscrupulous businessman to accelerate the terms and take delivery immediately.*

That Does Not Compute

After Dr. Smith creates his artistic masterpiece and proudly displays it to John and Maj. West, John grabs the canvas, turns it around in an attempt to figure out what the painting represents, and then returns it to Smith, who replaces it on the easel. However, the top of the canvas is now pointing to Smith's left instead of straight up.

During the opening scene, in which the condensation unit crashes against some large boulders, shadows from the props are clearly visible on the set's backdrop landscape painting due to the artificial lighting.

Also during the pre-credits sequence, viewers can catch a glimpse of the Robot beginning to topple over as the mechanical man goes up the *Jupiter 2*'s ramp during the storm. When the camera cuts back to him, his bubble is sitting crooked on his plastic collar.

As Will and Dr. Smith approach The Trader's camp for the first time, the camera follows them as they go behind an enormous rock and appear on the opposite side where the merchant's dogs charge them. The shadows of the actors' two stunt doubles waiting behind the rock formation can be seen as Will and Smith approach. The difference in body shapes between Mumy/Harris and their doubles are painfully obvious, especially Harry Monty, the dwarf-stuntman standing-in for Mumy.

Trivia Challenge

1. What type of device did The Trader use which allowed him to speak English to Will and Smith?
   A. Language replicator
   B. Galactic language translator
   C. Language duplicator

2. According to the merchant, what were the two things a trader loved?
   A. A good deal and even better profits
   B. Something for nothing and a satisfied customer
   C. Good company and good business

3. What did The Trader request from Don in exchange for the cooked turkey he materialized on the space family's outside dinner table?

4. Which word did The Trader use to describe the Robot?
   A. "Antediluvian"
   B. "Outdated"
   C. "Antique"

5. When Will went searching for the Robot at The Trader's campsite, what did the boy find attached to his mechanical friend's legs section?

6. According to the alien merchant, what was the secret of success in business?

MEMORY BANKS OVERLOAD

What did "artist" Dr. Smith state that his "master-piece" represented?

SPACE AGE FAST FACT

The *Lost in Space* cast became known throughout Hollywood as the "Goons" because of their attempts to intimidate any guest star who appeared on the series. Tactics by the show's regulars would include whispering and pointing while an actor was filming a scene, drawing nipples and writing graffiti on costumes, and changing scenes or dialogue without advising the guest star. Ironically, Jonathan Harris, who played the show's villain, was a perfect gentleman on the set, often taking the time to rehearse scenes with actors making guest appearances and giving them advice on how to interact with his character.

1.24
HIS MAJESTY SMITH

Original Airdate: 03.16.66
Earth Year

Ship's Log: *Dr. Smith is crowned king by visitors from another planet, not realizing the aliens always selected useless beings as monarchs for their annual ceremony of sacrifice.*

That Does Not Compute

When the androids are suddenly "frozen" in suspended animation aboard the alien spaceship, the blond woman standing behind Dr. Smith with a basket blinks her eyes and has difficulty holding her hands steady.

During the scene when the duplicate Smith exits the alien vessel and is "reunited" with John, Maj. West and Will, the alien activates his visual projection screen to demonstrate to the real Dr. Smith how easily the *Jupiter 2* crew would accept his impostor. The spaceship door opens all the way to the top and the duplicate Smith prepares to walk down the ramp when the alien simultaneously switches on the viewscreen. The projected images, however, show the door just beginning to rise.

After Dr. Smith breaks a flask over the alien's head, he turns to run from the spaceship and encounters what is obviously a poorly constructed dummy version of one of the actors playing an android.

Trivia Challenge

1. How many light years had Nexus and his "companions" crossed space in search of a being "worthy" of wearing the crown?
   - A. 7.2
   - B. 10
   - C. 19

2. According to Nexus, why did the aliens go off-world to look for a new king?
   - A. "To prevent weak rulers"
   - B. "To find the best stock and leadership abilities available"
   - C. "To bring new beings and fresh ideas to the planet"

3. (True or False) Dr. Smith told the aliens that royalty always descended from Ireland on Earth and that he was Irish on his paternal grandmother's side.

4. Which planet was the homeworld of the visiting aliens?
   - A. Laconia
   - B. Andronica
   - C. Tellorina

5. What was Smith's title when he ascended to the throne?

6. Whom did he wish to name heir apparent to the throne?

7. What was the name of the aliens' annual ceremony in which the "useless" king was sacrificed?
   - A. Festival of Sacrifice
   - B. Celebration of the Monarch's Sacrifice
   - C. Royal Day of the Ceremonial Sacrifice

8. (Fill in the Blank) The alien created the duplicate Dr. Smith from the _____ of the original "useless" Earthling.

MEMORY BANKS OVERLOAD

(Fill in the Blanks)

After Will declined to wear the crown and become king, the Nexus android stated that another "candidate" would have to be selected, one of sublime _____, extraordinary _____, judicial _____, and royal _____.

SPACE AGE FAST FACT

During the series' first year, Dick Tufeld was paid a combined salary of $400 per episode, $200 for narration and an equal amount for supplying the voice of the Robot.

1.25
THE SPACE CROPPERS

Original Airdate: 03.23.66
Earth Year

Ship's Log: *The Jupiter 2 expedition encounters a hill-billy family of space farmers whose matriarch Dr. Smith romances in hopes of securing transportation back to Earth.*

That Does Not Compute

In the cliffhanger seen at the conclusion of the previous episode, "His Majesty Smith," the Robot identifies the werewolf howling as that of a *hanus lupus*, not a *canus lupus* as heard at the beginning of this episode.

When Effra demands that Will bring her a lock of Don's hair, the Robot is standing next to them deactivated. After she leaves, Will replaces the automaton's power pack and the boy asks for his assessment of the alien's strange request. Remarkably, the Robot was able to hear Will and Effra's entire conversation even though he wasn't activated at the time.

Trivia Challenge

1. How many times had Effra visited Earth?

2. According to Sybilla, what type of fuel did the space farmers' galactic vehicle use for propulsion?

3. Why did Effra want a lock of Don's hair?

4. (Fill in the Blank) After studying samples of the space croppers' "little green things," John concluded that the plants contained the "deadliest _____" he'd ever seen under a microscope.

5. Who did Dr. Smith choose as his best man for his wedding rehearsal to Sybilla?

6. Which weapons did the *Jupiter 2* crew successfully use to kill the crop of attacking plants?
   A. Freezing units
   B. Gas guns
   C. Neutron guns

7. What was the destination of the galactic space farmers after they departed the Robinsons' planet?
   A. The Little Dog Star System
   B. The Wild Cat Nebula
   C. Constellation of the Big Quail

MEMORY BANKS OVERLOAD

Name the three items that Will, Penny, and Dr. Smith were seen placing in their time capsule at the beginning of the episode.

SPACE AGE FAST FACT

Mercedes McCambridge, who played Sybilla, was quoted in a September 1966 issue of *TV Guide* as stating that "Jonathan [Harris] certainly ruled the roost" on the set of *Lost in Space*.

ALPHA CONTROL INTELLIGENCE DOSSIER

#1-57566-185-3
Major Donald West

1. (True or False) Don West was born on July 24, 1973 in New York City.

2. What was the name of his father, a retired Air Force pilot with the rank of colonel?
   A. Bruce
   B. Mark
   C. Anthony

3. (Fill in the Blank) Although more interested in athletics, Don received above average grades while attending Brooklyn's Robert C. _____ High School.
   A. Elliott
   B. Amsterdam
   C. Ingersoll

4. At what age did Don earn his pilot's license?

5. Captivated by the unimaginable advances in space travel technology, he applied to the Air Force Academy and with the help of his congressman was accepted in the fall of 1991. Because he had completed two years of ROTC training in high school, what rank did he immediately receive upon admission?

6. (Fill in the blank with the correct number) Don earned a bachelor of science degree from the Academy after successfully completing a _____-year program

designed for officers requesting entrance into the United States Space Corps.

7. (True or False) After displaying a combination of aviation skill in both simulators and advanced jet trainers and high grades while assigned to the USSC Pilot Training Center in Houston, Texas, Don was rapidly promoted to the rank of captain in 1995 at the age of twenty-two.

8. Including Don, how many trainees were chosen as pilots of the Alpha Centauri colonization program, only a year after the *Jupiter 1*'s tragic destruction?
   A. Ten
   B. Fifteen
   C. Twenty

9. When did Don first begin dating Judy Robinson?
   A. During his first semester of the astronaut training program
   B. While attending the Air Force Academy
   C. After he was chosen by the Robinsons to be the pilot of the *Jupiter 2*

MEMORY BANKS OVERLOAD

On what date was it announced that the recently promoted Major West had been selected to be pilot for the *Jupiter 2* colonization mission?

TECH SPECS #3

Match the letter to the correct parts and equipment on the Parajets.

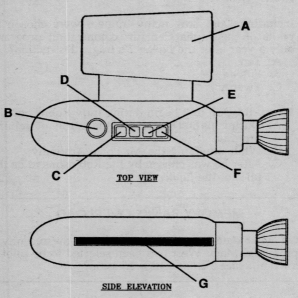

TOP VIEW

SIDE ELEVATION

PARAJETS

Technical drawing by Edwin E. Echols.

1. _____ Timer
2. _____ Intensity
3. _____ Maintenance access
4. _____ Braking
5. _____ Pilot arm access
6. _____ Release/secure
7. _____ Thrust control

1.26
ALL THAT GLITTERS

Original Airdate: 04.06.66
Earth Year

Ship's Log: *A galactic thief on the run from an intrepid law enforcement officer entrusts Penny with a small disk, the key to a priceless treasure that appeals to Dr. Smith's covetous nature.*

That Does Not Compute

In the episode's opening scene, narrator Dick Tufeld erroneously calls Dr. Smith "Professor."

In several instances, the metal ring's power cord is clearly visible trailing behind Smith.

Trivia Challenge

1. Who shot one of Security Officer Bolix's hunting "animals" with a laser gun, although to no effect?

2. Where were John, Maj. West, Will, and the Robot during this episode?

3. As a demonstration of his abilities as a "professional thief," what did Ohan steal from Dr. Smith?

4. Which organization employed Bolix?
   A. The Galactic Bureau of Investigation
   B. The Central Intergalactic Security Department
   C. The Galaxy Law Enforcement Agency

5. (True or False) When Maureen asked him to leave the *Jupiter 2*, the security officer boasted that he was "the sole representative of the law in over three million miles" and could do anything he pleased.

6. According to Bolix, what was a policeman called on Earth?
   A. "A bluecoat"
   B. "A flatfoot"
   C. "A cop"

7. (True or False) Dr. Smith told the galactic police officer to give the reward for Ohan's capture to charity.

8. Identify the planet which served as the base headquarters for the galactic law enforcement agency that employed Bolix as an officer.
   A. Kranus
   B. Tauron
   C. Quotox

MEMORY BANKS OVERLOAD

(Fill in the Blanks)

The small disk's voice stated that it was required to warn Dr. Smith before he was awarded the "greatest treasure in the whole galaxy": "Use what you shall receive with _____. Do not let _____ be your master."

SPACE AGE FAST FACT

Practical jokes abounded on the set. After locking Bob May in the bulky Robot suit during a lunch break, Mark Goddard and Billy Mumy returned later only to discover him happily hunkered down inside the outfit, smoking a cigar and reading one of the Hollywood trade papers with a small flashlight.

1.27
THE LOST CIVILIZATION
Original Airdate: 04.13.66
Earth Year

Ship's Log: *After escaping an erupting volcano, John, Maj. West, Will and the Robot investigate a cave and discover an ancient civilization that has been stockpiling armies of soldiers in hopes of one day conquering the universe.*

That Does Not Compute

During the opening scenes when the Chariot and its passengers are almost engulfed by lava in an uncharted valley of volcanoes, the all-terrain vehicle easily brushes aside one of the large, prop boulders as it passes by.

After entering the cave, Will invites the Robot to take a walk with him and stretch his legs. The automaton responds, "That does not compute," but when he continues with "My legs do not stretch," the Robot's chest light doesn't flash.

It's reported as one hundred and thirty-one degrees inside the Chariot, but why are the men still wearing their heavy, long-sleeved tunic tops instead of the T-shirts they have worn so often when working around the *Jupiter 2* campsite or drilling for fuel or water sources?

Trivia Challenge

1. Why was the Chariot's air-conditioning system non-operational?

2. Whose idea was it to bypass the Chariot's ignition system after the exploratory rover stalled during the volcano eruption?

3. What were the Robot's first words after he recovered from his fall inside the cave?
   A. "Beware the first step"
   B. "I'm not programmed for short-cuts"
   C. "Danger, Will Robinson"

4. Why did the Robot order Will to "kiss the girl"?

5. What was the name of a cat Penny once had as a pet?

6. (Fill in the Blank) The Major Domo informed the marooned colonists that the lost civilization's immense warrior army consisted of "over a thousand _____ of soldiers" frozen in suspended animation, awaiting the day to conquer the universe.

7. (Fill in the Blank) John lectured the Major Domo, "You're all the same, you would-be conquerers. Whether it's a continent, the _____, or the universe—a few pages in history in exchange for millions of lives."

MEMORY BANKS OVERLOAD

What were the Princess' last words before she went to sleep again?

SPACE AGE FAST FACT

Every day after lunch, Jonathan Harris distributed a Tootsie Roll Pop to every member of the cast and crew.

1.28
A CHANGE OF SPACE

Original Airdate: 04.20.66
Earth Year

Ship's Log: *Will returns from a multi-dimensional trip aboard an alien extragalactic vehicle with his intelligence greatly enhanced, but when Dr. Smith attempts the same test flight he is transformed into an old man.*

That Does Not Compute

The alien craft is capable of faster-than-light travel in various dimensions with "unlimited thrust, scope, and speed," yet when the extragalactic vehicle blasts-off and reaches space in less than two or three seconds, Will and Dr. Smith are not strapped into the capsule seat (the Robinson boy is even seen wandering around the interior during lift-off).

When the alien ship lands, John and Maj. West note that the spacecraft looks "different" and probably isn't the same extragalactic vehicle that Will commandeered for his second test flight. However, compare the two ships after Will returns and you can see that they are exact replicas of each other, identical in size, shape, design, and color schemes.

Trivia Challenge

1. What did Dr. Smith fall into while he and Will were on

a plateau investigating the source of a strange glowing light?

2. Who described the interior of the alien ship as "compact as a protein pill"?

3. (Fill in the Blank) The Robot's analysis of the spacecraft indicated that it was capable of "_____ the universe."

4. (Fill in the Blank) After being transformed into a supergenius, Will lectured his father and Don, "To understand me, the first thing you'll have to do is discard everything you know about _____ conversion factors."
   A. light-speed
   B. energy
   C. interdimensional

5. Who called Smith "a crazy, old fool" after he was transformed into an elderly, white-haired man in a wheelchair?

6. What position of importance did the gill-covered alien assume Dr. Smith held among the stranded colonists?
   A. Commander
   B. King
   C. Supreme Ruler

7. Identify the 19th-century "master of the written word" whom Dr. Smith paraphrased after the alien reduced his age.

MEMORY BANKS OVERLOAD

(Fill in the Blank)

According to Will, Dr. Smith believed he would become "some sort of _____ of the galaxies" if he somehow learned how to navigate the alien vehicle.

SPACE AGE FAST FACT

Irwin Allen and the series writers originally plotted to kill off the Zachary Smith character during the first season, but fan mail and telephone calls to the network were strong indicators of his popularity and the cunning doctor's death sentence was revoked.

1.29
FOLLOW THE LEADER

Original Airdate: 04.27.66
Earth Year

Ship's Log: *After a planet quake traps John in a cave, he discovers the tomb of an ancient warrior and becomes possessed by the alien's disembodied spirit.*

That Does Not Compute

Searching for the senior Robinson, Don, Maureen, and Judy make their way to the catacomb, where the possessed John appears to them in the alien's warrior garb after a small explosion. Look closely and you will see that John materializes a split second before the actual blast heralds his triumphant appearance.

As the burial mask-clad John approaches Will and the Robot to take his son to the climactic scene on the cliff, his shadow can clearly be seen on the backdrop painting.

Just before the episode's last commercial break, Will says to his alien-possessed father, "You're going to push me off, aren't you?" to which John replies, "Yes, Will Robinson, I am." When action resumes after the commercial, the same two lines are repeated.

Trivia Challenge

1. What type of creature appeared and scared Dr. Smith into running and dropping his laser pistol to the floor of the cave?

2. Within a week, Will had twice recharged the Robot's power pack. Why was the mechanical man expending so much energy?

3. According to Dr. Smith, who was more suited to eating carrots for breakfast?

4. (Fill in the Blank) When John tried to pry open the rock door to the cavernous tomb, the voice of the alien warrior warned him that "not even the _____ of a hundred men" could remove the obstruction from the portal.

5. Who speculated that John's unpredictable behavior was caused by "a complete mental breakdown"?

6. How long had the incorporeal alien spirit dwelt in the cave?
    A. "A millennium"
    B. "Three hundred years"
    C. "Many centuries"

7. Who remarked that John's eyes seemed "to look right through you"?

8. What was John referring to when he observed, "In all the worlds and galaxies of this universe, there is nothing stronger"?

9. What was the name of the alien spirit?

MEMORY BANKS OVERLOAD

(Fill in the Blank)

Maj. West instructed the Robot to "tune Smith out" by shutting off his _____ unit.

SPACE AGE FAST FACT

Although there are conflicting stories detailing tension among the cast during filming of the series, everyone involved is in agreement that Angela Cartwright's and Billy Mumy's mothers were always demanding script changes and fighting over the number of lines of dialogue their kids had.

PICK A NUMBER

*Note: Because of the difficulty of the following questions,
each correct answer will count as a 5-point MEMORY
BANKS OVERLOAD*

1. (Fill in the Blank) Dr. Smith's "mission" in "The
   Reluctant Stowaway" was to reprogram the *Jupiter
   2*'s environmental control robot to destroy the spaceship _____ hours after liftoff.

2. In "The Android Machine," how many minutes did
   Mr. Zumdish allow the Robinsons to discuss the
   return of Verda before he made good on his threat
   to destroy their spacecraft?

3. (Fill in the Blank) John Robinson was 6'3" in height
   and weighed _____ pounds.

4. (True or False) The alien warrior Gromack ("The
   Deadly Games of Gamma 6") could lift _____
   times his own weight.

5. How much pressure were the *Jupiter 2*'s space helmets
   designed to withstand?

6. (Fill in the Blank) The Robinsons were intended to
   be the first of as many as _____ million families per year launched into deep space, "man's newest
   frontier of colonization."

7. What was the automatic hair setter design number Judy ultimately decided on after a little persuasion from her mother in "My Friend, Mr. Nobody"?

8. In "The Oasis" episode, how many gallons of water were in the storage tanks before the two-week supply was depleted by Dr. Smith's shower?

9. How many sons did Sheriff Baxendale have in "Return from Outer Space"?

10. (True or False) Earth was 5.3 light years to the Alpha Centauri star system.

11. What was the price of a bottle of carbon tetrachloride in the Hatfield Four Corners General Store?

12. (Fill in the Blank) Sir Sagramonte's seemingly unattainable quest for the Gundemar creature had lasted for _____ years.

13. (True or False) In "Rocket to Earth," Dr. Smith stated that he weighed 180 pounds.

14. How much did it cost to use a pay phone in San Francisco's Chinatown, circa late 1990s?

15. In "Visit to a Hostile Planet," the *Jupiter 2* returned to Earth in 1947. What was the Michigan license plate number of the car in which John and Maj. West tuned in the radio?

16. (True or False) The designation number of the Xenian Space Probe was XL73.

17. How many words did the Robot calculate were contained in Will's history book in "Space Creature"?

18. In "Deadliest of the Species," what was the serial

number of the female robot's space imprisonment capsule?

19. (Fill in the Blank) The Robot calculated that the Tauron "visitors" in "The Sky is Falling" were approximately 1.8 meters in height and weighed _____ kilograms.

20. According to John in "The Keeper, Part II," how many years was the *Jupiter 2*'s food and power supply estimated to last?

21. What was the atmospheric density of "The Flaming Planet"?

22. (True or False) In "Junkyard in Space," the Robot remarked that Dr. Smith was "one-hundred percent fat."

23. What was Dr. Smith's prisoner number in "Fugitives in Space"?

24. How many planets in the Alpha Centauri star system could support terrestrial life?

25. At what time was the *Jupiter 2* scheduled to depart from Earth in "Visit to a Hostile Planet"?

26. (True or False) In "Trip Through the Robot," the mechanical man fixed his construction date as two-and-one-half years earlier.

27. How many years in Earth's time continuum had the revolutionist Morbus been imprisoned in the Hades-like fiery dimension?

28. In the episode "Curse of Cousin Smith," what number did Jeremiah pick on the gambling machine after betting his share of Aunt Maude's fortune?

29. How many flasks of cosmonium did Will discover the miner Nerim left behind in his hasty escape from the disintegrating Priplanus?

30. What was the *Jupiter 2*'s scheduled departure time in "Blast Off into Space"?

31. In "All That Glitters," how many berries did Dr. Smith eat that he and Penny were collecting for Maureen to bake a pie?

32. (Fill in the Blank) While Smith and Will went on a werewolf safari, the Robot was programmed for _____ thousand shovelfuls while digging the pipeline trench.

33. (Fill in the Blank) In a successful attempt to retrieve the Robot from "The Space Trader," Dr. Smith signed a contract stating that he would become property of the galactic merchant in _____ hundred years.

34. (True or False) Feeling guilty about the way he treated the mechanical man during the "War of the Robots," Dr. Smith agreed to polish him every day for three weeks.

35. How many watches was Dr. Smith seen wearing on his arm after demonstrating to Will the duplicating abilities of the cyclamen plants?

36. What was Don's prisoner number in "The Fugitives in Space"?

37. What was the range of the force field projector?

38. What did the Space Pod's serial number 277-2211 IA stand for in reality?

39. How many episode titles of the series featured the word "space"?

40. Identify the first season episode which was rated number six for the week it aired (the highest ranking of any *Lost in Space* installment in its entire three-year run on CBS).

41. How many segments of the series featured no guest stars?

42. How many episodes ended with the cliffhanger: "To be continued two weeks from tonight"?

FANDOM EPISODE RANKING:

Season One

The following ranking of Lost in Space's *first season episodes (with 10.0 being the highest) have been posted in various manifestations at science-fiction conventions and in cyberspace on fan-based websites.*

Ranking		Episode Title
1.	10.0	"The Reluctant Stowaway"
2.	9.07	"The Keeper, Part I"
3.	9.05	"The Keeper, Part II"
4.	8.88	"Follow the Leader"
5.	8.80	"The Hungry Sea"
6.	8.75	"My Friend, Mr. Nobody"
7.	8.63	"There Were Giants in the Earth"
8.	8.57	"Invaders from the Fifth Dimension"
9.	8.50	"The Derelict"
10.	8.45	"Island in the Sky"
11.	8.43	"Return from Outer Space"
12.	7.98	"War of the Robots"
13.	7.88	"One of Our Dogs is Missing"
14.	7.80	"Wish Upon a Star"
15.	7.75	"The Challenge"
16.	6.90	"The Magic Mirror"
17.	6.76	"Attack of the Monster Plants"
18.	6.50	"Welcome Stranger"
19.	6.44	"A Change of Space"
20.	6.38	"All that Glitters"
21.	6.33	"Ghost in Space"
22.	6.15	"The Lost Civilization"

23. 6.03   "The Oasis"
24. 5.72   "His Majesty Smith"
25. 5.43   "The Raft"
26. 5.25   "The Sky is Falling"
27. 5.01   "The Sky Pirate"
28. 4.79   "The Space Croppers"
29. 4.37   "The Space Trader"

2.1
BLAST OFF INTO SPACE

Original Airdate: 09.16.66
Earth Year

Ship's Log: *The Jupiter 2 crew prepare for a hurried departure from the planet after discovering that a miner's blasting has caused a chain-reaction of cataclysmic quakes that will disintegrate their entire world.*

That Does Not Compute

When Dr. Smith dedicates the monument of himself during the opening scenes, the Robot's elliptical head sensors are rotating for the first time since early in season one, but by the end of the scene they have ceased working again.

Dr. Smith is assigned by John and Maj. West to go to the drill site and collect the equipment before their lift-off from the planet. Close-up shots show Smith wearing his black tunic while maneuvering the Chariot, but an exterior view of the roving vehicle reveals at least two occupants dressed in parkas in the front seats.

The Chariot's windows have withstood meteor storms and molten rock from volcanic eruptions, but a statue come-to-life easily shatters one of the side window's Plexi-glas.

In first season's "Island in the Sky," the *Jupiter 2* sailed over the rocky ridge and disappeared from view as we heard the unmistakable sound of the spaceship's crash on the planet. Had the craft been able to slow its descent and extend its landing gear, they would have been destroyed by the lateral force as the *Jupiter 2* struck the ground. Yet, during this episode's climactic blast-off from the planet, a quick shot shows the perfectly intact landing gear being retracted.

Towards the end of the episode, when the *Jupiter 2* is nearly engulfed by a mushroom-shaped fireball, the fusion core lights at the bottom of the spaceship actually come loose on one end and then magically reattach in the following scene.

Trivia Challenge

1. According to Nerim, how long had he been mining the planet?
    A. "Since I ran out of money and my wife ran out on me"
    B. "Longer than I care to remember"
    C. "Long enough to get my bearings"

2. (True or False) The scruffy miner was a dozen light years from his homeworld.

3. (Fill in the Blank) Dr. Smith and Nerim referred to Cosmonium, a rare, sparkling liquid and the subject of the miner's excavation, as the "_____ of the living force."

4. (Fill in the Blank) John warned the *Jupiter 2* crew that the planet was going to "disintegrate into _____ dust" in a matter of hours.

5. Boasting that prospecting was in his blood, what did Smith say his Uncle Thaddeus had discovered "all by himself"?

6. Identify the "busted" part that had disabled Nerim's spaceship?
    A. Primary ignition switch
    B. Thruster control
    C. Fusion core stabilizer

7. What was Nerim's nickname for Smith?
   A. Zach
   B. Zach boy
   C. Zacharoo

8. Where was the Robot secured during the *Jupiter 2*'s hasty liftoff from the planet?

MEMORY BANKS OVERLOAD

At what time was the *Jupiter 2* scheduled to blast off?

SPACE AGE FAST FACT

Although the relationship between Dr. Smith and the Robot was considered one of the main reasons that the series was building a loyal fan base of viewers, the off-screen association between Jonathan Harris and Bob May was not cordial. By this point in the show's run, Harris had barred the younger man from his dressing room.

2.2
WILD ADVENTURE
Original Airdate: 09.21.66
Earth Year

Ship's Log: *The relentless Dr. Smith once again sabotages the Jupiter 2 expedition in his endless quest to return to Earth and in the process brings the spaceship and its crew dangerously close to their homeworld's sun.*

That Does Not Compute

While attempting to trick Penny into changing the *Jupiter 2*'s course, Smith is essentially accused of lying by the Robot. Smith quickly removes the automaton's power pack and he slumps over in his traditional deactivated posture. After Penny climbs up the ladder to the upper level control room, Smith turns to make some snide comment to the Robot and we can plainly see that the mechanical man is now erect. Smith walks away, but when he returns the Robot is slumped even *more* than he was when his power pack was initially removed.

Jupiter 2's pilot, Maj. West, mentions that they should be seeing Earth soon since the spacecraft just passed "Uranus and Arturus" inside the solar system. As Isaac Asimov noted in a *TV Guide* article about the accuracy of such shows as *Lost in Space* (citing this episode as an example), Arturus is not a planet, but a star. No wonder they were lost in space!

During Smith's space walk scene with the green lady, Bob May's feet are visible when he exits the ship's elevator and walks behind John.

Trivia Challenge

1. What did Mr. Smith covertly use to alter the *Jupiter 2*'s course from Alpha Centauri to Earth?

2. (Fill in the Blank) The Robot advised Smith that a new course required reprogramming of fuel consumption _____ ratios.

3. How many hours of power did the *Jupiter 2* have remaining after Dr. Smith accidentally dumped the reserve fuel cells into space?
    A. 8–10
    B. 12–18
    C. 20–25

4. (Fill in the Blank) In 1996, Alpha Control launched a succession of fuel barges to be used basically as service stations in space for the _____ probe 22.

5. Dr. Smith diagnosed Don as suffering from which illness?
    A. "Space fever"
    B. "Space rapture"
    C. "Galactic viral infection"

6. (Fill in the Blank) The green alien's sing-song language was based on _____ progression.
    A. euphonic
    B. melodious
    C. mathematical

7. Identify the metallic chemical element that was used in the construction of the *Jupiter 2*'s hull.

8. (True or False) Alpha Control informed the *Jupiter 2* that they could only track the spacecraft with a radio-telescope.

MEMORY BANKS OVERLOAD

According to the Robot's exact calculation, how many ways were there "to skin a cat"?

SPACE AGE FAST FACT

Dick Tufeld originally met Irwin Allen when he was a nineteen-year-old college student. The future narrator of *Lost in Space* and voice of the Robot was announcing on a radio station where he introduced Allen's Hollywood gossip show.

2.3
THE GHOST PLANET

Original Airdate: 09.28.66
Earth Year

Ship's Log: *Believing that they have "gone in circles" and returned to Earth, Dr. Smith and Will direct the Jupiter 2 to a planet that is in reality populated only by cybernetic creatures intent on making the lost colonists their human slaves.*

That Does Not Compute

The tow cable used by stage crew members to pull the Robot along is clearly visible during the scene in which the mechanical man takes Will to join Dr. Smith on the assembly line.

Trivia Challenge

1. What did Space Control utilize to physically manipulate and tow the *Jupiter 2* to the surface of the alien planet?
    A. Linear graviton force beam
    B. Tractor beam
    C. Magnetized field

2. (Fill in the Blank) Dr. Smith boasted to Maureen that he knew the _____ in South America like "the back of my hand."

3. Whose idea was it to send the Robot to report on the "ghost" planet's atmospheric and biological composition?

4. What was Dr. Smith's theory on the "lack of humanity" at the spaceport?

5. Who said, "In space I doubt everything but the evidence of my own eyes, senses, and instruments"?

6. What did Dr. Smith say was in the bag the Robot was carrying, rather than telling Will the truth that he was surrendering the *Jupiter 2*'s weapons to the Officer 03 Robot?
   A. Maureen's breadsticks
   B. Canned rations
   C. Penny's classical music tapes

7. What was Smith's "reward" for delivering the spaceship's weaponry to the cybernetic aliens?

8. What was the Robot's model number?

MEMORY BANKS OVERLOAD

Identify the four places in the spaceport where the number 115 ("double one five") appear in this episode.

SPACE AGE FAST FACT

Guy Williams and June Lockhart became close friends during the filming of the series. The two stars would play classical music in their dressing rooms between scenes and other members of the cast and crew would come by to sit for a few minutes and relax while listening to Tchaikovsky or Rachmaninoff.

2.4
FORBIDDEN
WORLD

Original Airdate: 10.05.66
Earth Year

Ship's Log: *The Jupiter 2 crashes on yet another unknown planet, this one inhabited by a large alien bird and its master, an eccentric hermit who tricks Dr. Smith into drinking a liquid explosive.*

That Does Not Compute

During the pre-credits sequence, the *Jupiter 2* narrowly evades a missile fired at them from the surface of the automated planet, but the spaceship is damaged as a result of the missile's explosive impact on another nearby planetary world. Stock footage used from the *Jupiter 2's* launch from Priplanus in the second season premiere, "Blast Off Into Space," once again shows the fusion core lights at the bottom of the spaceship actually coming loose on one end as it is nearly engulfed by a mushroom-shaped fireball.

Watch carefully as the *Jupiter 2* makes its crash landing through the planet's atmosphere and you'll notice the guide wires reflecting in the sun as the ship flies over the mountains.

After the galactic vehicle crashes in a valley on the planet's surface, Will runs to get a fire extinguisher and you can clearly see the prop man's arm as he hands it to the boy.

The Robot informs John and Maureen that he will

escort Will as he delivers a home-cooked meal to the highly-explosive Dr. Smith to insure that the young Robinson remains "at a safe distance," but the automaton allows him to walk right up to Smith and hand him the container of food.

Trivia Challenge

1. What type of missile did the automated planet fire at the *Jupiter 2* as a protest for the spaceship's escape from the world of robots?
    A. Antimatter
    B. Proton-scattering warhead
    C. Hyperatomic

2. What explanation did John give for refusing to allow the Robot to venture outside of the ship to report on the new planet's atmospheric conditions?

3. Which character was the source of the comment, "Patience, Dr. Smith. All things come to he who waits"?

4. According to the Robot, what did the planet's fog contain that rendered it hazardous to human breathing?
    A. Hydrogen chloride
    B. Cosmic dust
    C. An unidentified, flammable, colorless, odorless, and gaseous chemical element

5. (Fill in the Blank) Capt. Tiabo alleged that he was assigned to the Army's Special _____ to investigate the crash of the *Jupiter 2*.

6. How long had the alien hermit lived on the planet to escape the hurry of civilization?
    A. "Over 100 years"
    B. "Just a decade over a century"
    C. "Over 200 years"

7. Who philosophized that "the highest tribute one

human can pay to another is the sacrifice of personal safety"?

8. What was Capt. Tiabo's secret superweapon?

MEMORY BANKS OVERLOAD

In what sector was the new planet located?

SPACE AGE FAST FACT

Jonathan Harris discussed with Irwin Allen the possibility of giving the Robot a name and recommended "Clawed." The series producer, who was notorious for his lack of a sense of humor, questioned why anyone would want to call the mechanical man "Claude."

THE ONE AND ONLY

*Test your knowledge of equipment, weapons, etc.
which only appeared once in the series and then
seemingly became* Lost in Space.

1. Name the only segment of the series in which the Robot's audio unit served as a short-distance receiver.

2. (True or False) The one and only time Priplanus' two moons were shown was in "Wish Upon a Star."

3. In which episode did the Chariot's neutron gun make its single appearance?
   A. "Ghost in Space"
   B. "Attack of the Monster Plants"
   C. "There Were Giants in the Earth"

4. (Fill in the Blank) The only time the Space _____ was used by the *Jupiter 2* expedition was in "The Raft" when John and Maj. West used the equipment in an attempt to locate the small spacecraft.

5. (True or False) At the conclusion of "The Raft," John arrived just in time to save Will and Dr. Smith by shooting and killing an alien monster with a slender laser pistol that had never been seen before nor would ever be used as a weapon again.

6. Identify the only episode in which the Robot fired laser bolts rather than a continuous electrical charge.
   A. "War of the Robots"
   B. "The Anti-Matter Man"
   C. "Invaders from the Fifth Dimension"

7. In which episode did the plant purifying unit make its one and only appearance?

8. What kind of drill arrived on the scene in "The Thief from Outer Space" and then was never seen again during the series' three-year run.

9. Which episode was the only one to begin without any action before the opening credits?
   A. "The Reluctant Stowaway"
   B. "Blast Off into Space"
   C. "The Derelict"

10. (True or False) "Island in the Sky" was the only segment during the first season in which the *Jupiter 2*'s extended landing legs were seen.

11. Identify the only episode in which the *Jupiter 2*'s Vector Control Tapes were used to decode the *written* word.

12. (True or False) "The Hungry Sea" was the only installment in the series in which the force field was used without the familiar hardware set up.

13. Which episode marked the only appearance of the Parajets?

14. The *Jupiter 2* crew's negative electro-magnetic beam unit was used only once to pull an alien ship back to the planet. Name the episode.

MEMORY BANKS OVERLOAD #1

Which installment of the series was the only one to show John and Maj. West welding?

---

15. (True or False) In "The Mechanical Men," the *Jupiter 2*'s utility room between the elevator and the freezing tubes made its one, briefly glimpsed appearance. (Note: During the third season the storage room became the Space Pod bay.)

16. In which episode was the radio-telescope used by the *Jupiter 2* crew?
   A. "There Were Giants in the Earth"
   B. "The Girl from the Green Dimension"
   C. "The Sky Pirate"

17. Name the episode in which the Robot was blasted by a laser weapon, resulting in the only time the mechanical man's legs deflated and his torso came to rest on top of them.

18. (True or False) The only occurrence of the *Jupiter 2*'s Vector Control Tape unit being used to decipher *vocalized* alien language was in "Kidnapped in Space."

19. Which series segment marked the only time that the Robot displayed his ability to make things disappear?

20. Which third season episode was highlighted by the only appearance of the expedition's rain-making device?
   A. "Space Beauty"
   B. "Space Creature"
   C. "Space Destructors"

21. Name the installment in which the *Jupiter 2*'s atomizing units were shown for the first and last time. (Note: In "Junkyard in Space," John was attempting to repair the units, but they looked completely different.)

22. (Fill in the Blank) The _____ tower made its solo appearance in "Castles in Space."

23. (True or False) During the events chronicled in "Space Destructors," John and Maj. West's latest creation, an electronic net, was used to disintegrate a cyborg and then was never seen on the series again.

24. Name the only episode in which it was mentioned that Dr. Smith wore eyeglasses (although he was never seen sporting them).

25. (True or False) "The Flaming Planet" was the one and only segment which showed John and Maj. West flying in the Space Pod together.

26. Identify the episode which marked the single time the viewing audience was able to glimpse the *Jupiter 2*'s power core.

27. (Fill in the Blank) "The Reluctant Stowaway" was the first and last installment of the series in which the extra vehicular _____ (E.V.A.) thrusters were used.

28. Name the only episode in which the *Jupiter 2* set was not used at all.

29. During the final act of one of the shows, the action froze and the left side of the screen moved inward, revealing the following, "Back in a minute . . . Don't go away." After the commercial break, the screen reversed itself and the action resumed. Which episode marked this singular occurrence during the series' entire three-year run on CBS?

MEMORY BANKS OVERLOAD #2

(All three questions must be answered correctly to be awarded the 5-point bonus)

Name the episodes in which the following made their one and only appearances:

1. The force field's energizer and the power grid hardware;
2. The Space Pod's auto pilot; and
3. The Robot drinking through his computer tape compartment.

2.5
SPACE CIRCUS

Original Airdate: 10.12.66
Earth Year

Ship's Log: *The only traveling circus in the galaxy puts on a free show for the stranded colonists, but the owner sees a fortune in Will's mysterious new "mind powers" and plots to take the boy away with the troupe.*

That Does Not Compute

In several scenes the bottom section of the detachable head mask of the large, furry Cosmic Monster costume can clearly be seen, especially when the actor wearing it turns his head sharply, displaying the dark area between the head and body part of the white outfit.

Trivia Challenge

1. Which chemical element was needed to operate the *Jupiter 2's* plant purifying unit?
    A. Cobalt magnesium
    B. Carbon neptunium
    C. Cesium polonium

2. (Fill in the Blank) According to Dr. Marvello, the space circus' Cosmic Monster, one of the wonders of the universe was "the fiercest specimen from Super _____ 12."

3. (True or False) Marvello boasted that his traveling galactic circus was the "Greatest Show in the Universe."

4. (Fill in the Blank) The circus ringmaster and curator referred to Earth as one of "the _____ places in the galaxy."

5. (Fill in the Blank) Dr. Marvello introduced himself as "Professor extraordinaire, galactic _____, and bringer of joy to the crowned heads of the universe."
   A. illusionist
   B. magician
   C. entrepreneur

6. Per Marvello's circus introduction, who was "the strongest man in any universe"?
   A. Quacho
   B. Vicho
   C. Zeno

7. She was the "mistress of the occult" and the "queen of mystery." What was her stage name?

8. Identify the once popular Earth song whose lyrics were stored in the Robot's memory banks.

9. What did Dr. Marvello give to Will as a going-away present before he and his circus troupe departed for parts unknown in the galaxy?
   A. A free "any time, anywhere" season pass
   B. "A celestial Annie Oakley"
   C. "A hearty thank you" and a pat on the back for making him feel young again.

MEMORY BANKS OVERLOAD

Identify the four items that Will materialized with his mind powers during the course of this episode.

SPACE AGE FAST FACT

Many *Lost in Space* fans blame the popular influence of *Batman*, which debuted on ABC in January 1966, for drastically changing the direction of the series from serious science fiction to "camp"—a classic example being this episode!

2.6
PRISONERS OF SPACE

Original Airdate: 10.19.66
Earth Year

Ship's Log: *A galactic court accuses the lost expedition of committing a variety of crimes in outer space, but testimony reveals that Dr. Smith was responsible for each of the offenses.*

That Does Not Compute

While Dr. Smith digs a hole under the electronic fence in a successful attempt to escape from the imprisoned *Jupiter 2* campsite, the Robot acts as a sentry to guard against discovery by the alien judge. Although Smith's tunnel is on the far side of the camp, when the judge's communications module appears to question the Robot, the audio device is sitting on the same rock amid the same surroundings as when it was positioned by the beast a few yards from the *Jupiter 2*'s ramp at the beginning of the episode.

When the one-eyed beast appeared at the outset of the episode with the judge's voice machine, Dr. Smith's wine-making apparatus seemed to be only a few short yards from the *Jupiter 2* camp. But when Will and the Robot go searching for Dr. Smith after his escape, it takes them over an hour to make their way to the still's secret location.

It is painfully obvious that the electronic fence is nothing more than stretched cellophane and the testimony seat simply a high-back, leather executive chair with the wheels removed.

The aliens seemingly planned ahead for the Robinsons' testimony. When they instantly transport Will to the courtroom, there is a pillow in that same executive chair to raise him to ear level of the memory machine.

Trivia Challenge

1. What was the name of the official court "responsible for judging and punishing all crimes committed in interstellar space"?
   A. Supreme Court of the Galaxy
   B. Galactic Court of Justice
   C. The Galaxy Tribunal of Justice

2. (True or False) According to the Robot's analysis, the moving lights atop the energized fence acted as a radar pickup.

3. What was used to instantly transport the *Jupiter 2* crew from the campsite to the courtroom?
   A. Matter-energy converter
   B. Molecular transfer beam
   C. Annular confinement transporter

4. When the memory machine looked into John's mind and displayed the past, who was shown conducting Will's final physical exam before the launch of the *Jupiter 2* from Earth?

5. Who referred to the alien memory machine as a "truth serum with pictures"?

6. How many hours did the judge allocate Will to locate Smith after the doctor escaped from the camp?

7. Although Smith was found guilty of all crimes, why were the charges against him dropped?

MEMORY BANKS OVERLOAD

Per the sentencing guidelines of the galactic court, what was the penalty for aiding a witness to escape?

SPACE AGE FAST FACT

When Jonathan Harris first asked Irwin Allen for "special guest star" billing at the tail end of each episode's opening credits, the *Lost in Space* producer initially refused, stating that viewers would assume that Harris wouldn't be returning every week. Allen eventually relented and Harris' "special guest star" status was the first of its kind on any television show.

2.7
The Android
Machine

Original Airdate: 10.26.66
Earth Year

Ship's Log: *While experimenting with an intergalactic department store's ordering machine, Dr. Smith accidentally requests an unemotional android who quickly finds her way into the space colonists' hearts.*

That Does Not Compute

In the pilot and initial episodes of the series' first season, the Robot was a true threat to the *Jupiter 2* crew (with the exception of Dr. Smith), an automaton of impressive physical strength who crushed Maj. West's helmet, which was rated to resist 10,000 pounds of force. This episode is a classic example of the transformation that the Robot has undergone: from a mobile arsenal of electrical blasters to a comic straight-man to Dr. Smith. His whining about Verda the android "embarrassing" him in front of the Robinson children is a sad commentary on the deterioration of the Robot's character.

Trivia Challenge

1. How many cans of deutronium did John and Maj. West estimate was needed for the *Jupiter 2*'s launch?
   A. Four

    B. Five
    C. Six

2. Who manufactured the metallic android, Verda?
    A. Unit 12, R.D.S. Remote Unit
    B. Beto II, S.I. 7 Supreme Unit
    C. The Galaxy Manufacturing & Shipping Co., Ltd.

3. Which historic event did the Robot recount in Will and
   Penny's "classroom."
    A. The first manned U.S. space flight
    B. Columbus' discovery of America
    C. The Wright Brothers first airplane flight aboard
       the *Kitty Hawk*

4. (True or False) The Robot's computer was both analog
   and digital.

5. How did Verda "embarrass" the Robot?

6. What was the name of the intergalactic department
   store that owned and operated the ordering machine?
    A. The Universal Department Stores, Inc.
    B. Celestial Department Stores
    C. Intergalactic Mail Order Company

7. Identify the department store's complaint manager for
   Area 17.

MEMORY BANKS OVERLOAD

(Fill in the Blank)

Possessing human qualities by the episode's conclusion, Verda was transformed into Special Deluxe Android, Model _____, and would be used in the future to train other androids.

SPACE AGE FAST FACT

Dee Hartford, the actress who played Verda the android, was the sister-in-law of Groucho Marx, one of Irwin Allen's major financial backers for *Lost in Space* and a frequent visitor on the series set.

2.8
THE DEADLY GAMES OF GAMMA 6

Original Airdate: 11.02.66 Earth Year

Ship's Log: *John is invited to compete in a galactic fighting match against alien warriors, but the real reason for the games is to determine whether Earth can be attacked and conquered.*

That Does Not Compute

After Dr. Smith volunteers to fight in the galactic games, John orders the Robot to use any means necessary to insure that Smith doesn't leave the campsite. In the very next scene we see him behind bars in a padlocked cage that could hold at least ten humans. Just before the *Jupiter 2* blasted-off from Priplanus in this season's premiere episode, John told the crew to discard any unnecessary items due to the ship's weight problem for launch. Suddenly we find out they are carting around an enormous cage. Did anyone see the U-Haul trailer behind the *Jupiter 2* when they left Priplanus?

Trivia Challenge

1. What was Myko's profession?

2. How many viewers watched the televised Gamma Games throughout the galaxy?

    A. Tens of millions
    B. Hundreds of millions
    C. Over a trillion

3. (Fill in the Blank) Myko snidely commented: "It is said throughout the galaxy that Earthmen are _____ and without courage."

4. What was Dr. Smith's alleged "payoff" if he successfully recruited John to fight in the Gamma Games and he was crowned galactic champion?

5. Who said Earth people were "strange and unpredictable"?
    A. Myko
    B. Gromack
    C. The gray-bearded alien leader

6. What was inscribed on the back of Dr. Smith's blue fighting robe?
    A. NEVER FEAR, SMITH IS HERE
    B. TIGER SMITH
    C. SNAKEBITE SMITH

7. What type of cameras were used to televise the Gamma Games throughout the galaxy?
    A. Duranium
    B. Digitized
    C. Solarized

8. Identify the "weapon" that John used to win in the contest against the dematerialized Geoo.

9. What was the name of the Russian roulette-type revolving laser turret?
    A. Wheel of Life
    B. Spin-of-Death
    C. Circle of Destiny

MEMORY BANKS OVERLOAD

Believing Smith to be overmatched by the midget, Geoo, who threw a towel onto the fight mat?

SPACE AGE FAST FACT

Jonathan Harris once played a guest villain on Guy Williams' *Zorro* television series, but interestingly enough the two actors never mentioned or discussed their original meeting during the entire three-year period they worked together on *Lost in Space*.

ALPHA CONTROL INTELLIGENCE DOSSIER

#1-57566-233-7
Judy Robinson

1. What was Judy Robinson's middle name?
   - A. Marie
   - B. Elana
   - C. Eileen

2. (True or False) She was born on February 26, 1978 in Los Angeles, California USA.

3. Which description best fit Judy as a child?
   - A. Gregarious and outgoing
   - B. Brilliant and moody
   - C. Backward and shy

4. Identify her cousin with whom she maintained a close relationship right up to the day of the *Jupiter 2*'s launch?
   - A. Janice
   - B. Jane
   - C. Joan

5. (Fill in the blank with the correct number) During her teenage years, Judy's blue eyes and blond hair caught the attention of several boys. Maureen, however, refused to allow her to go on a date until the age of _____.

6. In which field did she plan to pursue a career?
   - A. Photography and film-making

   B. Acting, singing, and dancing
   C. Botany and hydroponic gardening

7. Emotional and slightly rebellious by nature, Judy initially voiced her opposition to joining her siblings and parents as the first family in space. Why did she change her mind about accompanying them on the colonization mission?

MEMORY BANKS OVERLOAD

Where did Judy complete her high school education?

TECH SPECS #4

Match the letter to the correct parts and equipment on the E.V.A. Thruster.

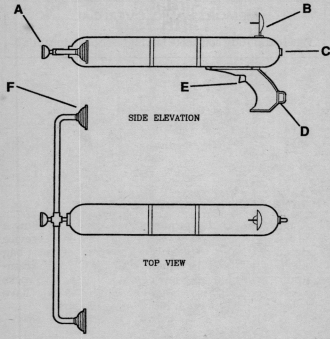

SIDE ELEVATION

TOP VIEW

E.V.A. THRUSTER

Technical drawing by Edwin E. Echols.

1. ____ Beacon
2. ____ Thruster exhaust
3. ____ Thrust control
4. ____ Braking thruster
5. ____ Line coupling
6. ____ Propellant intake

2.9
THE THIEF FROM
OUTER SPACE

Original Airdate: 11.09.66
Earth Year

Ship's Log: *Will becomes an apprentice to a galactic thief who has roamed the cosmos for centuries in search of a beautiful princess.*

That Does Not Compute

During the pre-credits sequence, close-up shots show a thief who can barely get his hand through a small crevice between two rocks to steal Will's wrench and tool bag while he is repairing the mineral drill. But when the camera pulls back for a full view of the scene, the two rocks are separated by a gap large enough for Will to have crawled between them on his hands and knees.

Trivia Challenge

1. What was the Thief's self-proclaimed title?
     A. "The Supreme Thief of the Galaxy"
     B. "The Terror of the Cosmos"
     C. "Galactic Thief Extraordinaire"

2. Stating that his face looked familiar, where did the Thief believe he had met Dr. Smith before?
   A. In jail or at a thieves' market
   B. Quonos III's prison planet
   C. At Sheik Abul-Kabba's bachelor party

3. How long had the Thief been searching the galaxy for his lost princess?
   A. "The life-span of six lions"
   B. "Over two hundred years"
   C. "A millennium"

4. What was the first rule of a thief?
   A. "Never steal anything on an empty stomach"
   B. "Eat while you think, think while you eat"
   C. "Everything can be stolen *once*"

5. What did the Thief use as a compass to point the way to the Princess' location?

6. Identify the interdimensional space vehicle that the Thief used to transport himself and others from his asteroid home to the surface of the Robinsons' planet.

MEMORY BANKS OVERLOAD

What was the thief's rule #21?

SPACE AGE FAST FACT

A new father, Malachi Throne accepted the role as "The Thief from Outer Space," solely for the opportunity to play a character who established a relationship with a child.

2.10
CURSE OF COUSIN SMITH

Original Airdate: 11.16.66
Earth Year

Ship's Log: *Dr. Smith's cousin lands on the Robinsons' planet in an attempt to murder his relative, making him sole heir of the family fortune.*

That Does Not Compute

If the *Jupiter 2* crew is indeed lost in the cosmos and Alpha Control back on Earth can't locate the missing space colonists, then how is it possible for Dr. Smith's cousin to find them so easily?

Trivia Challenge

1. How did Will cut his chin?

2. (Fill in the Blank) Jeremiah Smith referred to himself as a "citizen of the _____."

3. Which planet did Jeremiah "touch upon" during his "wandering" through the galaxy?

4. Identify the new piece of equipment that John and Maj. West were installing in the Chariot.
   A. Transistor unit
   B. Guidance system
   C. Scanner antenna

5. What type of weapon was Jeremiah originally hiding under his clothing (and dropped on the ground)?

6. Name the deceased "rich, arrogant, and untrustworthy" matriarch of the Smith family whose fortune created the blood feud between Dr. Smith and his cousin, Jeremiah.

7. What intergalactic gangster did Jeremiah contact to request a universal gambling machine to be delivered to the planet?

MEMORY BANKS OVERLOAD

What was Col. Jeremiah Smith's middle name?

SPACE AGE FAST FACT

During the long breaks between the filming of his scenes, Jonathan Harris did needlepoint or worked crossword puzzles on the set to help focus his concentration.

2.11
WEST OF MARS
Original Airdate: 11.30.66
Earth Year

Ship's Log: *A galactic gunslinger who looks exactly like Dr. Smith arrives on the Robinsons' planet to hide from a relentless space enforcer bent on taking him back to be executed for his crimes.*

That Does Not Compute

When Zeno first encounters his doppelganger, he forces him at gunpoint to back against a huge, encompassing rock. Yet, when a front shot of Zeno is required in the scene, the camera peers over Dr. Smith's left shoulder as if only half of his body is positioned against the boulder.

When the space enforcer's cage-like ship lifts-off, it immediately engages an energized field that surrounds the exterior of the bars. Although the props department utilizes the same cellophane wrap as with the charged fence in "The Prisoners of Space" episode, this time it hangs like a loose shower curtain about the ship. At one point, the enforcer even pulls it apart to stick his hand-held telescope out into space to determine his position in the cosmos.

Where did our intrepid space family Robinson get a mine car and the iron rails for it to travel on to the smelter?

Trivia Challenge

1. Who described a "superswift" as "one who can draw and fire his space weapon in the blinking of an eye"?

2. (Fill in the Blank) Dr. Smith referred to the desperado as "the great, the illustrious Zeno, the peerless, fearless, noble knight _____ of outer space."

3. Which one of the following was Zeno's profession before he "took up killing" as a superswift?
   A. Esteemed scientist
   B. Brilliant mathematician
   C. Galactic bounty hunter

4. Which organization employed the space enforcer?
   A. The United Federation of Galaxies
   B. The Galactic Federation
   C. The United Alliance of Planets

5. The faux Smith threatened to rip out the Robot's wires, smash his transformer, and vaporize his electrodes. What did the space outlaw promise to do with what was left of the automaton?
   A. Turn him into a trash can
   B. Melt him down into beer cans
   C. Roll him down a hill

6. What was the space enforcer's name?

7. Which *Jupiter 2* crew member called Dr. Smith "our conquering hero"?

8. (True or False) When confronted about his six-shooter, the Smith impersonator explained that he found the pistol in Lost Springs Canyon.

9. How many space credits was the reward for Zeno's capture?
   A. 10,000
   B. 20,000
   C. 50,000

MEMORY BANKS OVERLOAD

What was the name of "the scourge of outer space" who challenged "Zeno" to a duel?

SPACE AGE FAST FACT

After the monkey that played Debby the Bloop not only bit Angela Cartwright several times but also her baby brother, Christopher, Irwin Allen refused to hire the chimpanzee for any further episodes. He changed his mind after the series' animal trainer had her teeth extracted.

2.12
A VISIT TO HADES

Original Airdate: 12.07.66
Earth Year

Ship's Log: *Dr. Smith experiments with an alien harp and is instantly transported to what he thinks is Hades, but in reality is nothing more than a jail cell for an imprisoned political revolutionist.*

That Does Not Compute

The monsters and alien creatures on the series are typically very frightening in appearance, especially considering the budgetary restraints and the legendary frugality of Irwin Allen; unfortunately, the dragon-like creature in this episode certainly wins the award for the most *fake*-looking monster to have ever appeared in *Lost in Space*. It is painfully obvious that the creature is constructed of nothing more than papier-mâché, and pales in comparison to the bulbous-headed monster with the webbed feet and hands.

During the fight scene between Don and Morbus, the major repeatedly connects with his fists only a fraction of a second before the alien dematerializes and then Don swings wildly as if he strikes at nothing but air.

Trivia Challenge

1. During a flashback to his youth, Smith was seen pilfering exams from a teacher's desk. How much money did he receive in exchange for the purloined test papers?
   A. "Fifty bucks"
   B. "A hundred dollars"
   C. "Twenty dollars and a couple of cheeseburger baskets from the drive-in"

2. Whose birthday cake did Smith steal a slice from while nobody was looking?

3. What did Dr. Smith promise to do in order to have all of his "sins" forgiven and an opportunity to receive a "second chance" at life?

4. According to the Robot, what in actuality was the place that Smith believed was "Hades"?

5. (True or False) Smith used a sledgehammer from the *Jupiter 2* in an unsuccessful attempt at destroying the harp.

6. (Fill in the Blank) Morbus considered the musical instrument "a sort of _____ keylock and jailer."

7. (Fill in the Blank) Morbus couldn't find any reference in his big book for "women _____."

8. Identify the "pure of heart" character who was finally able to break the harp, thus opening Morbus' prison gates?

MEMORY BANKS OVERLOAD

Identify Morbus' peaceful homeworld.

SPACE AGE FAST FACT

June Lockhart, who was acting in the play *Steel Magnolias* at the time of Guy Williams' death in 1989, saw a figure with a black coat and a white scarf in one of the makeup mirrors after a performance, but when she spun around no one was in the room. After returning home, she called Williams' wife, who confirmed that the black and white ensemble was the actor's favorite outfit.

LASTING IMPRESSIONS

All good things must come to an end . . . Match the series events or Jupiter 2 equipment with the episodes in which they made their final appearance.

1. _____ Black & white telecast
2. _____ John *heard* logging their voyage
3. _____ The Chariot
4. _____ The Space Pod
5. _____ Ended series run on CBS
6. _____ John *writing* in his logbook
7. _____ Smith wears his beige outfit top
8. _____ The Robot plays Will's guitar

A. "The Oasis"
B. "A Visit to Hades"
C. "Ghost in Space"
D. "Follow the Leader"
E. "Junkyard in Space"
F. "The Magic Mirror"
G. "Castles in Space"
H. "One of Our Dogs is Missing"

MEMORY BANKS OVERLOAD

Identify the last episode to be helmed by frequent *Lost in Space* director Don Richardson.

VOICE ACTIVATED

Match the robots, alien creatures, and galactic devices with the actors who provided the voices.

1. _____ "Deadliest of the Species" Female Robot
2. _____ "The Questing Beast" Gundemar
3. _____ Alien Judge in "Prisoners of Space"
4. _____ Cybernetic Leader on "The Ghost Planet"
5. _____ "All That Glitters" Disk
6. _____ Little Joe in "The Curse of Cousin Smith"
7. _____ Purple Leader of "The Mechanical Men"
8. _____ "Space Destructors" Alien Machine
9. _____ "Space Creature"

A. Michael Fox
B. Joey Tata
C. Allan Melvin
D. Bartell LaRue
E. Sue England
F. Gregory Morton
G. Ted Lehmann
H. June Foray
I. Ronald Gans

MEMORY BANKS OVERLOAD #1

Who supplied the voices for Zalto's dummy in "Rocket to Earth" and the robot judge in "Hunter's Moon"?

MEMORY BANKS OVERLOAD #2

Which actor provided the vocal track for the possessive, disembodied alien spirit, Canto?

2.13
WRECK OF THE ROBOT

Original Airdate: 12.14.66
Earth Year

Ship's Log: *Three black-robed aliens dismantle the Robot in hopes of learning the principle behind all Earth machines as part of a diabolical plot to attack and subjugate the human race.*

That Does Not Compute

During the pre-credits bowling sequence, Dr. Smith's pink ball rolls past the pins and over a small mound, but when a black ball with a lit fuse comes back neither Dr. Smith nor Will notice it is a different color. Even when the ball is only a few feet from them as it rolls backwards on the bowling lane, Will says, "It's coming back."

Why does John need to drill holes in the Robot's waist plate atop the leg section prior to reattaching the mechanical man's body? Wouldn't the screw holes already be there from when the aliens dismantled the Robot?

During the climax when the Robot is trying to destroy the alien machine-controlling device, the wind defense almost blows one of the alien's derby off his head, but in the following scene the hat is squared perfectly on his head.

Trivia Challenge

1. What was Don's "deep, dark secret"?

2. Who referred to Dr. Smith as a "cruel, cold man"?

3. Identify the title of the book that Will was reading in his cabin when his father entered and told him that the Robot had been found, but dismantled.
   A. *Beyond the Solar System*
   B. *Intergalactic Space Flight*
   C. *The Complete Space Atlas*

4. What "strange sensation" did the Robot register in his sensors?

5. Which piece of equipment's hose was used by the aliens in an attempt to choke Judy?
   A. The plant purifying unit
   B. The compressor unit
   C. The automatic laundry

6. Who made the comment that "nothing is perfect . . . neither man nor machines"?

MEMORY BANKS OVERLOAD

Identify the alien race to which the three black-robed, derby-wearing life-forms belonged?

SPACE AGE FAST FACT

Although Guy Williams was originally hired to be the star of *Lost in Space*, by the second season Jonathan Harris' salary was $2,750 an episode, compared to Williams' $2,500.

2.14
THE DREAM
MONSTER

Original Airdate: 12.21.66
Earth Year

Ship's Log: *To make his golden, faceless android more human, a Dr. Frankenstein-like biophysicist steals the Robinsons' finest human qualities, leaving the Jupiter 2 crew dispassionate and apathetic.*

That Does Not Compute

After Dr. Smith and Maj. West free themselves from the magnetic manacles in the laboratory, they make their way to the quietly sleeping Sesmar. As Smith and Don turn the corner, the pursuing Raddion (played by Dawson Palmer) mistakenly misses his cue and takes one step forward. Quickly realizing his error, he retreats behind a wall immediately.

Trivia Challenge

1. Who assumed Penny was suffering from "heat stroke" after she began "babbling" about her encounter with Sesmar and the android Raddion?

2. Why was Dr. Smith banned from the *Jupiter 2* campsite?

3. What did Sesmar call his pair of small-sized golden androids?

MEMORY BANKS OVERLOAD #1

Match the following *Jupiter* 2 crew members with the "cardinal virtues" they possessed (according to Dr. Smith).

1. _____ John
2. _____ Maureen
3. _____ Will
4. _____ Judy
5. _____ Penny
6. _____ Don

A. Warm and sensitive
B. Solid, technical know-how
C. Hope, courage, loyalty and love
D. Aggressiveness
E. Great capacity for love
F. Full of enthusiasm and eagerness for learning

4. According to Earth "reckoning," how long had Sesmar lived on the planet?
   A. "Six months"
   B. "Almost a year"
   C. "Going on two years"

5. Identify the miniature device worn on Sesmar's wrist which he used to make immediate repairs to the *Jupiter* 2's "atmospheric modifier."
   A. Matter materializer
   B. Molecular replicator
   C. Matter-energy conversion unit

6. What did the biophysicist utilize as a means of transportation from the planet surface to his "flying laboratory"?
   A. Maser beam
   B. Molecular transporter
   C. Conveyor tube

7. What was Raddion's life span?
   A. "Practically eternal"
   B. "More than a human brain can comprehend"
   C. "Thousands of years"

MEMORY BANKS OVERLOAD #2

Identify the small device that Sesmar gave John and Maj. West to "increase the efficiency" of the Robot.

SPACE AGE FAST FACTS

Guest star John Abbot had never seen an episode of *Lost in Space* prior to his appearance on the series, nor did he ever watch any of the shows afterwards, later commenting in interviews that he didn't approve of Jonathan Harris' "stupid kind of acting."

2.15
THE GOLDEN MAN
Original Airdate: 12.28.66
Earth Year

Ship's Log: *The Robinsons and Dr. Smith learn a valuable lesson about outward appearances when a handsome, golden-skinned humanoid and an ugly, frog-like alien land on the planet to wage war against each other.*

That Does Not Compute

It's a stretch of the imagination to believe that Judy is actually trapped in an electronic mine field when half-buried, inflated and multi-colored beach balls are used as the explosive charges, especially when the air stems can be seen as Keema carries Judy out of the mined area in his arms. In addition, why couldn't she simply walk between the balls (which were two to three feet apart) as Keema did when he "saved" her?

Trivia Challenge

1. Who assumed that an alien ship spotted entering the planet's atmosphere was "a falling star"?

2. What did Dr. Smith fear was in the elegantly-wrapped gift box?

3. Who covertly traveled to Keema's camp to determine his "true motives"?

4. What were the terms of the golden-skinned alien's "mutually advantageous deal" with Dr. Smith?

5. Who called Keema "as handsome in spirit as he is in appearance"?

6. Who made the character evaluation: "Mr. Keema is much too handsome and charming to lie"?

MEMORY BANKS OVERLOAD

Identify the "very deadly and destructive" weapon Keema intended to use in his war against his frog-like nemesis?

SPACE AGE FAST FACT

Mr. Keema was originally scripted to transform into a werewolf at the conclusion of the episode, rather than the hideous monster with an oversized pumpkin-shaped head and distorted figures.

2.16
THE GIRL FROM THE GREEN DIMENSION

Original Airdate: 01.04.67 Earth Year

Ship's Log: *The age old dilemma of one woman and two men takes on new meaning when the green alien lady comes calling on Dr. Smith again and in the process infuriates her old lover.*

That Does Not Compute

When she made her first appearance in "Wild Adventure," Athena was referred to simply as the "green lady" or the "green alien," even at the conclusion of the episode after a hypnotized and space-suited Dr. Smith frolicked with her in the cosmos. When she is first recognized in this episode, Dr. Smith and everyone else immediately calls her "Athena," as if they're on a first-name basis. We can only assume that they exchanged cards and letters since their first encounter.

In "Wild Adventure," the Robot said Athena originated from the "Green Mist," but in this episode she states that she is from the "Green Dimension." Could the Robot (who was noted in an earlier episode as "never being wrong") have erred in his original report?

Trivia Challenge

1. Identify the meteorological event that transformed the electron telescope.

2. How many canisters of deutronium did Smith steal from the drill site to quench Athena's "thirst"?
   A. Two
   B. Three
   C. Four

3. Who turned Will green "as a pickle"?

4. According to John, why were the fuel canisters not stored for safekeeping in the *Jupiter 2*?

5. (True or False) As foreseen by the newly prophetic Dr. Smith, Judy injured the middle finger of her right hand on a thorn.

6. Who offered to teach Dr. Smith a "few karate tricks" in preparation for his fight with Urso?

7. After Urso forced Smith to peer into the telescope, the doctor glimpsed a future scene of the *Jupiter 2* crew conducting a funeral. Thinking that he was going to die, what did Smith plan to leave Will?
   A. His "taped memoirs"
   B. The "priceless collection of self-portraits"
   C. His "masterpieces of artwork"

MEMORY BANKS OVERLOAD

How many minutes did it take Dr. Smith to "run" three hundred yards back to the *Jupiter 2* after Athena originally materialized on the planet?

SPACE AGE FAST FACT

Series costume designer Paul Zastupnevich attempted to give each of the main characters an individual costume color and always tried to avoid having extras or guest stars wear the same color schemes as the show's regular cast.

ALPHA CONTROL INTELLIGENCE DOSSIER

#0-7860-0315-4
Penny Robinson

1. What was Penny Robinson's birthdate?

2. (True or False) Her middle name was Marie.

3. Identify the newly-formed program established by Alpha Control to recruit young people for future colonization missions which Penny joined after the Robinson family relocated from California to Houston.
   A. Space Cadets
   B. Space Scouts
   C. Future Astronauts of America (FAA)

4. (True or False) Shortly after becoming a member of the Houston chapter of the junior space program, Penny was elected president.

5. According to Alpha Control's psychological tests, which of the following best described the youngest daughter of the Robinson family?
   A. Tomboyish with a tendency to indulge in fantasy
   B. Feminine and overly concerned with physical appearance
   C. Immature and interested in listening to popular music rather than socializing

6. How old was Penny at the time of the *Jupiter* 2 launch?
   A. Ten

B. Twelve
C. Fourteen

MEMORY BANKS OVERLOAD

(Fill in the blank with the correct number)

A brilliant and gifted child, Penny was advanced several grades in school and was tested as having an I.Q. of _____ when she and her family embarked on their colonization mission to Alpha Centauri.

TECH SPECS #5

Match the letter to the correct equipment or room aboard the Jupiter 2.

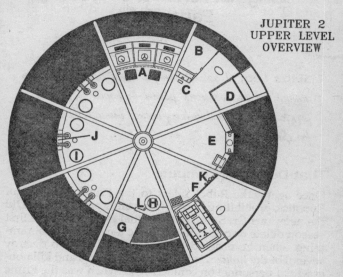

JUPITER 2
UPPER LEVEL
OVERVIEW

Technical drawing by Edwin E. Echols.

1. _____ Air lock
2. _____ Space Pod communications
3. _____ Flight control
4. _____ Elevator
5. _____ Communications/ aux control
6. _____ Suspended animation control
7. _____ Storage
8. _____ Systems control
9. _____ Freezing tubes
10. _____ Hatch
11. _____ Cabin pressure controls
12. _____ Space Pod bay

2.17
THE QUESTING
BEAST

Original Airdate: 01.11.67
Earth Year

Ship's Log: *A galactic knight on a quest for honor arrives on the Robinsons' planet in hopes of slaying a ferocious dragon that he has pursued through the universe for years.*

That Does Not Compute

Once again, the Robot refers to the Prime Directive of Robotics, prohibiting him from harming any humans. Did the nefarious Dr. Smith in the initial episodes of the first season delete or override this basic tenet of his programming when he ordered the mechanical man to destroy several of the *Jupiter 2*'s life support systems and kill nonessential personnel on contact? If so, when was the Prime Directive's inhibition against harming human beings reinstated in the automaton's programming?

Trivia Challenge

1. Identify the piece of equipment that the Robot was attempting to repair from behind the safety of a lead shield.

2. When a ransom could not be paid, whose head did Sir Sagramonte threaten to cut off per the Rules of Chivalry?

3. Which one of the following was the name of the knight's homeworld?
    A. Zebed
    B. Praetor
    C. Antare

4. What was the name of Sagramonte's bespectacled canine companion?
    A. Barkley
    B. Bayer
    C. Baxter

5. Identify the "scurrying" and "annoying" creatures that frightened even the fire-breathing Gundemar dragon.

6. The lady dragon asserted that "teleportation" was her method of interstellar travel. What was the one word Sagramonte used to explain his transportation from planet to planet and galaxy to galaxy?

7. (Fill in the Blank) What did Smith tell Will he regretted "for the first time" in his "miserable life"?

MEMORY BANKS OVERLOAD

(Fill in the Blank)

Sir Sagramonte explained to Dr. Smith about his homeworld: "We are a people so old in civilization and so wise in science that in order to maintain our _____ we've returned to an earlier, simpler age . . . the age of innocence and childhood."

SPACE AGE FAST FACT

Carey Wilbur wrote this and many other episodes of *Lost in Space*, including a story planned for the fourth season called "Malice in Wonderland," featuring Will, Penny, the Robot, and Dr. Smith as both themselves and as characters from the classic childrens' story, including Jonathan Harris in drag as the Queen of Hearts.

The entire cast in a first season publicity photo

"The Reluctant
Stowaway"

Never fear,
Smith is here

Will Robinson examining the fungus creatures surrounding Jimmy Hapgood's ship in "Welcome Stranger"

Will and the "Invaders from the Fifth Dimension"

Space parents John and
Maureen Robinson

A 1965 Christmas card
from the gang

Maureen, Penny and
Will with some
"Monster Plants"

The "Ghost in Space"
whom Dr. Smith was
convinced was his
Uncle Thaddeus

Those fabulous
Robinson women
model the latest
space fashions

Torin Thatcher as
"The Space Trader"

John Robinson after being possessed by the spirit of Canto in "Follow the Leader"

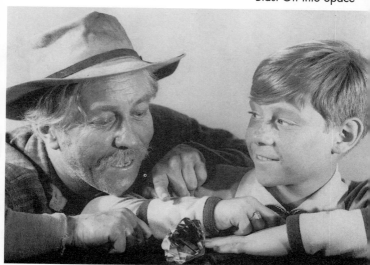

Will and Nerim (Strother Martin) in "Blast Off Into Space"

Verda (Dee Hartford) and the Robot in "The Android Machine"

The Enforcer (Allan Melvin) mistakes Dr. Smith for Zeno the gunslinger in "West of Mars"

Vitina Marcus as Athena, "The Girl from the Green Dimension"

The Robot pilots Zahrk's space cutter in "Mutiny in Space"

Smith makes a point to Thor (Bern Hoffman) in
"The Space Vikings"

Al Lewis, better known as Grandpa Munster, gueststars as
the Great Zalto in "Rocket to Earth"

Smith and Niolani
(Francine York), leader
of the Condor Nation of
female warriors

The miniature "Mechanical Men" take Dr. Smith prisoner

Mr. Archon (John Carradine) eyes Judy in "The Galaxy Gift"

Space cadets Will and Penny in their second season

Smith with one of the cyborgs he planned to use to conquer the universe in "The Space Destructors"

Penny with the mischievous J-5 (Lou Wagner) in "The Haunted Lighthouse"

The very model of a 1998 family:
The Robinsons in Season Two

Penny assumes her role
as "Princess of Space"

Dr. Smith with Chronos
"The Time Merchant" (John Crawford)

Maureen pursued by the Hairy Mutant
(aka the Horny Mutant) in "One of Our Dogs is Missing"

Grizzled convicts
ponder escape in
"Fugitives in Space"

Stanley Adams as Tybo,
lead carrot in "The
Great Vegetable
Rebellion"

2.18
THE TOYMAKER
Original Airdate: 01.26.67
Earth Year

Ship's Log: *Dr. Smith and Will become trapped in an abandoned Celestial Department Store's ordering machine which is being operated by one of the company's retired toymakers.*

That Does Not Compute

During several scenes involving Mr. O.M.'s wind-up monster guard, the furry creature's front key sporadically stops and starts rotating. In one instance, when the key mechanism comes to a standstill, the monster gives it one brief turn itself. When Will removes the key completely, the wind-up creature sags forward, then suddenly raises its arms and growls one last time before collapsing from lack of power.

As Will and Dr. Smith remove the boards to the doorway back to Earth, they turn and see the monster growling and gaining on them from across the large, open room. But in the next scene, Mr. O.M. and the wind-up monster turn a sharp corner and enter the room through a narrow passageway between two shelf units.

When the toy soldier grabs John, the wind-up key in its back isn't rotating at all.

Trivia Challenge

1. What did Dr. Smith call the abandoned department store ordering machine?
   - A. "Intergalactic mail order catalog"
   - B. "Universal mail order machine"
   - C. "A get-anything-you-want android machine"

2. Who called the Robot "just a machine"?

3. What did Mr. O.M.'s initials represent?

4. (Fill in the Blank) The Robot's analysis determined that the department store ordering machine "operated on a _____ dimensional process."

5. What did Dr. Smith order from the device but didn't receive?

6. Mr. O.M. planned to ship Smith to a planet in Andromeda where the children had a particular preference for animated toys. How many feet tall were the boys and girls on that world?
   - A. Fifty
   - B. Seventy-five
   - C. One hundred

7. Why did Mr. O.M. close down his toy outlet on Earth?

8. Why was the Robot whistling while searching for Will and Dr. Smith inside the toy factory?

9. Which type of device did Mr. Zumdish use to destroy the obsolete ordering machine?
   - A. Fusion grenade
   - B. Vacuum activator
   - C. Atomic detonator

MEMORY BANKS OVERLOAD

Identify the shape-conforming plug from the Celestial Department Stores that Mr. Zumdish offered to the *Jupiter 2* crew as a "free sample" to seal the potentially dangerous fissure.

SPACE AGE FAST FACT

Episode writers Bob and Wanda Duncan actually had a two-part story titled "The Great Space Race" approved for *Lost in Space*'s fourth season, but the series was canceled after its third year and the teleplay was never filmed.

2.19
MUTINY IN SPACE

Original Airdate: 01.01.67
Earth Year

Ship's Log: *Once again banned from the Jupiter 2 campsite, Dr. Smith discovers an alien space cutter manned by a revenge-seeking admiral who was set adrift by a mutineering former crew mate.*

That Does Not Compute

During one scene aboard Zahrk's ship, the Robot makes a raspy comment while steering the vessel and the admiral asks if the automaton is losing his voice. The Robot quickly replies that his "computers are dry." Since when does the mechanical man require water or other liquids to lubricate his computerized systems?

When John and Maj. West activate the negative electromagnetic beam and pull Zahrk's ship back to the planet, the alien vessel is actually shown in the atmosphere going backwards. Aboard the craft, however, the Robot notes that an "unidentified planet is dead ahead," indicating that they are still in outer space as the beam reverses their course.

Trivia Challenge

1. What rank did the admiral appoint Will after he was first captured aboard the vessel?

2. How often did Zahrk expect Will to write his mother after they set out on their voyage to seek revenge against the admiral's mutineer?
   A. Once a week
   B. Twice a month
   C. Once a month

3. (Fill in the Blank) Impressed with the young Robinson boy's nautical skills aboard the ship, Zahrk promoted Will to the rank of _____ and promised to advance him to first mate "in a year or two."

4. Who discovered the alien ship's logbook?

5. What was the "standing order" aboard the admiral's ship, which cleared the head, toned the muscles and stimulated the nerves?

6. Where did Zahrk hide the written combination to his pantry locker?
   A. Under his mantle chronologer
   B. On his left wrist
   C. Under his hat

MEMORY BANKS OVERLOAD

Name Admiral Zahrk's mutineering former mate.

SPACE AGE FAST FACT

Many of the characters' names in frequent *Lost in Space* writer Peter Packer's teleplays were anagrams of what they were portraying in the episode. Nerim in "Blast Off into Space" was Miner, Raddion for Android in "The Dream Monster" and so on. Anyone care to solve the puzzle of Zahrk's name in this episode?

2.20
THE SPACE VIKINGS
Original Airdate: 02.08.67
Earth Year

Ship's Log: *While rehearsing a play, Will, Penny, and Dr. Smith accidentally summon the ancient Norse Gods from the void of interstellar space.*

That Does Not Compute

When Dr. Smith throws Thor's golden hammer toward the *Jupiter 2*, the crew assumes that the subsequent explosion is an "earth tremor." Obviously the space pioneers are not on terra firma, so why do they almost always insist on referring to any planetary shaking of volcanic or tectonic origin as "earthquakes" or "earth tremors"?

Trivia Challenge

1. What did Dr. Smith utilize to reproduce "a perfect facsimile" of Thor's gloves?
    A. Electronic Synthesizer Unit
    B. Servomatic Replicating Device
    C. Central Reproduction Terminal

2. What was the name of the singing Valkerie who appeared on a flying horse and transported Dr. Smith and the Robot to the feast hall of Valhalla?

3. Identify the "terrible creatures" that attacked Asgard, the home of the Gods?

4. Which nickname did Thor give to Dr. Smith?
   A. "Zach"
   B. "Smitty"
   C. "Doc"

5. According to the Robot, what were the two "weapons" that Smith commanded "best"?

6. (Fill in the Blank) In a desperate attempt to convince Thor that he possessed inhuman strength, Dr. Smith squeezed water from two _____ that resembled rocks.

MEMORY BANKS OVERLOAD

Name the frozen underworld inhabited by taunting elves and trolls.

SPACE AGE FAST FACT

CBS commissioned a survey and discovered that teachers in schools around the country were using Dr. Smith's alliteratives for the Robot as learning tools to increase students' vocabulary.

THE NAME GAME
PART I

We hope you are one of those unique and talented persons who never forgets a name.

1. Name the two episodes in which Will, Dr. Smith and the Robot discover an apparently aged version of the *Jupiter 2* spaceship.

2. What was the name of the Beach Boys tune sung by Will and Judy around a campfire in "Castles in Space"?

3. He was the alien judge presiding over a galactic tribunal in "Prisoners of Space." What was his name?
   A. Ekmah
   B. Iko
   C. Vax

4. Identify the two episodes in which the *Jupiter 2* crew were threatened by erupting volcanoes.

5. The cowardly Dr. Smith actually fired a laser in four installments of the series during its three-year run. Name the episodes.

6. In "The Reluctant Stowaway," Dr. Smith rendered a military police officer unconscious and dumped his body through the *Jupiter 2*'s waste disposal chute. What was the MP's name?

7. Identify the ancient Canto's homeworld in "Follow the Leader."

    A. Praxis
    B. Benzar
    C. Quasti

8. What were the names of the two episodes that showed John turning against the rest of the *Jupiter 2* crew?

9. The director of first season's "There Were Giants in the Earth" has two sons who are now well known actors. What are their names?

10. Which Woody Allen movie used props from *Lost in Space*?
    A. *Bananas*
    B. *Sleeper*
    C. *Everything You Ever Wanted to Know About Sex, But Were Afraid to Ask*

11. In which series installment could Will not pronounce the word "ostracized"?

MEMORY BANKS OVERLOAD #1

Name the episode in which Maureen used an automatic device to instantly prepare potato chips.

---

12. Who was the Alpha Control officer Will attempted to contact from Hatfield Four Corners?
    A. Col. Mason
    B. Gen. Saxon
    C. Lt. Gen. Wellington

13. Name the planet Will suggested the *Jupiter 2* had crash landed on in "The Hungry Sea."

14. Which western series appeared opposite of *Lost in Space* on another network during its entire three-year run?
    A. *Bonanza*
    B. *The Virginian*
    C. *Big Valley*

15. What nickname did Jimmy Hapgood give Don?
    A. "Sonny"
    B. "Fly Boy"
    C. "Flyin' Man"

16. Name the four episodes in which the *Jupiter 2* was forced to make a crash landing.

17. In three separate series segments the galactic vehicle had to make an emergency liftoff from a planet. Name this trio of episodes.

18. The June 28–July 4, 1997 Special Collectors' Issue of *TV Guide* named the "100 Greatest Episodes of All Time." Which installment of *Lost in Space* was chosen as number 76?

19. Identify the product the Robot pitched in commercials during the early 1970s?
    A. Diehard batteries
    B. Snack Pack pudding
    C. Brute cologne

20. What did Penny name the puppy in "One of Our Dogs is Missing"?

21. (True or False) The alien boy in "The Magic Mirror" called Dr. Smith "goofy."

22. Who was Don referring to when he remarked, "Beneath that tough, militant exterior is a twelve-year-old boy"?

MEMORY BANKS OVERLOAD #2

In "The Anti-Matter Man," Will read to Dr. Smith from an old book of strange folklore. What was the title of the chapter the young Robinson stumbled upon concerning a parallel world inhabited by evil duplicates?

23. What was the name of the anti-matter Don?

24. Name Maureen's imaginary childhood friend who lived inside her teddy bear.
    A. Skittles
    B. Mr. Noodles
    C. Max Zero

25. What was the name of Capt. Tucker's hometown back on Earth where he was a "nuisance" before being kidnapped by aliens?
    A. Humboldt, Tennessee
    B. Punxsatawney, Pennsylvania
    C. Fairbury, Nebraska

26. Who was the wife of Dr. Smith's Uncle Thaddeus?

27. In "A Change of Space," to whom was Judy dictating a letter to on her tape recorder?

28. What was the name of Nerim's burro?
    A. Saskar
    B. Rohbur
    C. Ginny Mae

29. In "A Visit to Hades," Morbus (whom Smith believed was the Devil) reviewed the record of the scheming doctor's life and showed him some of the petty, nefarious deeds of his past. According to Smith, what was the name of the boy who was whispering in the classroom in the video replay from the doctor's youth?

30. What fleet was Admiral Zahrk a member of in "Mutiny in Space"?

MEMORY BANKS OVERLOAD #3

What were the names Dr. Smith gave to the two rock monsters in "The Cave of the Wizards"?

MEMORY BANKS OVERLOAD #4

Name the old French folksong the duplicate Judy and Penny sang to keep from being afraid in "The Phantom Family."

31. In the third season series segment "Princess of Space," what popular TV show was spoofed?

32. Name the four episodes in which the *Jupiter 2* expedition encountered meteors.

33. Identify the famous baseball player whom Dr. Smith claimed to have taught "the dipsy doodle" pitch.

34. Name the only two episodes which featured narration before the cliff-hanging ending?

35. Who was also known as "The Mighty Mite"?

36. Identify the tune Hamish played on his bagpipes in "The Astral Traveler."

37. (True or False) Not only is a Saticon a derby-wearing, constantly swaying alien, but it is the name of a type of television camera.

MEMORY BANKS OVERLOAD #5

Name the episode featuring Maureen's humorous attempt at imitating the Robot's waving arms and "Warning! Warning!" alert.

THE NAME GAME
PART II

Match the series events to the name of the episode in which they occurred.

1. _____ Dr. Smith was seen eating caviar

2. _____ Don & Smith bonded as temporary friends

3. _____ Maureen decided the J2 needed a general cleaning

4. _____ Don taught Judy how to bake a Boston cream pie

5. _____ Smith stole a piece of birthday cake

6. _____ Child labor laws were referenced

7. _____ Smith took credit for a ditch dug by the Robot

8. _____ The Robot baked Dr. Smith a surprise cake

9. _____ Smith made wine from kookaberries

10. _____ Smith attempted to formulate a special rocket fuel

11. _____ John's professional football offer was mentioned

12. _____ An alien suggested Smith drink Gloog

A. "Mutiny in Space"

B. "A Visit to Hades"

C. "The Mechanical Men"

D. "His Majesty Smith"

E. "Prisoners of Space"

F. "The Golden Man"

G. "Space Primevals"

H. "Wreck of the Robot"

I. "Deadly Games of Gamma 6"

J. "Fugitives in Space"

K. "The Keeper, Part I"

L. "The Time Merchant"

MEMORY BANKS OVERLOAD

"The Keeper" was the only *Lost in Space* two-part episode. Name the director for each installment.

2.21
ROCKET TO EARTH

Original Airdate: 02.15.67
Earth Year

Ship's Log: *Dr. Smith volunteers as a magician's assistant to the Great Zalto in hopes of stealing the sorcerer's spaceship and returning to Earth.*

That Does Not Compute

Zalto erroneously calls Smith "Professor." The fight promoter, Myko, made the same mistake in "The Deadly Games of Gamma 6," as did Dick Tufeld in his pre-credits narration in the episode, "All That Glitters."

When Zalto does the great disappearing act, his shadow can still be seen moving across the room on the left side of the split-screen.

Trivia Challenge

1. What did Zalto transform into an egg?

2. Who theorized that Dr. Smith was suffering from "space fatigue"?

3. (True or False) The alien magician threatened to turn Dr. Smith and Will into laughing hyenas.

4. What did Zalto call his ability to appear "to just one person out of a group" as he did with Dr. Smith?

    A. "Selective Visual Transformation"
    B. "Limited Optical Materialization"
    C. "Restricted Ocular Manifestation"

5. (Fill in the blank with the correct number) The ventriloquist dummy boasted that Zalto had been working diligently for _____ years to become "the greatest magician in the galaxy."

6. What was Zalto's "greatest feat of magic"?

7. (True or False) After John ordered the magician to be off the planet by dawn the next morning, Zalto complained that he would be reduced to performing his magic at space sideshows, planet county fairs, and asteroid circuses.

8. What type of highly-explosive missiles did Will and Dr. Smith fire at Earth from Zalto's spaceship?

9. Which military agency's headquarters assumed that Will and Smith's small spaceship was a hostile alien vessel and fired upon it in retaliation?
    A. Strategic Air Command
    B. U.S. Space Surveillance
    C. United Defense Command

MEMORY BANKS OVERLOAD

Where did the missiles launched from the nose cone of Dr. Smith and Will's space pod-sized craft detonate on Earth?

SPACE AGE FAST FACT

Although Jonathan Harris wore the same dark uniform shirt for almost the entire three years *Lost in Space* was on CBS, he was constantly arguing with costume designer, Paul Zastupnevich, who wanted the actor to wear a lighter color to make him look thinner.

2.22
THE CAVE OF THE WIZARDS

Original Airdate: 02.22.67
Earth Year

Ship's Log: *After months of repairs to the Jupiter 2's control system, the spaceship appears ready for blastoff, but an alien-transmuted Dr. Smith complicates the fast-approaching launch window.*

That Does Not Compute

Dr. Smith attempts to gain entrance to the *Jupiter 2* by pressing the "hatch button" on the exterior of the spaceship (also see "The Time Merchant"). What purpose does it serve if some alien monstrosity or malevolent planet creature can simply wander up to the spaceship and open the hatch from the outside with the simple touch of a button?

Trivia Challenge

1. Who recommended Dr. Smith return to the *Jupiter 2* for "hot food" and "bed rest" in an effort to restore his temporary loss of memory?

2. (Fill in the Blank) With his mind suddenly open to external suggestions, Smith was placed in a hypnotic trance and drawn to a cave containing an ancient, alien computer of the _____ civilization.

3. How many generations earlier had the aliens' ancestors abandoned human life forms?

4. What name did the Robot request Will call him after he was given a plating of gold?

5. Why did the computer brain ultimately reject Smith as the new leader of their alien civilization?

MEMORY BANKS OVERLOAD

(All three questions must be answered correctly to achieve the 5-point bonus)

1. What type of propellant did the *Jupiter 2* use?
2. Who remarked, "Clothes make the man"?
3. What did the Robot use to hit Dr. Smith in the head to successfully restore his temporary memory loss?

SPACE AGE FAST FACT

Jonathan Harris considers this imaginative and creative episode to be his favorite of the series, providing him with an opportunity to "stretch" as an actor and demonstrate the many facets of Dr. Smith's character.

2.23
TREASURE OF THE LOST PLANET

Original Airdate: 03.01.67
Earth Year

Ship's Log: *Will's old friend, Captain Tucker, and a band of treacherous cutthroats search for a priceless treasure after Dr. Smith discovers a mechanical head that mistakenly believes he is its former pirate master.*

That Does Not Compute

During the pre-credits sequence, as Dr. Smith climbs out of the dark pit after finding the hideous alien head, it is obvious that he is ascending concealed steps.

Trivia Challenge

1. What two words did the mechanical head keep repeating as a form of greeting?

2. Identify the one-eyed reptilian pirate who suggested that Dr. Smith "make Sleemoth."

3. (Fill in the Blank) The Robot's analysis of the mechanical head determined it to be a _____, a device that when properly directed could lead someone to all sorts of treasure.

4. Who called the Robot "iron pants"?

5. Which one of Tucker's treasonous crewmates ate "lasers for breakfast"?

6. What was the name of the furry, horned pirate creature who was destroyed in a trap during the search for the buried treasure?

MEMORY BANKS OVERLOAD

(Fill in the blank to complete the name)

The mechanical head mistakenly believed that Dr. Smith was a pirate named _____, who came from a very rich world.

SPACE AGE FAST FACT

Bob May, who wore black raccoon-type makeup and a solid dark outfit inside the Robot, went to the bank in the garb during his lunch hour and was arrested even though he explained, "Hey, I'm the Robot on *Lost in Space!*"

ALPHA CONTROL INTELLIGENCE DOSSIER

#1-48781-888-2
William Robinson

1. What was Will Robinson's middle name?
   A. Howard
   B. Edward
   C. Thompson

2. In which American city was he born?
   A. Los Angeles, California
   B. San Gabriel, California
   C. New York, New York

3. (True or False) Will's birthdate was February 1, 1987.

4. (Fill in the blank with the correct number) By the age of _____, people were already calling the youngest member of the Robinson family "the little genius."

5. Because of his high I.Q., what grade in high school had Will been advanced to at the time of the *Jupiter 2*'s launch?

6. (True or False) At the age of eight, to the Robinsons' astonishment, the boy dismantled the family's video-cassette recorder and then put it back together again in working order.

7. Will's hobbies and interests included geology, electronics, singing, and playing what musical instrument?

8. Intensely curious, Will often endangered both himself and the *Jupiter 2* expedition by going off on his own without either parent's permission. After the spaceship became hopelessly lost in space, what was Will's first exploration which got him into trouble with his family?

MEMORY BANKS OVERLOAD

What was Will's I.Q. at the time of the *Jupiter 2*'s colonization mission to Alpha Centauri?

TECH SPECS #6

Match the letter to the correct room or equipment aboard the Jupiter 2.

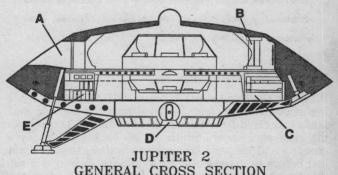

JUPITER 2
GENERAL CROSS SECTION
FRONT VIEW

Technical drawing by Edwin E. Echols.

1. ____ Stateroom
2. ____ Lab
3. ____ Freezing tube
4. ____ Air lock
5. ____ Reactor chamber

2.24
REVOLT OF THE ANDROIDS

Original Airdate: 03.08.67
Earth Year

Ship's Log: *After an android revolt at the Celestial Department Stores, the human-like Verda returns to the Robinsons' planet pursued by a Super Android programmed to destroy the rebel.*

That Does Not Compute

When Dr. Smith attempts to prove to IDAK that he is not fast enough on his feet, he dives past the android and lands in the middle of the mat on his stomach. The following close-shot shows Smith on his back with his eyes crossing and his head falling backwards against the mat just before he passes out. As Will runs to him, we see that Smith is now lying unconscious on his back in the dirt with only his head resting on the mat.

During the battle between the second IDAK and the Robot, watch closely and you will see pieces of the automaton's plastic collar fly off after being hit by the Super Android.

Trivia Challenge

1. Which precious stones was the furry, white monster eating?
    A. Diamonds

B. Rubies
C. Emeralds

2. What three words did the IDAK Super Androids constantly repeat when they were in pursuit of Verda?

3. (Fill in the Blank) IDAK was the abbreviation for "Instant _____ And Killer."

4. Where was the original IDAK's service port located?
   A. Behind his IDAK chest plate
   B. In his back
   C. On his belt

5. (Fill in the Blank) The original IDAK unit's weakness was that he was "susceptible to _____."

6. What did John use to destroy the CDS Intergalactic Generator?
   A. Neutron grenade
   B. Disintegrator capsule
   C. Atomic mine

7. (True or False) According to IDAK, Verda was known as Target Android 110.

MEMORY BANKS OVERLOAD

(Fill in the blanks with the correct numbers)

The original IDAK Super Android unit was model Alpha _____, but after he failed to destroy Verda, his creators replaced him with the superior IDAK Omega _____.

SPACE AGE FAST FACT

Guy Williams, recognized by his fellow cast members as a savvy stock market player, was continually on the phone between the filming of scenes, ordering his broker to sell shares in a company, buying more a half hour later, and then selling the same shares, two hours later because the stock went up half a point.

2.25
THE COLONISTS

Original Airdate: 03.15.67
Earth Year

Ship's Log: *The Jupiter 2 male crew members are enslaved by the ruler of a female warrior race who has come to the planet to establish a colony.*

That Does Not Compute

John and Maj. West are recaptured by Niolani and her male guards after Maureen deactivates a section of the labor camp's force field. Will, though, manages to escape to the drill site with the Robot and return with a detonator and plastic explosives. It's highly unlikely that the force field sector would have still been deactivated by the time Will made his way back. It also defies logic to believe that no one notices Will is missing for such a lengthy period of time. Although the sentries constantly patrol the camp, they must have taken their coffee breaks at the same time because none can be seen while Will wires the archway with the explosives.

Trivia Challenge

1. (Fill in the Blank) Niolani was nobly born of the _____ Nation of female warriors.

2. (Fill in the Blank) The *Jupiter 2* males were forced to work night and day clearing a landing pad and erecting

an electronic _____ arch which all colonists would have to pass through before breathing the planet's air.

3. (True or False) Niolani referred to the Robot as a "repulsive creature, class M-3."

4. Which decoration of bravery did the female ruler state that she was recommending Smith for after he foiled John and Maj. West's escape?
    A. The Condor Merit Badge
    B. The Diamond Cluster of Courage
    C. The Warrior's Medal of Honor

5. Which device did Penny mention to Will as the source of her newfound education concerning the superiority of women?
    A. Indoctrination unit
    B. Conditioning machine
    C. Thought transformer

MEMORY BANKS OVERLOAD

Match the radio relay stations with the *Jupiter 2* crew members who were assigned to make them network operational)

1. _____ R.T.S. 001   A. John
2. _____ R.T.S. 002   B. Judy & Penny
3. _____ R.T.S. 003   C. Don & Dr. Smith
4. _____ R.T.S. Central   D. Will & the Robot

SPACE AGE FAST FACT

Actress Francine York competed against six other statuesque women for the role of Niolani, including Edy Williams, who would later portray Non in the third season episode, "Two Weeks in Space."

2.26
TRIP THROUGH THE ROBOT
Original Airdate: 03.22.67
Earth Year

Ship's Log: *Losing power and unable to be recharged, the Robot wanders into a restricted area of the planet where alien gas vapors transform him into a mechanical giant.*

That Does Not Compute

Not only does the Robot shrink back to his normal size in fits and spurts during the climax, some of his body parts remain enlarged while others diminish quickly. As John, Maj. West, and Dr. Smith make their way back to the opening in the Robot's tread, some of the internal mechanisms begin to get smaller. The aperture, however, is still the same size as when Will and Smith initially removed the tread plate and entered. As soon as the men exit and realize that Will is still trapped inside, John immediately attempts to reenter through the opening but discovers that it has now shrunk too small for his body. Unbelievably, the men use a tree limb as leverage to keep the tread opening from reducing any further until Will makes it safely through just as the Robot returns to normal size.

Trivia Challenge

1. Who called Dr. Smith "the jinx of the Robinson family"?

2. Identify the forbidden and gaseous area of the planet where the Robot collapsed.
   A. Rock Canyon
   B. The Badlands
   C. The Valley of Shadows

3. Believing that he was about to "die" from lack of power, what were the Robot's final words when he fell to the ground?
   A. "Think of me often, my friends"
   B. "Farewell, beautiful world"
   C. "Why did it have to end like this?"

4. (Fill in the Blank) After discovering that the Robot had become a gigantic mechanical man, Dr. Smith described the automaton "as big as a _____."

5. What was the purpose of the Robot's interior infrared heat-seeking laser unit?

6. (Fill in the Blank) Will and Dr. Smith were able to repair the Robot's _____ timer, which acted like a heart to the human-like machine.
   A. sensory
   B. cybernetic
   C. diode

MEMORY BANKS OVERLOAD

How were Will and Dr. Smith able to reduce the Robot to his normal size?

SPACE AGE FAST FACT

After an executive at CBS decided that any demonstrative affection between John and Maureen Robinson would embarrass the young viewing audience, an edict was issued from the network that Guy Williams was not to touch his co-star in any manner, including taking June Lockhart's hand to help her out of the *Jupiter 2*.

2.27
THE PHANTOM FAMILY

Original Airdate: 03.29.67
Earth Year

Ship's Log: *Don, Judy, Penny, and Dr. Smith are replaced with mechanical facsimiles by an alien who demands that Will teach the duplicates to behave like humans or the real Jupiter 2 crew will be destroyed.*

That Does Not Compute

It seems that Billy Mumy and Dick Tufeld had difficulty in pronouncing or remembering Lemnoc's name (even though it was written in big letters on a nameplate above his chair in the cave control station). In one scene the Robot warns Will that "Lennoc" is approaching and Will introduces the alien to the duplicates as "Lumnac" in another.

Trivia Challenge

1. Where were John and Maureen during most of this episode?
   A. Observing volcanic activity
   B. Determining the extent of cosmic storm damage to the weather relay stations
   C. Making final adjustments to the network of radio transmission units

2. (Fill in the Blank) Lemnoc referred to the Smith duplicate as "the _____ one."

3. What did Lemnoc freeze and then shatter as a demonstration to Will of the cryogenic tubes' effects?
   A. Test tube
   B. Daisy
   C. Glove

4. Identify the two duplicates who were temporarily damaged by outside exposure to a passing cosmic storm.

5. What was the ultimate "symbol of survival" that Lemnoc wanted to take back to his homeworld?

6. What would happen to the duplicates if they were confronted by their real identities?

7. (Fill in the Blank) In the end, Lemnoc learned from Will that "more can be achieved through_____ than by fear."

MEMORY BANKS OVERLOAD

What was the maximum timeframe the real *Jupiter 2* crew could survive cryogenically frozen in Lemnoc's suspended animation tubes?

SPACE AGE FAST FACT

Billy Mumy absolutely detested the color and style of his character's outfits after the first season. During the second and third years, the young artist repeatedly sent Paul Zastupnevich design sketches for a Bucky Barnes (Captain America's partner) type of uniform he wanted to wear on the show, but the series costume designer turned down every request.

COMMUNICATION CHANNELS

Season Two

The radio transmission relay stations are still not operating at full capacity. Perhaps you should use the Vector Control Tapes to decipher the following transcripts.

1. Who said of "The Girl from the Green Dimension," "I thought she was anything but sinister"?
   A. Judy
   B. Maureen
   C. Penny

2. In which episode did Judy ask, "You mean you don't feel the earth tremor?"

3. Identify the series segment in which Dr. Smith shrieked, "There's a monster in my bed!"
   A. "The Galaxy Gift"
   B. "The Dream Monster"
   C. "The Ghost Planet"

4. In "Mutiny in Space," which character remarked, "I think it smells like the Fourth of July!"

5. (True or False) In "Wild Adventure," the always hungry Dr. Smith sadly commented, "I'm going to miss our hydroponic garden."

6. In which episode did John say, "It's been raining flak!"?
   A. "Space Circus"
   B. "The Deadly Games of Gamma 6"
   C. "Mutiny in Space"

7. In "Mutiny in Space," who noted the obvious, "You are in hot water, Dr. Smith—up to your neck!"?
   A. Don
   B. John
   C. The Robot

8. In which installment of the series did Penny remark, "I've seen strange looking alien beings before"?

9. Identify the source of the quote: "She slips a little in second stage."

10. Name the episode in which the Robot complained, "I no longer compute."

MEMORY BANKS OVERLOAD #1

(Fill in the Blank)

In "Wild Adventure," Dr. Smith noted, "Dreams are the true _____ of our desires."

---

11. Who compared Smith's explanations to "a box of magic tricks"?

12. What were the first words out of Dr. Smith's mouth when he saw that his statue had become a living stone creature?
    A. "Cease and desist!"
    B. "It's alive!"
    C. "Oh, no!"

13. In which episode did Smith attempt to assume his self-proclaimed "rightful destiny as a star"?

14. In "The Deadly Games of Gamma 6," who sarcastically called Smith a "man of action"?

15. Identify the series segment in which Smith referred to Maj. West as "the criminal type."
    A. "The Prisoners of Space"
    B. "Treasures of the Lost Planet"
    C. "The Thief from Outer Space"

16. In "Wild Adventure," which *Jupiter 2* crew member noted, "There are no service stations in space"?
    A. The Robot
    B. Dr. Smith
    C. Maj. West

17. (Fill in the Blank) In "The Ghost Planet," Will admitted to Dr. Smith, "I can't tell _____ as good as you can."

18. In which episode did the Robot state the obvious: "I am not a man. I am also not quite a machine. I must be something in between"?

MEMORY BANKS OVERLOAD #2

(Fill in the Blank)

After the *Jupiter 2* blasted off from "The Ghost Planet," the Cybernetic Leader ordered them to "Come back! Come back!" to which John responded, "Another time, _____."

---

19. In "The Astral Traveler," who was the source of the snide remark, "Better get Dr. Smith inside before he melts"?

20. In which episode did John happily say about the doctor, "I wouldn't have him any other way than his old mean, cunning, conniving self"?
    A. "Curse of Cousin Smith"

    B. "The Mechanical Men"
    C. "A Visit to Hades"

21. Identify the alien who confessed that his race of beings were becoming extinct due to a "lack of will to survive."

22. (Fill in the Blank) In "Trip Through the Robot," Dr. Smith noted of the mechanical man: "He walks, he talks, he experiences a minimum of _____, but with all that he is still a MACHINE."

23. In which installment of the series did the Robot complain, "I do not like to work on foreign imports"?

24. Identify the alien who remarked, "Home is where you happen to be at the moment."

25. Name the episode in which Dr. Smith advised the youngest Robinson, "Don't be in such a hurry to grow up, dear William. It isn't really worth it."

26. Who told Will to "roll with the punches" in "The Ghost Planet"?

27. Identify the character who said, "Ask me no questions and I'll tell you no lies, Earth creature."

28. In which episode did the Robot sarcastically refer to Dr. Smith as "my mentor as well as a great, decent human being and a credit to our expedition"?
    A. "Forbidden World"
    B. "The Android Machine"
    C. "West of Mars"

29. Who noted in "The Ghost Planet" that Benedict Arnold was an American traitor who "sold George Washington down the river" in 1780?

30. Name the conspiring alien who observed that Will was "bright as a penny."

MEMORY BANKS OVERLOAD #3

(Fill in the Blank)

Dr. Smith informed the galactic fight promoter, Myko, that John was "a man of _____, not battles."

---

31. In "Curse of Cousin Smith," which character philosophized that "all of living is a gamble"?
    A. Jeremiah
    B. Little Joe
    C. John

32. Who said Smith was a "miserable little snitch" when he was a boy?

33. (True or False) In "The Toymaker," John commented that the "nice thing" about having a son was watching "him become a man and grow up with him all over again."

34. In which episode did a dejected and disappointed alien sigh at the conclusion, "Well, back to the drawing board"?

35. In "Forbidden World," which *Jupiter 2* crew member said, "He was a big guy and he hit me when I wasn't looking"?

36. Who snidely referred to Dr. Smith as "a brave man" in "The Golden Man"?

37. In which series installment did Smith engrave the words "GONE BUT NOT FORGOTTEN" on his own tombstone?

MEMORY BANKS OVERLOAD #4

Identify the source of the quote: "People can work miracles when they're happy."

38. Name the episode in which the Robot remarked about a sleeping Dr. Smith, "He is catching eighty winks—forty with each eye!"

39. In "The Mechanical Men," which member of the Robinson expedition complained that Dr. Smith was "behaving like a spoiled child"?

40. "You can't learn what you can't feel" observed who in "The Phantom Family"?

41. (Fill in the Blank) Morbus described the meals in Hades as "_____, but slightly overdone."

42. (Fill in the Blank) After they were captured by Mr. O.M.'s toy monster, the Robot informed John, "I'm not programmed to warn against _____ dangers."

43. In "The Colonists," who told Smith, "Sabotage is your favorite sport," alluding to the doctor's activities before the *Jupiter 2*'s launch from Earth?

MEMORY BANKS OVERLOAD #5

Identify the source of the quote: "A great leader crushes his opposition."

2.28
THE MECHANICAL MEN

Original Airdate: 04.05.67
Earth Year

Ship's Log: *An invading force of miniature mechanical men lay siege to the Jupiter 2 camp and demand that the Robot take his place of destiny as their "supreme majestic leader."*

That Does Not Compute

During the pre-credits sequence, an angry Dr. Smith stomps off to take a nap away from the campsite. Lying down on the ground with his lab coat used as a pillow, he must have been utterly exhausted because he never wakes up while the noisy little mechanized beings place a platform under his body, restrain him with several chains, and place two silver pillows under his head.

When the personality-altered Robot returns to the *Jupiter 2* campsite to demand the *Jupiter 2*, John asks, "What can we do for you?" to which the mechanical man illogically replies, "As a matter of fact there is."

Trivia Challenge

1. Identify the two pieces of equipment that were sabotaged by the little mechanized invaders.

2. (Fill in the Blank) Compared to the tiny Robots, the

purple leader remarked that Dr. Smith was "a physical and mental _____."

3. (Fill in the blank with the correct number) For _____ thousand years the mechanical men had known that some day a "great warrior" would appear and lead them to power and glory.

4. Who referred to the tiny Robots as "mechanical freaks" and "monsters"?

5. Which planet was the miniature beings' homeworld?
    A. Idini
    B. Industro
    C. Iccobar

6. (Fill in the Blank) The Robot and Dr. Smith were forced to undergo an "operation of character _____ and substitution" to switch their minds.
    A. relocation
    B. readjustment
    C. reformation

7. Name the famous presidential address that Dr. Smith quoted from while possessed with the mind of the Robot.

8. What was responsible for the re-transference of the Robot's and Dr. Smith's characters?

MEMORY BANKS OVERLOAD

Identify the "few necessities" that the Robot packed in his suitcase.

SPACE AGE FAST FACT

Ironically, before William Hurt was chosen for the part of John Robinson in the 1998 movie version of *Lost in Space,* Jonathan Harris had commented in interviews that Hurt was one of his favorite actors and his critically-acclaimed performance in *Kiss of the Spider Woman* was one of only two roles (the other being Peter O'Toole's in *Beckett)* he would have accepted in the latter years of his acting career if afforded the opportunity.

2.29
THE ASTRAL TRAVELER

Original Airdate: 04.12.67
Earth Year

Ship's Log: *Trapped in a cave, Will is transported via a space warp to an ancient Scottish castle on Earth where he encounters a ghost and a moat monster.*

That Does Not Compute

During the climax, the hooded executioner pushes Smith's head down on the chopping block while Will runs outside to the moat to implore Angus to spare the doctor's life. The boy argues his case passionately for a few moments to both the lake monster and the ghostly Hamish. Because they both show mercy, the executioner dematerializes just as he is about to decapitate Smith. Considering the length of time it takes for Will to plead for Smith's life, the executioner should have already finished his grisly task and sat down to sharpen his axe for the next victim.

Trivia Challenge

1. What type of storm caused the landslide that sealed the cave entrance?
   A. Cosmic
   B. Electric
   C. Ion

2. In which year was Hamish Rue Glamis executed?

    A. 1497
    B. 1585
    C. 1602

3. Identify Hamish's "lord and master" who commanded that he be beheaded for "high treason."

4. No longer a ghost, which painful ailment came back to "torment" Hamish after 400 years.
    A. An aching back
    B. Gout
    C. A rheumatic arm

5. How many years had Angus been living in his "watery grave"?
    A. 400
    B. 600
    C. 900

6. What musical instrument did Hamish play to keep Angus "calm"?

7. Who called the two Scots "home" to the eternal rest they earned after being found "guilty of charity"?

MEMORY BANKS OVERLOAD

(Fill in the blank with the correct family name)

When Hamish discovered that Smith was a direct descendant of the _____ clan on his maternal side of the family, the vengeance-seeking Scot planned to have the doctor beheaded since one of his ancestors was responsible for betraying him centuries earlier.

SPACE AGE FAST FACT

Billy Mumy's first season stand-in, Harry Monte, a cigar-chewing, foul-mouthed midget, was replaced during the second and third year with a young, single mother who later became a stuntwoman on the series.

2.30
THE GALAXY GIFT

Original Airdate: 04.26.67
Earth Year

Ship's Log: *Penny's loyalties are severely tested when she must either watch her family die or surrender an amulet, a protective belt of great power entrusted to her by an alien being known as Mr. Arcon.*

That Does Not Compute

Where do Dr. Smith, Penny, Will, and the Robot obtain their play rehearsal attire and stage props such as western jackets and cowboy hats, bonnets, wigs, handlebar mustaches, capes, dresses (big enough for the Robot), framed pictures, wooden doors and walls? It's absolutely amazing, the endless "supplies" that just happen to appear when needed by the *Jupiter 2* crew. It reminds us of the old *Gilligan's Island* joke: "If they could make a radio out of a coconut, why couldn't they *fix the boat?*"

In an obvious continuity oversight, no one recognizes the black-clad, derby-wearing Saticons as the malevolent aliens who dismantled the Robot in an attempt to control all of Earth's machines in the episode "The Wreck of the Robot."

How is it possible for Dr. Smith's and the Robot's molecules to be transported to another location if they are not completely enclosed in the tube-shaped chambers when the device is in operation. Everyone else closes the translucent doors tightly, but Smith hangs halfway out of the tube as if he is riding on a merry-go-round and the Robot is simply too bulky to fit into any of the transportation chambers.

Trivia Challenge

1. (Fill in the Blank) Mr. Arcon described the Saticons as "cruel and vicious creatures from a _____ planet."

2. (True or False) According to the Robot, the evil aliens "communicated by high-frequency cosmic signals."

3. What was the "greatest gift in the galaxy"?

4. As a "test pilot," Dr. Smith sent Debby the Bloop through the molecular transporter. What did she bring back after her *first* trip?

5. What two identifiable objects from Earth did Debby return with after her *second* voyage through the transporter device?

6. In which section of San Francisco did Dr. Smith's aunt reside?
   A. Pacific Heights
   B. Knob Hill
   C. Chinatown

7. (Fill in the Blank) Families did not exist on Mr. Arcon's homeworld; instead each being was hatched from eggs in the _____ incubator.

8. Where did Mr. Arcon threaten to banish Dr. Smith as punishment for attempting to surrender the amulet in exchange for his return to Earth?
   A. Nagus XI's mining colony
   B. The Saticon's "dead" homeworld
   C. A dead star

MEMORY BANKS OVERLOAD

What was the name of Dr. Smith's favorite restaurant in San Francisco's Chinatown?

SPACE AGE FAST FACT

At the end of the second season, Irwin Allen planned to fire Jonathan Harris, but was persuaded by frequent *Lost in Space* director Don Richardson to reverse his decision. Richardson argued that Allen was the show's "P.T. Barnum" and Harris was a performing "lion" who simply needed a "crack of the whip."

FANDOM EPISODE RANKING:

Season Two

The following ranking of Lost in Space's *second season episodes (with 10.0 being the highest) have been posted in various manifestations at science-fiction conventions and in cyberspace on fan-based websites.*

Ranking		Episode Title
1.	10.0	"Trip Through the Robot"
2.	9.08	"Blast Off into Space"
3.	8.45	"Wild Adventure"
4.	8.30	"Wreck of the Robot"
5.	8.12	"The Golden Man"
6.	8.10	"The Prisoners of Space"
7.	8.06	"The Ghost Planet"
8.	7.94	"A Visit to Hades"
9.	7.90	"The Android Machine"
10.	7.86	"The Colonists"
11.	7.81	"The Mechanical Men"
12.	7.41	"The Phantom Family"
13.	6.98	"Revolt of the Androids"
14.	6.87	"Rocket to Earth"
15.	6.66	"The Dream Monster"
16.	5.25	"Space Circus"
17.	5.10	"The Cave of the Wizards"
18.	5.02	"The Galaxy Gift"
19.	4.89	"The Toymaker"
20.	4.23	"Curse of Cousin Smith"
21.	4.15	"The Astral Traveler"
22.	4.04	"Deadly Games of Gamma 6"

23.	3.88	"The Forbidden World"
24.	3.62	"Girl from the Green Dimension"
25.	3.31	"The Questing Beast"
26.	3.12	"The Space Vikings"
27.	2.92	"West of Mars"
28.	2.73	"The Thief from Outer Space"
29.	2.32	"Mutiny in Space"
30.	1.63	"Treasure of the Lost Planet"

THE WRITE STUFF

"Last week, as you recall . . ." Match the Lost in Space wordsmiths with the episodes they penned.

1. _____ Bob & Wanda Duncan
2. _____ Peter Packer
3. _____ William Welch
4. _____ Carey Wilbur
5. _____ Robert Hamner
6. _____ Jack Turley
7. _____ Shimon Wincelberg
8. _____ Margaret Brookman Hill
9. _____ Michael Fessier
10. _____ William Read Woodfield & Allan Balter
11. _____ Norman Lessing
12. _____ Jackson Gillis
13. _____ Barney Slater

A. "One of Our Dogs is Missing"
B. "Space Beauty"
C. "The Space Vikings"
D. "Ghost in Space"
E. "Wreck of the Robot"
F. "Wild Adventure"
G. "Island in the Sky"
H. "Two Weeks in Space"
I. "The Time Merchant"
J. "West of Mars"
K. "Hunter's Moon"
L. "There Were Giants in the Earth"
M. "Invaders from the Fifth Dimension"

MEMORY BANKS OVERLOAD

What was frequent *Lost in Space* writer Shimon Wincelberg's one-time pseudonym and the singular pen name for the writing duo of Barney Slater and Robert Hamner?

SPACED OUT TITLES

Match the original, working episode titles to their final, aired name designations.

1. _____ "The Cyclamen"
2. _____ "Gateway to Alpha Centauri"
3. _____ "Creature of the Vacuum"
4. _____ "Mechano Monsters"
5. _____ "Twinkle, Twinkle Little War"
6. _____ "Carnival in Space"
7. _____ "The New Planet"
8. _____ "Twinkle, Twinkle Little Star"
9. _____ "Home Sweet Home"
10. _____ "The War World"
11. _____ "The Migrants"
12. _____ "The Robinson Monster"
13. _____ "O Brave New World"

A. "The Great Vegetable Rebellion"
B. "The Flaming Planet"
C. "The Golden Man"
D. "Collision of Planets"
E. "The Dream Monster"
F. "The Keeper, Part I"
G. "Attack of the Monster Plants"
H. "Return from Outer Space"
I. "The Mechanical Men"
J. "The Promised Planet"
K. "Forbidden World"
L. "Space Creature"
M. "Island in the Sky"

MEMORY BANKS OVERLOAD

What were the original episode titles for "The Haunted Lighthouse" and "Invaders from the Fifth Dimension"?

3.1
CONDEMNED OF SPACE

Original Airdate: 09.06.67
Earth Year

Ship's Log: *To avoid collision with a fast approaching comet, the Jupiter 2 makes an emergency liftoff into outer space where the crew discovers a mammoth prison ship full of frozen inmates.*

That Does Not Compute

When Will climbs down into the automated prison vessel, he peers through one of the door windows and you can clearly see one of the "frozen" criminals adjust his position on the pedestal and move his hand to tighten the grip on his weapon. Come to think of it, why would these dangerous prisoners be frozen with their machetes, laser rifles, and an assortment of other weapons in-hand?

During the scene when Phanzig fires his rifle at Will and the Robot in the prison ship's corridor, explosives fly but no animated laser effect is shown.

Although the prisoners are supposed to be frozen in place aboard the vessel, almost all of them noticeably sway or move slightly while stationed on their pedestals.

Trivia Challenge

1. (Fill in the Blank) While enduring intense heat inside the

Jupiter 2, the Robot complained that his _____
were beginning to "melt."

2. Who was Dr. Smith hoping would discover his S.O.S.
   message adrift in space?
   A. "An astral traveler or cosmic benefactor"
   B. "A rescue party sent from home, sweet home"
   C. "A compassionate space soul or an explorer with
      a heart of gold"

3. Which type of beam did the automated prison vessel
   use to physically manipulate the *Jupiter 2?*
   A. Focused linear graviton
   B. Magnetic
   C. Tractor

4. According to the Robot's calculations, how many
   galactic convicts were incarcerated in frozen animation
   aboard the ship?
   A. 5,345
   B. 7,624
   C. 9,874

5. What was the name of the automated prison vessel?

6. Which planet was prisoner Phanzig's place of birth?
   A. Tauron
   B. Quarx
   C. Vera

7. How many centuries had Phanzig been sentenced to
   "frozen sleep"?

8. Identify the game of looped strings which Phanzig
   used as a weapon against Dr. Smith.

MEMORY BANKS OVERLOAD

What was Phanzig's prison number?

SPACE AGE FAST FACT

For the third season, costume designer Paul Zastupnevich once again created all new outfits for the cast regulars. Although a wardrobe change was in order to give the show a new look, and possibly a new approach, it was also true that the previous year's costumes were tattered and literally coming apart at the seams due to constant use by the show's stars, their stunt doubles and repeated trips to the cleaners.

3.2
VISIT TO A HOSTILE PLANET

Original Airdate: 09.13.67
Earth Year

Ship's Log: *A space warp returns the Jupiter 2 and its crew to Earth fifty years in the past where they are mistaken for invading aliens.*

That Does Not Compute

The emergency radio station announcer informs his listening audience of the *Jupiter 2*'s landing location, but only a handful of armed vigilantes attempt to defend the town. It's hard to believe that a military unit from a nearby base or the National Guard didn't respond, especially in light of the fact that the damaged spaceship sits in the parking lot of a sawmill for several hours. Remember, the *Jupiter 2* has traveled back in time to 1947, the same year that the U.S. government rapidly responded to (and allegedly covered-up) reports of a crashed UFO in the Roswell, New Mexico desert.

The Robot is shot near his chest light by the trigger-happy law enforcement officer Grover, but when the mechanical man turns around to make a quick retreat to the *Jupiter 2*, the bullet damage has disappeared.

Judy's hairdo changes noticeably from scene to scene throughout this episode.

After the *Jupiter 2* lifts-off at the episode's end, one of Manitou Junction's citizens erroneously states that the "flying saucer" landed in Manitou Falls.

Trivia Challenge

1. (Fill in the Blank) While attempting to clear _____ in the *Jupiter 2*'s fuel system, runaway acceleration past the speed of light carried the spaceship into hyperdrive.

2. After looking at the Earth calendar, John assumed that they had returned to their home planet in October 1999, "give or take a week or two." In actuality, what was the month and day in 1947?

3. (Fill in the blank with the correct number) It was announced on the radio that all power and communication within a _____ -hundred mile radius of the station had failed.

4. Who referred to the gun-toting town vigilantes as "hostiles"?

5. Identify the auto body repair shop where Dr. Smith stole a fire chief's outfit.
   A. We-Fix-M Garage
   B. Bob's Auto Doctor
   C. Len's Garage

6. According to John, in what year did the United States first land a man on the moon?

7. (Fill in the Blank) The science-fiction reading Grover convinced the townspeople that the *Jupiter 2* crew were shape-shifting aliens called "_____."

8. What type of ancient weapon did the vigilantes unsuccessfully attempt to fire at the spacecraft?

MEMORY BANKS OVERLOAD

Over the skies of which Great Lake was the *Jupiter 2* spotted and reported as a UFO?

SPACE AGE FAST FACT

The full-size $30,000 mockup of the *Jupiter 2*, too large to fit through the studio doors, was disassembled and reconstructed on 20th Century Fox's back parking lot, which was redressed along with the surrounding buildings to simulate part of the 1947 Earth town. After completion of the episode's filming, the large-scale version of the spaceship was placed in a corner of the lot and remained there until it was demolished following the series' cancellation at the end of the season.

3.3
KIDNAPPED IN SPACE

Original Airdate: 09.20.67
Earth Year

Ship's Log: *After Dr. Smith responds to a medical assistance distress call, the Jupiter 2 is captured by a mammoth space probe inhabited by time-controlling aliens and their ailing leader.*

That Does Not Compute

During the escape attempt from the confinement cell, John removes a metal leg from a bench and whacks an android guard on the head with it. Unfortunately, the prop bends so significantly that Guy Williams glances at it in surprise, perhaps waiting for director Don Richardson to yell "cut!"

The androids sneak aboard the *Jupiter 2* to operate a noisy alien device over Will's face. How come the mechanism doesn't wake up the boy, but rouses Maureen in her cabin several yards away? Mother's intuition, we suppose.

Where was the Space Pod hidden for the series' first two seasons? A perfect opportunity for its exploratory use would have been during the first year episode "Island in the Sky," when John descended to the planet surface with the Parajets and was almost killed in the process.

Trivia Challenge

1. What did the Robot call electromagnetic space static?
   A. Galactic opera
   B. Cosmic melodies
   C. Space music

2. (Fill in the Blank) Smith bragged that he was a "full-fledged Doctor of Intergalactic _____ Psychology."

3. Identify the galactic origin of the massive space probe.
   A. Xenian
   B. Tarkassian
   C. Yareth

4. (Fill in the Blank) The Robot graduated first in his class after studying two semesters of premed at the _____ of Cybernetics, "one of the best medical schools in the galaxy."

5. Why did the Robot change his major at the educational institution?

6. Which device did the androids use to reveal the Robot's closest companion among the *Jupiter 2* crew?
   A. Personality Indicator
   B. Character Identifier
   C. Identity Enhancer

7. (Fill in the Blank) Alien 1220 was constructed in the _____ day of the twelfth year of her "noble and exalted" leader's rule.

8. (True or False) The Robot diagnosed the ailing machine leader as "suffering from a worn-out mechanism, complicated by twisted, electronic rotors and eroded counterweights."

MEMORY BANKS OVERLOAD

What did Dr. Smith and Will use aboard the *Jupiter 2* to decipher the androids' complex communication form which was based on metric-fractional units?

SPACE AGE FAST FACT

CBS had renewed *Lost in Space* for a third season with the stipulation that Irwin Allen trim the show's budget, which explains why episodes filmed later in the year used fewer special effects, the same alien monsters showed up time and time again (usually with a different coat of paint), and stock footage was recycled quite often.

3.4
HUNTER'S MOON

Original Airdate: 09.27.67
Earth Year

Ship's Log: *John and the Robot descend in the Space Pod to evaluate surface conditions of a nearby planet and are captured by Megazor, an alien hunter who wants to make John his quarry in a deadly game of cat-and-mouse.*

That Does Not Compute

The *Jupiter 2* crew used radio transmitters as personal communication devices for the first two seasons of *Lost in Space*, but in this episode Don refers to the possibility of John's "communicator" being "defective" when the spaceship fails to make contact with him on the planetary surface. Compact handheld "communicator" units were in wide use at the same time in 1967 on that *other* space exploration series on NBC.

We realize that episodes were not aired in the same order as they were filmed, but it is disconcerting to see Maj. West's and Penny's hair cut short the previous week and then long once again in this installment of the series. (Note: Actually, Angela Cartwright's real hair was put up under a hairpiece to make it appear short.)

Trivia Challenge

1. How many points were required for Megazor to complete the field tests to determine his leadership qualities?
   A. 500
   B. 750
   C. 1000

2. Identify the piece of handheld equipment that Dr. Smith used to scan the planet surface "more efficiently."

3. Which alien did John kill with a spear while caged by Megazor?
   A. Klaxxon
   B. Invisibo
   C. Demarko

4. As usual, Dr. Smith was responsible for the crash of the *Jupiter 2*. What did he misfire to cause the spaceship to forcibly land on the planetary surface?

5. (Fill in the Blank) The protective suit worn by John during the hunt was "impervious to radiation, heat, _____, and all similar destructive forces."

6. (Fill in the Blank) Megazor admitted to Will that he had no family, but was created instead by a synthesis _____, the Mach III advance model.
   A. replicator
   B. incubator
   C. regenerator

7. What type of feelings had been eliminated in the alien hunter's culture by genetic replacements?

8. How many points did John earn for "cleverness" after defeating Megazor at the quicksand pit?
   A. 100
   B. 150
   C. 250

MEMORY BANKS OVERLOAD

According to the Rules of the Hunt, how many Earth minutes did John receive as a "head start" before Megazor began the pursuit?

SPACE AGE FAST FACT

Episode writer Jack Turley was very dissatisfied with the casting choice of Vincent Beck in the central role of Megazor. Rather than a polished and articulate alien, Turley had envisioned the character as some sort of immense, "looming spectre," more in the spirit of actor Michael Ansara (The Ruler in "The Challenge"), who was originally cast in the role.

ALPHA CONTROL INTELLIGENCE DOSSIER

#1-48671-988-1
Dr. Zachary Smith

1. Dr. Smith was a United States Space Corps staff psychologist and environmental expert. What was his rank prior to his hasty and totally unanticipated departure from Earth?

2. What was his birthdate?

3. (True or False) Smith spent the early years of his youth in New York City's lower Manhattan, until his parents were tragically killed in an automobile accident in the Lincoln Tunnel.

4. Who raised the boy after his parents' untimely deaths?

5. (Fill in the Blank) Through one of his relative's social connections, Smith and his cousin, Jeremiah, were able to obtain _____ scholarships for entrance to the prestigious Oxford University in England.
   - A. Fulbright
   - B. Marshall
   - C. Rhodes

6. (Fill in the blank with the correct number) While working towards a degree in psychology, Smith became the Grand Master of the Oxford Chess Society for _____ consecutive years.

7. From which school of higher learning did he earn his doctorate degree?
   A. Harvard
   B. Yale
   C. MIT

8. What branch of the American Armed Forces did Dr. Smith join after graduation?

9. He served sixteen distinguished years as a staff psychologist at a number of military bases in the U.S. and Europe. In what year was he promoted to the rank of Colonel and transferred to the recently formed United States Space Corps at their training center in Houston, Texas?
   A. 1989
   B. 1992
   C. 1995

10. (Fill in the Blank) As one of only about two dozen people in the world specializing in the field of _____ Space Psychology, Dr. Smith performed the final stress/pressure-analysis examinations of the Robinson family before they departed Earth on their mission of colonization to Alpha Centauri.

11. (True or False) Smith was also actively involved in the artificial intelligence programming for the *Jupiter 2*'s environmental control automaton.

12. After Smith's suspicious disappearance at the time of the *Jupiter 2*'s ill-fated mission, intelligence operatives from both the United States Space Corps and Alpha Control began to assemble the true facts of Smith's life. How did he *actually* gain entrance into Oxford University?

13. After his prosperous aunt's mysterious death severed his comfortable income, Smith dropped out of college and drifted around Europe. Who contacted him during this period in his life and provided him with a forged degree from Oxford?

14. Dr. Smith was later used as an intelligence operative within the USSC for an enemy foreign government, along with several other spies already placed in strategic positions. What was the two-word code name for the group of infiltration agents? (Hint: The first word is Latin for "god of winds" and the second word translates to mean "ghost or spirit.")

MEMORY BANKS OVERLOAD

Identify the southern United States city and state where young Zachary was raised by relatives after the accidental deaths of his mother and father.

TECH SPECS #7

Match the letter to the correct equipment or room aboard the Jupiter 2.

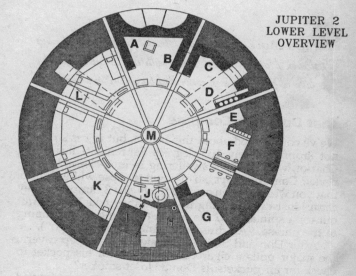

JUPITER 2
LOWER LEVEL
OVERVIEW

Technical drawing by Edwin E. Echols.

1. _____ Acceleration couch
2. _____ Emergency exit
3. _____ Storage
4. _____ Robot station
5. _____ Space Pod bay
6. _____ Landing gear bay
7. _____ Chariot lift
8. _____ Communication/controls
9. _____ Hatch
10. _____ Galley
11. _____ Laboratory
12. _____ Lavatory/storage
13. _____ Stateroom

3.5
SPACE PRIMEVALS
Original Airdate: 10.04.67
Earth Year

Ship's Log: *En route in the Chariot to cap a threatening volcano, Maj. West and Dr. Smith are taken captive by a tribe of primitive men controlled by an ancient computer.*

That Does Not Compute

We've complained about this before, but if it is so damn hot (approximately 100 degrees Fahrenheit) inside the Chariot, why sit there sweltering in long-sleeved turtlenecks? Come on, guys, strip down to those white T-shirts that you wear so often around the *Jupiter 2* campsite. They *always* insist on dressing up when they take the Chariot out for a spin around the planet (bringing new meaning to the phrase, "All dressed up and no place to go").

After Don and Smith are sealed in the deep cavern, the major pulls a cigarette lighter out of his pocket to check for air pockets. Is Don a closet smoker?

During the contest between the ancient computer and the Robot, watch closely as the Robot steps onto the platform in the tribal camp and you will catch a glimpse of Bob Mays' legs.

Trivia Challenge

1. What type of explosive charge was successfully used to cap the volcano?

A. Hyperatomic
B. Neutronic
C. Sonic wave mobilizer

2. Why were Don and Dr. Smith quarantined by the tribesmen?

3. Identify the leader of the primitive men.
   A. Baulok
   B. Rangah
   C. Sautok

4. (Fill in the Blank) The Robot admitted that Dr. Smith's "_____ can be infectious."

5. (True or False) Dr. Smith's great uncle's genuine gold hunter pocket watch was stolen by a tribal guard when he attempted to use the timepiece as a means to buy his way out of imprisonment in the cave.

6. What was the name of the powerful, ancient computer that governed the primitive tribesmen?

7. (Fill in the Blank) Don sarcastically called Smith "_____" when the doctor demanded that the major "fetch" the Chariot.

MEMORY BANKS OVERLOAD

Why did Don refer to the all-powerful computer as a "cracking plant"?

SPACE AGE FAST FACT

Jonathan Harris has repeatedly stated in interviews and at sci-fi conventions that the role of Dr. Smith on *Lost in Space* was his favorite part of all the numerous television, movie and theater productions he has performed in throughout his lengthy professional acting career.

3.6
SPACE
DESTRUCTORS

Original Airdate: 10.11.67
Earth Year

Ship's Log: *Dr. Smith discovers a cyborg-creating machine in a cave and sets out to conquer the universe with an army of half-human and half-machine creatures that possess his likeness and cunning.*

That Does Not Compute

During the fight between the first cyborg and the Robot, the mechanical man's back is dented *before* he falls to the floor of the cave.

After John uses a destructive capsule to disintegrate a cyborg that is about to kill Don, the remainder of the special effects charge can be seen burning out in a nearby bush next to a boulder.

John valiantly defends himself against dozens of sword-wielding cyborgs using his expert fencing skills. Afterwards, his hair is tousled and disheveled, but when he walks through a cave passageway and emerges on the other side, he looks as if he just stepped out of the coiffeur's chair, especially during the close-up shot of his confrontation with the cyborg version of Will.

Trivia Challenge

1. (Fill in the Blank) Without initially realizing the awe-

some capabilities of the cyborg-creating mechanism, Dr. Smith sarcastically referred to the device as an "oversized _____ machine."

2. Who called the half/man and half/machine creatures "mindless cyborgs"?

3. What did John and Maj. West use to destroy the first cyborg?
   A. Destructive capsule
   B. Electronic net
   C. Neutron grenade

4. Where did Dr. Smith dispose of the cyborgs who "couldn't make the grade" and measure up to his quality control standards?
   A. Reject pile
   B. Recycle bin
   C. Cybernetic trash compactor

5. With Will's assistance, how did the Robot escape from Smith's custody?

MEMORY BANKS OVERLOAD

(Fill in the Blanks)

In an attempt to create the "greatest mixture of generalship ever known," Dr. Smith programmed the cyborg's mental abilities and instincts with the cunning of _____, the _____ of Alexander the Great, the _____ of Genghis Khan, the strength of _____, and the _____ of himself.

SPACE AGE FAST FACT

The late, multi-talented comedian Red Skelton was one of Irwin Allen's financial backers for *Lost in Space* and his brother, Paul, was one of the series' prop makers.

3.7
THE HAUNTED LIGHTHOUSE

Original Airdate: 10.18.67
Earth Year

Ship's Log: *The Jupiter 2 crew, along with the recently discovered survivor of a space colony, blast off from yet another planet and encounter a galactic lighthouse.*

That Does Not Compute

As John initially explores the lighthouse, the computer repeatedly announces that the *Jupiter 2* departed Earth on September 18, 1997. Will comments "that's right," even though the spacecraft was actually launched on October 16, 1997 (according to the unaired pilot and "The Reluctant Stowaway" episode). Furthermore, the computerized voice also erroneously states that the *Jupiter 2*'s mission is one of "exploration" rather than "colonization," to which Don adds "It knows all about us."

The lighthouse was seen as the fuel barge in the "Wild Adventure" episode. You would think that Irwin Allen and company would care enough about the intelligence of the audience to at least change the spacecraft's color scheme (as he did with the derelict ship in "Kidnapped in Space") and the billboard-sized F-12 ship number emblazoned on its side.

Col. Foley introduces himself as an officer of the U.S. Air Force while on the lighthouse's control bridge, but during dinner John observes that the meal is "elegant" for a ranking officer assigned to the Space Force.

Trivia Challenge

1. Identify the two items J-5 misplaced in order to get Penny's attention.

2. How many years had the space colony survivor lived on roots and berries?

3. According to Colonel Foley, which two baseball teams competed in the 1984 World Series?

4. Who noted that J-5 had an "unusual scientific aptitude"?

5. How often did Col. Foley clean and test the space lightship's alarm bells?
   A. The first Monday of every month
   B. Every fourth Tuesday
   C. The first and last day of every month

6. (True or False) John told Foley that a cosmic storm was "sweeping the entire galaxy."

7. What happened to Foley's star maps?
   A. They were destroyed during an onboard fire
   B. The real colonel took off with them in his space raft
   C. They were burnt while Foley was cooking

8. Identify the two physical forms that the Zaybo invisible life force took during this episode.

9. What was Col. Foley's first name and middle initial?
   A. Bryan J.
   B. Tommy C.
   C. Silas J.

MEMORY BANKS OVERLOAD

A relief ship from Earth was due to visit the light-house in how many years?

SPACE AGE FAST FACT

The pointed ears worn by Lou Wagner's character, J-5, were actually an extra pair of Mr. Spock's from that *other* space series, *Star Trek*. *Lost in Space* makeup artist John Chambers (who later won an Academy Award for his work in *Planet of the Apes*) also designed the Vulcan's famous ears and "borrowed" a pair for this episode.

3.8
FLIGHT INTO THE FUTURE

Original Airdate: 10.25.67
Earth Year

Ship's Log: *Dr. Smith, Will, and the Robot accidentally land the Space Pod on an uncharted planet where everything they encounter may be an illusion designed to ward off intruders.*

That Does Not Compute

How is it possible for Dr. Smith, Will, and the Robot to initially overlook the statue of the mechanical man when it is in a clearing only a few yards from the aged and vine-covered *Jupiter 2*?

Why does Dr. Smith need Will's assistance in operating the Space Pod? In the episode "Kidnapped in Space," Smith pilots the small spacecraft to the Xenian space probe after the intercepted call for medical assistance promises great rewards.

Trivia Challenge

1. Who originally described the unknown planet as looking like an emerald?

2. What did Dr. Smith initiate aboard the Space Pod

which accidentally launched the exploratory vehicle towards the planet?
   A. Airborne guidance system
   B. Dual thrust controls
   C. Primary propulsion regulator

3. (True or False) Smith told Will that he never took naps that lasted longer than twenty minutes.

4. (Fill in the Blank) Astronaut Commander Fletcher stated that the Robot's "antique" model type became obsolete "with the end of the _____."

5. Which type of equipment did the "space historians" use to detect Dr. Smith, Will, and the Robot's presence on the planet?
   A. Space-Time Continuum Stabilizer
   B. Time Warp Scanner
   C. Ultrasensitive Perception

6. (Fill in the Blank) Sgt. Smith told his nefarious relative from the *Jupiter 2* that the only possible way to have the accusations against him erased was for him to appear in a face-to-face confrontation with members of the Supreme Court of the _____ Judiciary.
   A. Space
   B. Galactic
   C. Universal

MEMORY BANKS OVERLOAD

(Fill in the blanks from the inscription on the Robot's statue)

IN MEMORIAM

Erected to the memory of Earth's first _____ computer to traverse deep space. To the _____ hero of the Robinson expedition. Gratefully dedicated in the year two thousand two hundred and seventy a.d.

SPACE AGE FAST FACT

The dubbing of Dick Tufeld's voice tracks for the Robot was done rather imperfectly, typically using one audio mixer for part of an episode and a different one for the rest. One device might give a tinny, metallic sound, while the other might push the lower register, and with no explicit instructions on how to equalize the Robot's voice, the mechanical man sounded different from commercial to commercial and show to show.

GALACTIC CASTAWAYS

Test your behind-the-scenes knowledge of the Lost in Space *cast and crew.*

1. Billy Mumy has entertained a whole new generation of sci-fi television viewers in the role of a Minbari ambassadorial aide on the highly successful *Babylon 5* series. What is the name of his character?

2. In which holiday-themed movie did June Lockhart make her screen debut alongside her real-life parents?
    A. *It's a Wonderful Life*
    B. *A Christmas Carol*
    C. *Miracle on 34th Street*

3. Identify the former series co-star who confessed in a 1988 *Starlog* magazine (issue #135) interview: "I'm amazed by how many people are really interested and enthused about *Lost in Space*. I thought when I did the show it was a passing fancy. A silly show, but fun to do."

4. (True or False) Although he made a few appearances on TV talk shows, Guy Williams was never hired as an actor again after the cancellation of *Lost in Space*.

5. Throughout the early seventies, Williams' earlier swashbuckling television series, *Zorro*, began playing internationally in syndication. Name the famous

South American fan who asked the actor to come to Buenos Aires to appear in a charity show.

6. How old was Marta Kristen when her parents left her in a Norwegian orphanage?
   A. Four days
   B. A week
   C. Two weeks

MEMORY BANKS OVERLOAD #1

Identify the Paramount movie director to whom Mark Goddard wrote a letter after arriving in Hollywood, requesting advice on the best way to become an actor.

---

7. Which former *Lost in Space* regular has an actress sister who co-starred in the first *Alien* movie?

8. Jonathan Harris now considers himself the "king of voice-overs." Identify the robotic character from the ABC sci-fi series, *Battlestar Galactica,* whose vocalization he supplied.

9. Guy Williams died of a cerebral hemorrhage in Argentina in May of 1989. How long had he been dead before his body was discovered in his apartment?
   A. Three days
   B. One week
   C. Ten days

10. (True or False) Billy Mumy made his television acting debut on *The Loretta Young Show.*

11. Which *Lost in Space* star appeared in a *Gunsmoke* episode as Crazy Beulah, "an alcoholic nymphomaniac murderess with the mind of a twelve-year-old"?

12. Billy Mumy's television credits include the perennially popular 1960s series *The Twilight Zone.* Name the three episodes in which he appeared.

13. Although she was once called "a typical American girl" by an English newspaper, where was Angela Cartwright *actually* born?

14. Which of the series' stars finished a first motion picture role in *Rage to Live* just prior to getting the regular gig on *Lost in Space*?

15. (True or False) Billy Mumy's full name is Charles William Mumy, Jr.

16. Who made her professional acting debut at the age of eight in a Metropolitan Opera production of *Peter Ibbetson*, playing Mimsey in the dream sequence?

17. Name the well-received movie Guy Williams had recently starred in before being hired as the lead in *Lost in Space*.

18. As a ten-year-old fourth grader, who starred in an original comedy which she and two other elementary school students had written?

19. What was the name of Angela Cartwright's character on the long-running Danny Thomas show?
    A. Linda
    B. Tracy
    C. Nancy

20. On which TV game show did Guy Williams, June Lockhart, Angela Cartwright, Marta Kristen and Bob May make an appearance in 1983?

21. John Williams later achieved stardom as the conductor of the Boston Pops Orchestra and as the respected music composer for such box-office champs as *Jaws*, *Star Wars*, *E.T.* and *Jurassic Park* (to name only a few). What was different about the spelling of his name in the *Lost in Space* credits?

22. Who's a past spokesperson for International House of Pancakes (IHOP)?
    A. June Lockhart

B. Jonathan Harris
C. Angela Cartwright *and* Marta Kristen

23. On which soap opera were June Lockhart and Mark Goddard reunited in 1985, in which they danced with each other in the background during a wedding scene?
    A. *One Life to Live*
    B. *Days of Our Lives*
    C. *General Hospital*

MEMORY BANKS OVERLOAD #2

Name the ABC comedy series on which June Lockhart made a guest appearance immediately prior to beginning her starring role on *Lost in Space*.

---

24. By the time she was four, Angela Cartwright was well-known by the top photographers in the country and appeared in many advertisements. Which magazine's cover did she once grace?
    A. *Redbook*
    B. *Ladies' Home Journal*
    C. *McCall's*

25. What was the last project *Lost in Space* costume designer Paul Zastupnevich worked on for Irwin Allen?
    A. *Alice in Wonderland*
    B. *Swiss Family Robinson*
    C. *The Towering Inferno*

26. Who recommended Jonathan Harris for the role of Dr. Smith?

27. Whose adornment of "big dangling gold earrings" impressed Irwin Allen during casting interviews for the series' regulars?

28. (True or False) During *Lost in Space*'s first year, Guy

Williams was paid $2,000 per week to star as the lead of the series.

29. Who wasn't interested in starring in the space show, but only accepted the role in the pilot when he was assured the series would never sell?

30. Billy Mumy's agent at the time, his family, and Mumy himself, had decided against the child actor becoming a television series regular, preferring versatility in a variety of guest-starring roles. Why did Mumy "jump at the chance" to star in *Lost in Space?*

31. In which episode of Irwin Allen's *Voyage to the Bottom of the Sea* series did June Lockhart make a guest appearance prior to reading for the *Lost in Space* pilot script?

32. Identify the Walt Disney-produced television series which starred Guy Williams.

33. Name the 1950s series in which Jonathan Harris starred with Michael Rennie (who later appeared as the Keeper) as a pair of dashing adventurers.

34. Who was the make-up supervisor for *Lost in Space?*
    A. Ben Nye
    B. Nancy Wilhelm
    C. Dana Washburn

MEMORY BANKS OVERLOAD #3

What was the nickname the series cast gave to Mark Goddard?

---

35. Who were June Lockhart's famous parents?

36. Name the 1940 Betty Davis and Charles Boyer movie in which June had a supporting role.

37. Why did Jonathan Harris decline to be involved in the *Family Feud Lost in Space* game show reunion?

38. Which former star of *Lost in Space* owns a collection of comic books dating back to the late 1930s?

39. Who later starred as the 300-year-old Commander Gampu in the Saturday morning series *Space Academy*?

MEMORY BANKS OVERLOAD #4

Name the 1946 B-movie horror thriller starring June Lockhart.

---

40. After *Lost in Space* was canceled, which former series star worked with Irwin Allen once again in a 1969 episode of *Land of the Giants*, titled "Pay the Piper"?

41. Who drove to Florida to paint scenery and play bit parts in winter stock before being cast as a series regular on *Lost in Space*?

42. Which former cast member became a show business agent after the cancellation of the series?

43. Marta Kristen is an avid reader of the world's greatest literature. Who is her favorite author?
    A. Ernest Hemingway
    B. Erich Maria Remarque
    C. F. Scott Fitzgerald

44. Although a cartoonist and musician, in which movie did Billy Mumy portray a character color blind and inept at painting?
    A. *Bless the Beasts and Children*
    B. *Papillon*
    C. *Dear Brigette*

45. Which of the former *Lost in Space* stars was a brilliant musicologist?

MEMORY BANKS OVERLOAD #5

Name the series crew member who appeared briefly as a foreign interpreter during the Alpha Control scenes in the first episode, "The Reluctant Stowaway."

46. Who hosted the premiere of the previously unaired *Lost in Space* pilot on the Sci-Fi Channel?

47. Identify the former series star who acted as the official inspirational leader of Child Power, an organization devoted to spreading peace throughout the world.

48. Who made a guest appearance on *The John Larroquette Show* as his con artist mother?

49. This former *Lost in Space* star appeared in the movie, *Beyond the Poseidon Adventure*, which was produced by her former boss on the series, Irwin Allen. Name the actress.

50. (True or False) Described by one critic as "the complete man of the theatrical world," the versatile Jonathan Harris has portrayed an English bon vivant, Polish RAF pilot, Hindustani jewel thief, Chinese villain, and Jewish patriarch among his multitude of characterizations.

51. What was June Lockhart's real television ambition before she joined the *Lassie* series?
    A. Producer and director
    B. News reporter and analyst
    C. Episode writer

52. Who appeared as a regular cast member on the short-lived *Texas* series from 1979–80?

53. Where was Marta Kristen when producer Jimmy Harris "discovered" her and asked if she wanted the

opportunity to try out for *Lolita* (although she didn't get the part)?

    A. Eating a hamburger with her boyfriend at a drive-in restaurant

    B. Sitting on a bench at a bus stop

    C. Exiting a grocery store

54. Whose actress-daughter played Sheeba in the sci-fi series *Battlestar Galactica?*

55. (True or False) Mark Goddard appeared in the episode "Bang, You're Dead" for the briefly revived *Alfred Hitchcock Presents* in 1985.

56. Who is the owner of a gift shop in Toluca Lake, California called Rubber Boots?

57. Which former *Lost in Space* cast member's college professor father published the book, *The Person and Education*, which has been used in universities throughout America?

58. Who is the author of *My Book: A Child's First Journal*, which records a baby's first year of development?

59. Identify the *Lost in Space* star who portrayed the hilarious hotel manager eternally harassed by a frustrated bellboy named Jose Jimenez on *The Bill Dana Show.*

MEMORY BANKS OVERLOAD #6

What was the name of the 1986 *Gremlins*-like movie in which June Lockhart appeared with her actress-daughter who played the younger version of her white-wigged mother?

---

60. Who had a role as the daughter of Pier Angeli and Paul Newman in the movie *Somebody Up There Likes Me* when she was only three-and-a-half years old?

61. (True or False) Mark Goddard appeared with Liza Minelli in the Broadway play *The Act*.

62. Name the former series co-star who returned to space in the 1980 movie *Battle Beyond the Stars*.

63. Whose film debut was as a young Aladdin in *The Wizard of Baghdad?*

64. (Fill in the blank with the correct number) June Lockhart read an average of _____ newspapers a day, plus several newsmagazines, for three years (1952–55) to prepare for her appearances on the NBC-TV quiz show, *Who Said That?*

65. Whose grandfather was a concert singer?
    A. Marta Kristen
    B. June Lockhart
    C. Guy Williams

66. Which former *Lost in Sapce* star's screen credits include *The Prince and the Pauper* and *Damon and Pythias?*

67. Who was called a "happy nut" in a *TV Guide* article?

68. (True or False) Billy Mumy was quoted in a 1985 *Starlog* magazine (issue #96) as stating: "You don't get a great script every week in a series, but if you're lucky, you'll get a good script every fourth one."

69. Identify the movie in which June Lockhart played Gary Cooper's sister.

70. In 1947, Lockhart received critical praise (comparing her to Helen Hayes and Margaret Sullivan) for her portrayal of an ingenue in F. Hugh Herbert's Broadway comedy, *For Love or Money*. How many performances of the play did she act in before returning to Hollywood?
    A. 140
    B. 260
    C. 365

71. How many years did Lockhart star in the television series, *Lassie*?

MEMORY BANKS OVERLOAD #7

June Lockhart is best known for her portrayal of the mothers on *Lassie* and *Lost in Space*. What was the name of her character on the earlier, canine-classic television series?

---

72. Which former *Lost in Space* star later founded a theater company called the West Coast Ensemble?

73. Who later hosted a one-hour Saturday morning rap session with teens on Continental Cablevision called *Not So Strictly Speaking?*

74. Name the cast member who earlier in his professional acting career had a featured role in the Broadway play *The Heart of the City.*

75. After Joseph D'Angosta had a heated argument with series creator and producer Irwin Allen, who replaced him as the *Lost in Space* casting director?
    A. Mark Levine
    B. Chris Brooks
    C. Larry Stewart

76. (True or False) Although the "lead," Guy Williams' season three salary was only $2,850, compared to Jonathan Harris' $3,500.

77. Before becoming the Director of Music for CBS Entertainment, he wrote the musical compositions for the *Lost in Space* episodes "Forbidden World," "Thief From Outer Space," and "Curse of Cousin Smith." Who is he?

78. (True or False) Guy Della Cioppa was the executive in charge of Van Bernard Productions, the company

owned by Red Skeleton which served as one of Irwin Allen's investors in the series.

MEMORY BANKS OVERLOAD #8

Although the writers always submitted titles for their episodes, who frequently added something with "space, monster, creature, etc." to the names at the request of Irwin Allen (who ultimately decided on the final episode titles)?

---

79. Guy Williams' son, Steven, went on his first date with Angela Cartwright. What movie did they see together?

80. Name the series in which June Lockhart appeared for two seasons after the cancellation of *Lost in Space*.

81. Who appeared with Paul Muni and Marlon Brando in Ben Hecht's stirring Broadway play about Israel, *A Flag is Born?*

82. Identify the interfaith religious magazine that employed June Lockhart for almost two years.
    A. *Our Faith Today*
    B. *Guideposts*
    C. *God's Message*

83. (True or False) Before playing Dr. Smith in *Lost in Space*, Jonathan Harris portrayed an Army psychiatrist in the highly successful Broadway production *Teahouse of the August Moon* with David Wayne and John Forsythe.

84. Name the former series star who has appeared in commercials for such products as Sony TV, Tab, and Dr. Pepper.

85. Who appeared in the 1983 feature film, *Strange Invaders*, which spoofed the invasion B-movies of the past?

86. Whose screen credits include *Curse of the Black Widow*, *The Exterminator*, and *C.H.U.D. 2*?

87. Who once portrayed Charles Dickens on an episode of *Bonanza?*

88. What was the name of Billy Mumy's music group which recorded the now-classic fun/nonsense song "Fishheads"?
    A. Crooked and Steep
    B. Barnes and Barnes
    C. Zabaoabee

89. June Lockhart appeared in a 1951 *Robert Montgomery Presents* adaptation of Nathaniel Hawthorne's *The House of the Seven Gables.* What role did Jonathan Harris play in a screen version of the classic with Shirley Temple?

90. Identify the character from the old *Flash Gordon* serials to whom Irwin Allen compared Harris' portrayal of Dr. Smith?

91. With whom did Billy Mumy hope to co-produce a *Lost in Space* reunion movie titled "Epilogue," which he co-wrote with two friends?

92. Who provided voices for the Saturday morning animated series *Visionaries?*

93. (True or False) The background music for the original *Lost in Space* pilot, largely just passages from the soundtracks of the movies *The Day the Earth Stood Still* and *Journey to the Center of the Earth,* was credited to Bernard Hermann.

94. Who was the only star from *Lost in Space* to provide a voice in the pilot for an animated version of the series in 1973?

95. Which former star of the show became a school teacher in Boston?

96. Who appeared in an episode of the long-running ABC sitcom, *Roseanne?*

97. Whose son also became involved in the acting profession, recently appearing in the 1995 movie, *Three Wishes* with Patrick Swayze?

98. Name the former *Lost in Space* star who appeared in the 1976 TV version of the sci-fi film *Logan's Run.*

99. Who played Cully on the *Johnny Ringo* western series before starring in *Lost in Space?*

100. During interviews, who has labeled *Star Trek* "a kind of military show" and *Lost in Space* "a family fantasy show"?

101. Name the four former cast members who made cameo appearances in the 1998 *Lost in Space* movie.

MEMORY BANKS OVERLOAD #9

Who was the director of photography for the series' first season?

---

102. Although his "day job" was costume designer and assistant to Irwin Allen, in which episode did Paul Zastupnevich "moonlight" as the voice of one of the series' alien creatures?

103. Italian by birth, what was Guy Williams' real name?

104. (True or False) After *Lost in Space*, Debby the Bloop went on to play the wife of *Lancelot Link, Secret Chimp*, one of June Lockhart's favorite animal shows.

105. Name the actor with whom Billy Mumy formed the band "Seduction of the Innocent."

106. Which of the cast members was injured in a motorcy-

cle wreck just prior to filming the original series pilot?

107. Identify the *Lost in Space* star who was quoted as saying in a *TV Guide* profile, "Actually, if it hadn't been for Jonathan Harris we would have been off the air in thirteen weeks"?

108. Which cast member had a penchant for performing practical jokes on the set?

109. Name the popular early 1980s TV series in which Jonathan Harris was offered a role, but after reading a script realized the part was "totally wrong" for him.

110. Which former *Lost in Space* star appeared not once, but *three* times, on *The Dating Game*?

MEMORY BANKS OVERLOAD #10

Match the stand-ins and/or stunt doubles to the corresponding series stars.

(The entire section must be answered correctly in order to be awarded the 5-point bonus)

1. _____ Harry Monte
2. _____ Chuck Couch
3. _____ Ann Urcan
4. _____ John Hunt
5. _____ Henrietta "Hank" Silvey
6. _____ Donna Garrett
7. _____ Ralph Madlener
8. _____ Anne Merman
9. _____ "Handsome" Harry Carter
10. _____ Paul Stader

A. Guy Williams' stand-in
B. June Lockhart's space-walking double
C. Angela Cartwright's stand-in
D. Jonathan Harris' stand-in
E. Guy Williams' space-walking double
F. Billy Mumy's stand-in (1st season only)
G. Jonathan Harris' occasional stunt double
H. Mark Goddard's stand-in
I. Marta Kristen's stand-in
J. June Lockhart's stand-in

3.9
COLLISION OF
PLANETS

Original Airdate: 11.08.67
Earth Year

Ship's Log: *A demolition team consisting of four "useless" space hippies are assigned by their controller to destroy the planet the Robinson expedition has landed on before it collides with an inhabited world.*

That Does Not Compute

Instead of remaining at a safe distance during liftoff, Maureen and Dr. Smith stand within a yard or two of the Space Pod when John and Maj. West set off in the small spacecraft to find the demolition team.

Once again, the members of the *Jupiter 2* crew erroneously refer to a planetary tremor as an "earthquake."

The 515-pound box of demolition material lands on the planet's surface by parachute without so much as a "thud," but when Dr. Smith drops the box *twice*, the effect is similar to a ground-shaking planetary quake (or is that "earthquake"?).

Trivia Challenge

1. What had the planet developed that forced its destruction by the demolition team?

2. Identify the hardhat-wearing leader of the "useless" aliens.

3. What was the name of the demolition-targeted planet?
   A. Xeno
   B. Beto
   C. Kromah

4. (Fill in the Blank) Once Dr. Smith regained consciousness after inhaling the alien gas, the Robot stated,
   "Now I'll have to file your _____ away in my
   memory banks for future use."

5. What color was Smith's hair after he became endowed
   with Samson-like strength?

6. After Dr. Smith's strength diminished, which type of
   exercises revived the alien fumes that were still trapped
   in his lungs?
   A. Push-ups
   B. Deep breathing
   C. Running-in-place

7. (Fill in the Blank) The alien leader of the demolition
   team repeatedly referred to John as the "_____
   master."

MEMORY BANKS OVERLOAD

(Fill in the Blank)

Muscle-bound Smith proclaimed himself "the Mighty,
the Strongest Man in the _____."

SPACE AGE FAST FACT

An episode of the series typically took six days to film
and required the cast and crew to be on the set from
seven in the morning to seven at night.

3.10
SPACE CREATURE
Original Airdate: 11.15.67
Earth Year

Ship's Log: *While the Jupiter 2 is trapped in the orbit of a fog-shrouded planet, the crew disappears one-by-one to another dimension inhabited by a primitive, ghost-like alien who feeds on negative emotions.*

That Does Not Compute

Why don't John and Maj. West order the rest of the crew to secure themselves while they attempt to maneuver the *Jupiter 2* into the planet's orbit? When the two men fire the spacecraft's retro-rockets they are safely confined to their control seats (although their heads snap backwards). Dr. Smith, however, is awakened from a deep sleep in his cabin, visibly shaken to the point that he assumes the ship has been struck by a meteor and should be abandoned.

Why would John believe that Maureen and Judy would be in the spacecraft's power core?

After Maj. West departs in the Space Pod, John tells him to abort the search mission for the crew on the planet's surface if the atmosphere proves fatal, but the Robot had already announced that the planet was deadly to human life.

After encountering the ghost-like alien, Don asks, "What is that thing?" Unfortunately, it should be as obvious to him as it is to the viewing audience that the creature is nothing more than a man draped in a sheet.

Trivia Challenge

1. What was Dr. Smith's "code of honor"?

2. Which Earth year did the Robot consider "ancient" history?
   A. 1647
   B. 1865
   C. 1942

3. (Fill in the Blank) The Robot's analysis of the planet's atmosphere confirmed that it was equal parts _____ and an unidentifiable gas instantly fatal to humans.

4. Identify the equipment Maureen was in contact with when she abruptly vanished from the *Jupiter 2* galley?

5. Which two characters in this episode announced: "All I want is to be left alone"?

6. Identify the two negative emotions from which the evil alien organism derived nourishment.

7. (Fill in the Blank) During their final confrontation near the *Jupiter 2*'s power core, the creature informed Will that he was the boy's _____ from forty years in the future.

MEMORY BANKS OVERLOAD

Name the British author Dr. Smith quoted when he urged Will to search the power core by himself. (Hint: ". . . he travels fastest who travels alone.")

SPACE AGE FAST FACT

The Aurora Model Company, which had secured the rights to issue official *Lost in Space*-based plastic assembly kits such as the Robot and the Cyclops, rejected merchandising a *Jupiter 2* model kit because management believed that the flying saucer-shaped spacecraft was too "plain and simple."

3.11
DEADLIEST OF THE SPECIES

Original Airdate: 11.22.67
Earth Year

Ship's Log: *An alien space capsule containing a danger-ous, female automaton follows the Jupiter 2 to the surface of an uncharted planet where the Robot falls in love.*

That Does Not Compute

Why can't John and Maj. West hear the mechanical men report to their alien leader while they are standing behind a boulder only a few yards away from the *Jupiter 2* landing site?

The Robot demands the force field's subatomic ener-gizer from John and Maj. West in exchange for Will's life. John immediately goes inside the spacecraft and returns with the device in less than a minute. Wouldn't it take some time to remove the mechanism?

Trivia Challenge

1. Identify the malfunctioning piece of *Jupiter 2* equip-ment which forced the spaceship to land in order to be dismantled and repaired.

2. What did the Robot tell Will he saw through the ship's porthole as they descended to the planet surface?

3. Which police organization employed the two mechanical "space officers"?
   A. The Bureau of Intergalactic Law Enforcement
   B. The Central Galactic Police Agency
   C. The Intergalactic Law Enforcement Department

4. (Fill in the Blank) The Robot's "personality_____" computed that the female automaton was evil.

5. What was the *Jupiter 2*'s second line of defense against the "elephantine Eve"?

6. Who accused the Robot of having a "tawdry affair"?

MEMORY BANKS OVERLOAD

(Fill in the Blanks)

"Do you think I am just an _____ collection of computer-oriented nuts and bolts?" a lovesick Robot asked. "I have a central _____ mechanism that feels just like any other robots."

SPACE AGE FAST FACT

Dick Tufeld always names this episode as his favorite of the entire series, but Bob May considers it the worst.

3.12
A DAY AT THE ZOO

Original Airdate: 11.29.67
Earth Year

Ship's Log: *Most of the Jupiter 2's crew are captured, caged, and placed on exhibit in an intergalactic showman's traveling space zoo.*

That Does Not Compute

The giant lizard-like monster that Don kills with his laser pistol is obviously not the same fire-breathing dragon that threatens Will and Farnum B in the prehistoric world.

Where is John in this episode? Even at the conclusion, when the entire *Jupiter 2* expedition gathers on the spaceship's ramp, the Robinson patriarch is mysteriously missing.

It is never totally explained how Don gets out of the cage, obtains a laser pistol and closes down Smith's show.

Trivia Challenge

1. What was Mr. Farnum's "most valuable exhibit"?

2. Identify the Middle Ages' knight in armor.
   A. Lexxus
   B. Mort
   C. Vortox

3. (Fill in the Blank) Farnum proclaimed himself "the Greatest Showman in the _____."

4. According to Dr. Smith, what were the "sacred words"?
   A. "There is no business like show business"
   B. "The show must go on"
   C. "The only thing that matters is the show"

5. What was the life expectancy on Oggo's prehistoric homeworld?

6. How much did showman Smith charge the various alien species to view the zoo's caged humanoids?

MEMORY BANKS OVERLOAD

Who did Farnum B say was "the great monster tamer in all the outer heavens"?

SPACE AGE FAST FACT

Guest star Leonard Stone was allowed almost unprecedented creative control of his Farnum B character, selecting the wardrobe and designing his makeup and hairstyle as well.

DIRECTOR'S CUT

Match the director with the Lost in Space *episode he helmed.*

1. _____ Ezra Stone
2. _____ Nathan Juran
3. _____ Tony Leader
4. _____ Sobey Martin
5. _____ Harry Harris
6. _____ Seymour Robbie
7. _____ Alvin Ganzer
8. _____ Alex Singer
9. _____ Sutton Roley
10. _____ Don Richardson
11. _____ Irving Moore
12. _____ Paul Stanley
13. _____ Leonard Horn
14. _____ Justus Addiss
15. _____ Robert Douglas

A. "Space Beauty"
B. "My Friend, Mr. Nobody"
C. "War of the Robots"
D. "The Derelict"
E. "Curse of Cousin Smith"
F. "All That Glitters"
G. "Junkyard in Space"
H. "Ghost in Space"
I. "The Reluctant Stowaway"
J. "Welcome Stranger"
K. "Wish Upon a Star"
L. "Target Earth"
M. "The Toymaker"
N. "Invaders from the Fifth Dimension"
O. "The Mechanical Men"

MEMORY BANKS OVERLOAD

Who directed the original *Lost in Space* pilot "No Place to Hide"?

3.13
TWO WEEKS IN SPACE

Original Airdate: 12.13.67
Earth Year

Ship's Log: *While most of the Robinson expedition is away at the radar station, Dr. Smith converts the Jupiter 2 into a resort hotel to accommodate a group of vacationing aliens, not realizing that they are in reality fugitive space robbers.*

That Does Not Compute

Where does Smith procure (and on such short notice) a cash register, adding machine, ornate lawn furniture (with table umbrellas), and sports equipment such as shuffleboard, badminton, golf clubs, and ping pong tables? Perhaps the resourceful doctor found another abandoned Celestial Department Store ordering machine.

If the planet has two moons, then why is only one shown in the night sky when the aliens revert back to their original monster forms?

Trivia Challenge

1. Impersonating Earth astronauts, the alien criminals initially contacted the *Jupiter 2* and requested that the landing beam be activated. What did they claim was the name of their Class B-7 intergalactic spaceship?
   A. *Saturn 4*

    B. *Venus 5*
    C. *Mars 6*

2. What type of protective buffer did Don activate to impede the space robbers from landing their craft on the planet surface?
    A. Ionic particle field
    B. Defensive shield array
    C. Radiation shield

3. (Fill in the Blank) The alien criminals had hijacked Mr. Zumdish's spaceship for use as an escape vehicle after stealing a fortune in _____ from a bank.

4. What was the name of Smith's flagship resort hotel?

5. (Fill in the Blank) Dr. Smith wanted "to go down in history as the first intergalactic _____."

6. Identify the law enforcement troopers in pursuit of the alien robbers.
    A. Space Patrol
    B. The Galaxy Rangers
    C. Universal Police

7. Where did the space robbers intend to destroy the Robinson women?

8. In reality, what was the large, bejeweled ring that the alien female gave Smith?

9. What was the name of the new business Zumdish started at the end of the episode?
    A. Zumdish Fine Tailoring
    B. Galactic Travel Agency
    C. Zumdish Insurance Company

MEMORY BANKS OVERLOAD

What were the names of the two female alien space fugitives?

SPACE AGE FAST FACT

Mid-way through the third season, *Lost in Space* suffered a small but noticeable ratings drop. In response, Irwin Allen instructed the story department to introduce a new character into the series: a talking purple giraffe. A script was written, but the idea was quickly abandoned after it was discovered that the long-necked animal was too tall to fit into the *Jupiter 2* or appear in the same camera shots as the rest of the cast.

3.14
CASTLES IN SPACE

Original Airdate: 12.20.67
Earth Year

Ship's Log: *While setting up a radar tower, Don, Judy, Dr. Smith, Will, and the Robot discover a block of frozen fluid containing an ice princess in suspended animation.*

That Does Not Compute

After the princess is thawed from the alien sarcophagus, she walks away empty-handed. When she emerges from hiding in one of the campsite tents, however, she is wielding a long, pointed-tip shaft at Dr. Smith.

Chavo is able to get the Robot drunk by pouring fermented fluid into his computer tape compartment? And the mechanical man suffers from a hangover later? The Robot has become more and more human-like as the series has progressed from year-to-year, but this is going *too* far.

Where did Will, Dr. Smith and the Robot obtain the material to construct the mock-up "senorita" decoy of the ice princess?

Trivia Challenge

1. Why did the radio tower topple over with Don?

2. What did Dr. Smith carelessly leave atop the block of frozen fluid which caused it to thaw, effectively reviving the ice princess it encased?
    A. A thermal blanket
    B. The robot's power pack
    C. An energizer cell for the radar tower

3. (Fill in the Blank) The Robot snidely remarked to Dr. Smith, "I'm not programmed to interpret the language of the _____, only the language of windbags."

4. Identify the important piece of equipment that Chavo stole from the Robot after he got the mechanical man inebriated.

5. (True or False) Don sarcastically compared Chavo's paternal attitude toward Will to that of a "father alligator."

6. (Fill in the Blank) In departing, Chavo good-naturedly reminded the Robot, "The braver the _____, the harder he falls."

7. In addition to his knife, what else did Chavo accidentally drop to the ground?

MEMORY BANKS OVERLOAD

What was the ice princess' name?

SPACE AGE FAST FACT

Marta Kristen has repeatedly stated in interviews that if she had known *Lost in Space* would not develop the way Irwin Allen originally promised when he hired her, she would have refused to sign on for the series. Kristen's major regret: the lack of progress in the relationship between her character and Don West.

3.15
THE ANTI-MATTER MAN

Original Airdate: 12.27.67
Earth Year

Ship's Log: *While John and the Robot are working on the atomizing unit, an evil, anti-matter duplicate version of Prof. Robinson appears, dragging him in chains into a dark, parallel universe.*

That Does Not Compute

In the anti-matter world, trees cast shadows on a supposedly distant mountain range every time lightning flashes. You can also see a technician's shadow make an appearance as he manually pushes one of the moving boulders.

Why is Don reluctant to believe the battered Robot about John being an anti-matter version, despite the overwhelming evidence that had swayed him only a few scenes earlier?

As Will and the Robot approach the atomizing unit in an attempt to recreate the conditions of John's disappearance and follow after him in the anti-matter world, one of Bob May's feet can be seen momentarily to the right behind a large rock.

Although it has already been established that a violent electrical storm occurs when both Johns appear in either world, it is peaceful outside the *Jupiter 2*'s observation window when Don says that Will and John's duplicate have gone to the anti-matter world in pursuit of John.

Trivia Challenge

1. (Fill in the Blank) A somewhat overly-emotional Robot explained that a bizarre atmospheric disturbance was the result of two worlds whose _____ stability was out of balance.

2. According to the anti-matter Don, how long had he and the duplicate version of John been prisoners in the parallel universe?
   A. "Millenniums"
   B. "Thousands and thousands and thousands of years"
   C. "Centuries"

3. What did the Robot notice was unique about the impostor version of John when he appeared "even in strong sunlight"?

4. Identify the character who once noted, "In space, time isn't measured by the minutes or the hours, but by the millions of years"?

5. Who did the evil, anti-matter version of John brutally bludgeon with a lead pipe before following Will back to the parallel universe?

6. (True or False) The Robot's control mechanisms were self-repairing.

7. What was the only *physical* difference between the two versions of John?

8. In addition to Don's and Will's watches running backwards, what other weird phenomenon occurred after the anti-matter John arrived at the *Jupiter 2*'s campsite?

MEMORY BANKS OVERLOAD

Who called the Robot "punk"?

SPACE AGE FAST FACT

Mark Goddard considers the dark and serious "Anti-Matter Man" to be his favorite *Lost in Space* episode because it provided him with a rare opportunity to shine as an actor while playing both Maj. West and his evil double.

TECH SPECS #8

Match the letter to the correct room or equipment aboard the *Jupiter 2*.

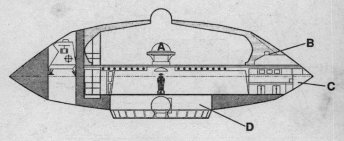

JUPITER 2
GENERAL CROSS SECTION
SIDE VIEW

Technical drawing by Edwin E. Echols.

1. _____ Power core   3. _____ Astrogator
2. _____ Flight controls   4. _____ Observation window

TECH SPECS #9

Match the letter to the correct equipment aboard the Space Pod

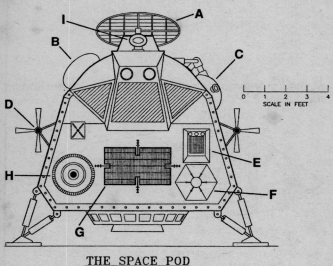

SCALE IN FEET

THE SPACE POD

FRONT VIEW

Technical drawing by Edwin E. Echols.

1. _____ Video sensor
2. _____ Sensor
3. _____ Reaction control
4. _____ Scanner
5. _____ Oxygen tank
6. _____ Radar antenna
7. _____ Atmosphere analyzer
8. _____ Hydrogen tank
9. _____ Solar screen

3.16
TARGET EARTH
Original Airdate: 01.03.68
Earth Year

Ship's Log: *Shapeless aliens assume the physical forms of the Jupiter 2 crew and travel to Earth aboard the spaceship in hopes of learning how to be individuals.*

That Does Not Compute

Why does the alien leader insist on opening and closing the hatch of the *Jupiter 2* every time he materializes and dematerializes aboard the spaceship?

After Dr. Smith knocks out his double and changes clothing, he points out the duplicate's webbed fingers to Will. But when the alien version of Smith regains consciousness and grabs a wall to steady himself, the webbing is noticeably missing.

At the beginning of the episode, the *Jupiter 2* is forced to land on the unknown planet to retrieve the accidentally-launched Space Pod. After the shapeless aliens physically replace the crew and steal the *Jupiter 2*, they also retrieve the small exploration vehicle after launch and store it in the Pod bay. During the trip to Earth, Will and Dr. Smith both use the radio in the Space Pod to notify Alpha Control and with the Robot's assistance, the alien duplicates of John and Maj. West are trapped in the Pod bay. However, when Will navigates the *Jupiter 2* back to the planet to rescue his family, the Space Pod is still sitting on the ground outside the alien city.

What would shapeless masses of protoplasm need with chairs at their control panels?

Trivia Challenge

1. Due to Dr. Smith's incorrigible antics, what vital component was trapped inside the runaway Space Pod?

2. Which *Jupiter 2* crew member theorized that the aliens "preferred intimidation to communication"?

3. What did the alien beings call Will?
   A. "Little Earth explorer"
   B. "Young Earth boy"
   C. "Small Earth traveler"

4. (Fill in the Blank) John's duplicate instructed the alternate version of Dr. Smith to act exactly as the original Earthling: "boastful, _____, and lazy."

5. According to the alien impersonators, what was John's "popular expression"?
   A. "I guess"
   B. "That's correct"
   C. "Of course, darling"

6. Which "Earth food" did Dr. Smith request the alien version of Maureen to prepare for him as nourishment?
   A. Pancakes
   B. Sandwiches
   C. Soup

7. (True or False) When Smith's duplicate was discovered bound and gagged in his cabin, the faux John demanded that Smith prove he was the real alien by "quickly" providing his true name, the planet of his birth, and his normal life span.

8. In which U.S. city did the *Jupiter 2* land on Earth?

MEMORY BANKS OVERLOAD

What was the name of the shapeless alien leader?

SPACE AGE FAST FACT

The stage-trained Jonathan Harris essentially created the character of Dr. Smith, brazenly rewriting his character's dialogue and ad-libbing lines during filming from week to week, transforming Smith from a murderous, hard-core villain to a cowardly, greedy, and selfish man the audience loved to hate.

3.17
PRINCESS OF SPACE

Original Airdate: 01.10.68
Earth Year

Ship's Log: *Penny is taken aboard an alien ship and trained to ascend to the throne of a space princess who was hidden on Earth years earlier.*

That Does Not Compute

The porthole view into space from Capt. Kraspo's alien ship shows the stars and nebulae going past the window from left to right, then abruptly reversing from right to left and sometimes not moving at all in other scenes.

Dr. Smith, Don, and Judy are all reduced to computer tape, but it is obvious that the strips are in actuality exposed camera film.

Trivia Challenge

1. How many years had Capt. Kraspo and his crew been traveling in space?
   - A. Five
   - B. Ten
   - C. Thirteen

2. Which planet was Princess Alpha's homeworld?
   - A. Cyrix
   - B. Beta
   - C. Urgo

3. What important governmental position did Dr. Smith want to hold while Penny reigned as Princess?

4. What nickname did the royal children call Aunt Gamma?

5. What magical instrument belonging to Capt. Kraspo rang whenever the Princess was near?

6. (True or False) Fedor was the ship's steward, tenth class.

7. In reality, Fedor was a computer. What did his "mother" make for him after he threw Capt. Kraspo into the brig?

8. (Fill in the Blank) The real Princess Alpha used her magical scepter to transform Fedor into a _____ card.

9. Where did Dr. Smith obtain a photograph of Penny at the age of six weeks?

10. Identify the mysterious code used to materialize the real Princess Alpha from computer tape.
    A. J48-78
    B. EL2-Z53
    C. K12-B6

MEMORY BANKS OVERLOAD

What were the names of the Archduke's three children?

SPACE AGE FAST FACT

In the early days before VCRs, episode music composers on *Lost in Space* were usually allowed only one opportunity to watch their assigned series segment, commit the episode to memory as best they could, and then go home and write music for the scenes.

3.18
THE TIME MERCHANT

Original Airdate: 01.17.68
Earth Year

Ship's Log: *While experimenting with cosmic particles during a storm, Will accidentally captures an angry time merchant named "The Great Chronos."*

That Does Not Compute

After Will is kidnapped by the time merchant at the beginning of the episode, Dr. Smith informs John that the boy was taken captive by "Chronos, Dr. Chronos." The alien, however, never introduced himself to Smith and Will in the cave as "doctor," only as "The Great Chronos" and "Chronos the Time Merchant."

When Dr. Smith steps into Chronos' cage-like time transporter, and the smoke begins to envelop his body, watch carefully and you will see that it is Jonathan Harris' stunt double. Also, during the climactic fight scene between John and the time merchant, it's effortless to distinguish between Guy Williams' stunt double and the actor himself in the long camera shots.

Trivia Challenge

1. Chronos destroyed an entire planet in which galaxy because the inhabitants wasted their time tapes?
   A. Andromeda

   B. Zentauri
   C. Omega

2. (True or False) Smith lied and told Chronos he was
    twenty-five-years-old in Earth years.

3. Which term did Smith affectionately use to refer to
    Earth when he was transported back in time to October
    16, 1997?
    A. "Terra firma"
    B. "Home, sweet home"
    C. "The Motherland"

4. (Fill in the blank with the correct number) The Robot
    was placed aboard the *Jupiter* 2 _____ minutes
    before liftoff.

5. (True or False) Chronos projected that if Dr. Smith's
    extra weight did not send the *Jupiter* 2 off course as
    it did previously, the spaceship would be destroyed
    within four months by an uncharted asteroid.

6. Chronos gave Will thirty electrocounters to return to
    Earth to repair the Robot and insure that Smith was
    placed aboard the *Jupiter* 2 before launch time. How
    many Earth minutes were equal to thirty electro-
    counters?
    A. Two
    B. Five
    C. Ten

7. Identify the launch pad number for the *Jupiter* 2.

MEMORY BANKS OVERLOAD

(Fill in the Blank)

Before the Robot traveled back in time to Earth in Chronos' transporter, the mechanical man said his good-byes to his friend Will: "New friends may be _____, but your old friend was titanium stainless-steel alloy with genuine chrome plate."

SPACE AGE FAST FACT

Director Ezra Stone, who helmed not only this episode but seven others in the series, was a noted actor and director at the time he was hired by Irwin Allen. The *Lost in Space* producer and creator had previously been turned down by several major directors who didn't want to be associated with what they considered a "second-rate" and "frivolous" television show. But Stone wrote Allen a personal letter and asked for the opportunity to direct an episode, stating "I want to be with a winner."

OUT OF THIS WORLD FX

*It's time to test your working knowledge of the series'
special effects and other tricks of the trade created
by technicians whom actor Jonathan Harris has
repeatedly called "the geniuses of Hollywood."*

1. In "The Reluctant Stowaway," what did FX techs
   use to create meteors for the scene of the *Jupiter 2*
   encountering the fierce and dangerous storm in deep
   space?
   A. Spray-painted cotton balls (with marbles inside)
   B. Pieces of tinfoil
   C. Pitted globs of dried mud

2. (Fill in the Blanks) The starry background of the
   spaceship traveling through space was accomplished
   by hanging a black _____ cloth on the back
   wall of the stage, spraying it with a sticky substance,
   and then throwing at it small shiny particles used
   in Christmas decorations known as _____,
   which stuck in random patterns.

3. (True or False) Small compressed gas bottles were
   remotely activated and a four foot miniature of the
   Jupiter 2 lifted by wires created the illusion of the spaceship blasting off from a planetary surface.

4. How many wires were used to fly the miniature galac-

tic vehicle over the Red Rock Canyon and Trona during the crash scenes?

5. In some third season episodes, a full-size mockup of the Space Pod was seen landing on a planet with the actors clearly visible inside. What did FX technicians use to lower the small exploratory pod?

6. When the miniature *Jupiter 2* model was filmed traveling through deep space, was it held up by wires or a pipe stand, or was some other method utilized?

7. How was the miniature model of the Space Pod lowered and returned to its docking bay in the mother ship?

MEMORY BANKS OVERLOAD #1

Name the classic sci-fi movie whose cinematic spaceship has been acknowledged as serving as the inspiration for the design of the flying saucer-shaped *Jupiter 2*.

---

8. How were effects such as lightning bolts and laser beams created?

9. What was used to supply the power for the miniature model's lights in scenes where the *Jupiter 2* was seen flying?
   A. Double A Batteries
   B. Small generators used in model cars
   C. Suspension wires

10. (True or False) Five feet in front of the black background wall used for space shots hung a bobinett treated with more sparkling Christmas decorations, which allowed FX technicians to obtain a third dimension when the camera was moved.

11. (Fill in the blank with the correct number) The ending to "The Keeper, Part I," in which it appeared that

dozens of alien monsters escaped his ship, was accomplished by simply filming the same _____ creatures exiting the vessel over and over again and then editing the scenes together.

12. Identify the actress whose character's headdress saved her life when an episode's climactic explosion caused a piece of the set's super structure to fly dangerously through the air.

13. How many hours were required to remove "The Golden Man" makeup from actor Dennis Patrick for his role as Mr. Keema?

14. Known formally as the "Experimental One Man Rocket Belt," the Jet Pack was an actual piece of practical hardware. Although careful film editing made the device appear as if John Robinson was flying it for an unlimited period, in reality how long was the rocket belt actually flown at a time during filming of the series?
    A. Less than thirty seconds
    B. Two minutes
    C. A little more than five minutes

15. (Fill in the Blank) The E.V.A. thruster was a variation of the type that was used by NASA's Project _____ astronauts when the first space-walks were taking place.

16. (True or False) The Jupiter 2 deck sets were on two separate levels and when the hydraulic elevator was lowered it went down into a hole, not the lower section of the spaceship.

MEMORY BANKS OVERLOAD #2

Identify the TV movie in which Irwin Allen modified the four-foot model of the Jupiter 2 for use as a futuristic building in an underwater city.

17. Who was responsible for enlarging the *Jupiter 2*'s original design of a simple, single-story pilotless space vehicle by adding a lower level and other items necessary to the altered emphasis of the series after Dr. Smith and the Robot were added as members of the crew?

18. (True or False) Although the Chariot all-terrain exploratory vehicle was built from the undercarriage of an actual Snow Cat, a four-foot miniature was used for long shot filming.

19. Which career did *Lost in Space*'s Stu Moody abandon to become a special effects wizard?
    A. Corporate executive
    B. Court judge
    C. College professor

20. (True or False) In addition to being used on *Voyage to the Bottom of the Sea*, *Planet of the Apes* and *The Towering Inferno*, many significant props from *Lost in Space* were used as set dressing on ABC TV's 1996 election night coverage.

21. (Affirmative or Negative) The *Jupiter 2* consoles were actual computers used in data processing in the late 1950s and very early 60s, modified extensively so that the blinking on and off effect could be realized.

22. The radar panel was constructed with sheet metal, but where did technicians obtain the device's knobs?

23. In which episode did one of the *Jupiter 2* special effects models make a "guest appearance" as a small-scale replica of the spaceship?

24. Name the series segment in which several scenes were filmed in a way to blur the borders of the televised picture to create the illusion of another dimension.

25. The footage of the sun in "Wild Adventure" was tinted green and reused as an alien planet in which episode?

26. During the planet quake scene in the original pilot, "No Place to Hide," what did Irwin Allen bang with a hammer while hovering above the cast on a catwalk in an attempt to jolt them?
    A. A garbage can lid
    B. A metal wastepaper basket
    C. Sheet metal

27. What did FX technicians use to construct the astronaut helmet that the Robot crushed to demonstrate his strength in "Island in the Sky"?

28. For which season was L.B. Abbot nominated for an Emmy Award for his photographic effect work on the series?

29. Name the episode in which Dr. Smith wore an astronaut helmet, which in actuality had no backside in an effort to accommodate actor Jonathan Harris' severe case of claustrophobia.

30. Identify the actress who almost became seriously injured when an explosion was detonated too close to the tube in which her character arrived on a planet.

31. In which series installment was the dome of an alien's spacecraft constructed from an immense plastic champagne glass previously used in a Marilyn Monroe movie musical?

MEMORY BANKS OVERLOAD #3

Where were the director and cameraman during the filming of "The Haunted Lighthouse" scenes in which a lion roamed freely on the set?

---

32. Identify the series alien whose makeup was one of the prototypes from the *Planet of the Apes* movie.

33. Who was the makeup artist who, in a matter of hours, constructed the shapeless Proto blobs in "Target

Earth" with plaster heads and shoulders of manne-
quins, polyurethane foam, and plastic?

34. Name the *Lost in Space* cast regular who was "hung
like a puppet" by wires in a harness during the filming of "Space Beauty."

35. Which makeup artist created the Dr. Smith masks for
the multitude of cyborgs in "Space Destructors"?

36. In which episode was the viewing audience provided
a rare, overhead shot of the *Jupiter 2* as Smith dumped
all of the spacecraft's fuel cells into space?

37. A giant lizard was used in "Flight into the Future"
as one of the planet's illusions. Name the movie from
which the scene was "borrowed."

38. (Fill in the blank with the correct number) The
Cyclops suit in the original, unaired pilot, "No Place
to Hide," was constructed from the peeled off bark
of more than _____ palm trees.
   A. thirty
   B. fifty
   C. seventy

39. For which national magazine's cover were Guy Williams and June Lockhart posing when the wire of
Williams' special space-walking "flying suit" broke
and he fell twelve feet onto a cement floor?

40. What was camouflaged with aluminum foil and
blinker lights and utilized as the huge vacuuming
CDS Generating Machine in "Revolt of the Robots"?

41. (True or False) The more comfortable third season
silver jumpsuits were made of the strong, thin polyes-
ter material called Mylar.

42. In the Irwin Allen movie *Towering Inferno*, who was
the former professional football star turned actor seen
adjusting the controls on major props once utilized
on *Lost in Space*?

43. What was used to construct the huge, silver-painted, towering pillars often used on alien sets in many of the series' episodes?

MEMORY BANKS OVERLOAD #4

The scenes of the dragon in "A Day at the Zoo" were "borrowed" from which two films?

3.19
THE PROMISED PLANET

Original Airdate: 01.24.68
Earth Year

Ship's Log: *Aliens disguised as young humans lure the Jupiter 2 to what appears to be an Earth colony in the Alpha Centauri star system where Will and Penny undergo brainwashing to amplify youthful, rebellious characteristics.*

That Does Not Compute

Why would Edgar give Will memory cones while attempting to brainwash the Robinson boy into a new way of thinking? It is obvious that the chemical inducements would just erase the brainwashing/adjustment processing just as the cones did for John, Maureen, Don, and Judy after they had been successfully subjected to the influence of "memory washing fumes."

During the climax, John and Maj. West arrive just in the nick of time to stop Bartholomew from subjecting Penny and Will to the transfusion process. John picks his daughter up off the pool table, turns toward the door and, while beginning to run, sits Penny down on her feet. In the next shot, however, John is still carrying her in his arms as he exits through the door.

The Promised Planet 331

Trivia Challenge

1. Which British author did Dr. Smith quote while lying on his "deathbed" at the beginning of the episode?
   A. Charles Dickens
   B. Rudyard Kipling
   C. William Shakespeare

2. (True or False) Bartholomew informed the *Jupiter 2* crew that terrestrial life had existed on all habitable planets in the Alpha Centauri star system for the past two years.

3. How often did a shuttle transport passengers from planet Delta to its main colony on Gamma?
   A. Every other day
   B. Twice a week
   C. Weekly

4. (Fill in the Blank) The *Jupiter 2*'s arrival on planet Delta was hailed with a spectacular _____ display of pyrotechnics.

5. What did the chemical memory cones smell like when they were ignited?
   A. Vanilla ice cream
   B. Cotton candy
   C. Incense

6. Which type of impulses were used by the aliens to mislead the Robot into believing that the Robinson expedition had finally approached the Alpha Centauri star system?
   A. Ionic
   B. Gravitational
   C. Magnetic

15. Bartholomew and Edgar sarcastically called Dr. Smith the same name as the ancestor of Noah who reportedly lived to be 969 years old. Who was this Biblical character?

MEMORY BANKS OVERLOAD

Will and Penny were separated from the older family members to undergo a processing period of "adjustment." Identify the letter/number cubicle designations in which they were placed.

SPACE AGE FAST FACT

Ezra Stone, who helmed this episode, was a close friend of Jonathan Harris from their theater years when Stone directed him in *The Man That Corrupted Hadleyburg*, based on a story by Mark Twain.

3.20
FUGITIVES IN SPACE

Original Airdate: 01.31.68
Earth Year

Ship's Log: *Maj. West and Dr. Smith discover an unconscious alien convict and are sentenced by a computerized court to life in prison for allegedly helping him to escape.*

That Does Not Compute

Don and Dr. Smith refer to the prison planet as "an inferno," because of the blistering heat and lack of shade, but why are there only two or three small fires continuously burning in close proximity to the area where they are busting rocks? If the planet's temperature is so hot that it produces spontaneous combustion, then why are there not other fires burning across the landscape, especially in the Devil's Quadrant?

The electronic judge has no arm-like appendages, but he somehow pounds the gavel in his court.

John, Maureen and most of the Robinson family are at the radar station during the course of events in this episode, but Will can't radio them with important news that Dr. Smith and Maj. West, their spacecraft pilot, have unjustly been sentenced to hard labor on a prison planet for the remainder of their life spans?

Trivia Challenge

1. What was the name of the alleged escape-proof prison planet?

2. (Fill in the Blank) Suspected of assisting a cosmic convict to escape, Dr. Smith and Don were remanded by the prison warden to the Intergalactic Court for the _____ of Criminal Procedure to appear before the electronic Judge 71, revised model 94E.

3. (True or False) The Robot utilized his electronic scent analyzers to lock in on the escaped prisoner, thus activating his automatic track and secure system.

4. How many unsuccessful escapes had been attempted on the prison planet during the warden's tenure?
   A. 500
   B. 861
   C. 1042

5. What was the convict's reward for working hard all day in the blistering heat of the prison planet?
   A. A bottle of cold water
   B. A block of ice
   C. A sonic shower

6. Identify the three rewards that the warden bestowed on Don and Dr. West after Creech was vaporized by the electronic field in the Devil's Quadrant.

7. Who originally wanted the warden to pursue a career as a dentist rather than a prison superintendent?

8. How many years had the regenerative Creech been incarcerated on the prison planet?

MEMORY BANKS OVERLOAD

What was Creech's convict number as prominently displayed on his striped prison clothes?

SPACE AGE FAST FACT

Although "The Great Vegetable Rebellion" was aired later, it was filmed before this episode and the following one, "Space Beauty." Because of their constant laughing throughout the filming (and re-filming) of the talking carrot installment, Guy Williams and June Lockhart were suspended from the set and their characters written out of both "Fugitives in Space" and "Space Beauty."

3.21
SPACE BEAUTY

Original Airdate: 02.14.68
Earth Year

Ship's Log: *Farnum B, once the owner of the traveling space zoo, is now operator of the Miss Galaxy beauty pageant and has come to the planet looking for contestants.*

That Does Not Compute

Why do the black-clothed aliens use the *Jupiter 2* elevator to descend to the crew cabins on the lower level when it is obvious that they can materialize and re-materialize anywhere at will?

The close-up shot of Farnum's contract with the "mysterious dictator" shows the handwritten date as "1968" in the top left corner.

During the climax, the rain-making machine causes it to snow, extinguishing the dictator's flames. In one of the final scenes the ground is clear surrounding the characters (who only have a few flakes in their hair and on their shoulders), but in the next shot the *Jupiter 2* campsite is completely covered in snow.

Also during the climactic scenes, why isn't Farnum B frozen in suspended animation like everyone else when the dictator hypnotically draws Judy from the spaceship?

Trivia Challenge

1. What was the name of Farnum B's agent?
    A. Alicia Square Root
    B. Nancy Pi-Squared
    C. Penelope Percentage

2. Who said, "Never trust anyone in show business. That's my rule"?

3. What was the official name for the Miss Galaxy beauty pageant?

4. Identify the small "concession" Farnum's agent made to secure the contract for the showman from the "mysterious dictator."

5. (True or False) Two of the beauty contestants in the pageant were Miss Fishtail and Miss Teutonium.

6. (Fill in the Blank) Will and the Robot's analysis of the dictator's "dark planet," determined that the seemingly inhospitable world was surrounded by a _____ gas 67 layer with a radioactive surface.

7. What did Will use as "bait" to lure the dragon lady?

8. How many years had the armor-wearing, fiery dictator been searching for beauty?
    A. 2,000
    B. 5,000
    C. 10,000

9. What was the Robot's stage name in the Miss Galaxy beauty contest?
    A. The Mechanized Love Machine
    B. Miss Mechanical Marvel
    C. Miss *Jupiter 2*

MEMORY BANKS OVERLOAD

How many Fahrenheit degrees of heat could the Robot endure?

SPACE AGE FAST FACT

During year three, *Lost in Space* writers were instructed to take a different approach to the series. Irwin Allen, believing that the previous season had been too whimsical, established guidelines resulting in a season with fewer scenes among the Robinson family members, less interplay between Dr. Smith and the Robot, and more action-driven plots.

COMMUNICATION CHANNELS

Season Three

The radio transmission relay stations have been effectively sabotaged by Dr. Smith. Once again, attempt to use the Vector Control Tape unit to interpret the following space static.

1. (Fill in the Blank) In "Deadliest of the Species," the Robot issued the warning, "Intensely heated objects are extremely dangerous. Undue _____ would produce severely burned fingers."

2. In which episode did Dr. Smith cry, "I'm too old to be nine-years-old!"?

3. Identify the character who remarked, "Earth? Never heard of the place."

4. Who philosophized, "A journey of a thousand miles starts with one step"?

5. In which series segment did Smith thank his *Jupiter 2* crew mates, "... for standing the death watch at my bed"?
   A. "The Promised Planet"
   B. "Kidnapped in Space"
   C. "Fugitives in Space"

6. Who said he preferred to "rely on the winds of chance, not superstition"?
   A. Don
   B. Smith
   C. John

7. Name the episode in which the Robot issued the fashion statement, "In times of emergency, one may dispense with formal attire"?

8. In "The Great Vegetable Rebellion," who called Tybo "a regular plant surgeon"?

9. Who noted that the Junkman had "cornered the intergalactic junk market"?

10. In which episode did Don point a laser pistol at Smith's head after referring to the doctor as "the most expendable of the whole group"?
    A. "Space Creature"
    B. "The Flaming Planet"
    C. "Fugitives in Space"

11. (True or False) In "Condemned in Space," Dr. Smith acknowledged that the intrepid space colonists were "caught between the Devil and the deep, black space."

12. Identify the series installment in which Smith called Don "a militant moron."

13. In which episode did an alien creature refer to Dr. Smith as "nice and hateful"?

14. (Fill in the Blank) The space bike-riding female misfit in "Collision of Planets" radioed the *Jupiter 2* after they escaped the exploding planet, "Get that _____ off the road!"

15. In which series segment did the Robot advise Will that "offense is the best defense"?
    A. "A Day at the Zoo"

      B. "Anti-Matter Man"
      C. "Flight into the Future"

16. Who referred to the prison ship in "Condemned in Space" as a "chamber of horrors"?

17. (Fill in the Blank) In the episode "Visit to a Hostile Planet," the Robot informed Dr. Smith that he preferred "_____ to seafood."

18. Identify the episode in which Dr. Smith snidely observed of the Robot: "It's quite obvious you were never programmed for music appreciation."

19. In "Space Destructors," which member of the *Jupiter 2* crew warned, "Dr. Smith must be stopped. The universe is in enough of a mess as it is without him being in charge"?

20. Who called Farnum B "a wicked man" in "A Day at the Zoo"?

21. Identify the character in "Two Weeks in Space" who noted, "There is no accounting for taste."
      A. Mr. Zumdish
      B. Dr. Smith
      C. TAT

22. In which installment of the series did Will tell his mechanical friend, "You're a robot. You're supposed to be functional, not pretty"?
      A. "Deadliest of the Species"
      B. "Junkyard in Space"
      C. "The Anti-Matter Man"

23. Name the alien being who repeatedly called Dr. Smith a "deadbeat."

24. (Fill in the Blank) In "Kidnapped in Space" the Robot issued the warning, "The sight of broken _____ and leaking oil is only for strong stomachs."

25. (True or False) In "The Anti-Matter Man," the Robot

noted that "worrying is not a character trait of robots."

26. Identify the episode in which Don stated the obvious, "Same old Smith. Same old monkey business."

27. To whom did Dr. Smith admit, "I wish I could be as honorable as you. But I am a weak man, full of human frailty. I sometimes wish I could be different, but I cannot seem to manage it"?

28. In "The Time Merchant," who complained, "I do not enjoy time travel, especially in economy class"?

29. (Fill in the Blank) In "Collision of Planets," the Robot commented to the *Jupiter 2* crew, "It just goes to prove, there is nothing you can do with a really _____ misfit."

30. Identify the alien creature who referred to the *Jupiter 2*'s force field as "a warm welcome"?

MEMORY BANKS OVERLOAD

In which episode from *Lost in Space*'s third and final season did the ever-complaining Dr. Smith wail, "I loathe reptiles"?

3.22
THE FLAMING PLANET

Original Airdate: 02.21.68
Earth Year

Ship's Log: *After a giant plant attaches itself to the hull of the Jupiter 2 and blocks all of the air ducts, the crew attempts to burn it off the spaceship by entering the atmosphere of a nearby hostile plant.*

That Does Not Compute

As the *Jupiter 2* is tossed about after encountering the planet's radiation belt (more of the prop department's overused polyethylene wrap), Judy and Penny fall *uphill* in the lab as the camera sways back and forth.

Through the observation window, the missiles are viewed coming straight at the *Jupiter 2*, but the long camera shots show the missiles homing in on the spaceship from its rear.

Dr. Smith's plant grows to such gigantic proportions that it attaches itself to the top of the *Jupiter 2* after he deposits it into space. When the plant is later discovered on the planet and recruited by John and Dr. Smith to be a worthy opponent of the Sobram, the creature has been reduced to the size of a man once again.

Trivia Challenge

1. What variety of citrus fruit did Dr. Smith mistakenly believe that his tree produced?

2. (True or False) Will asked Smith to dispose of the plant by burning it up through the *Jupiter 2*'s jet exhaust, but the doctor floated it out into space through the escape hatch.

3. Which *Jupiter 2* crew member at one time studied to be an architect?

4. What happened to the spaceship after a laser beam was fired at it from the surface of the hostile planet?

5. (Fill in the Blank) The Sobram remarked that Dr. Smith certainly had "the sneaky look of a dirty _____."

6. Why did the Sobram eventually decide that Don was unsuitable as his replacement to tend to the planet's weapons?

7. (True or False) Dr. Smith bragged that he had beaten the Robot in twelve straight games of chess.

8. Which character described Maj. West as "an expert in military strategy," whose courage was "beyond question"?

MEMORY BANKS OVERLOAD

According to the Sobram's immense history book, how long did the planets and civilizations battle each other before the warrior race appeared?

SPACE AGE FAST FACT

For the coming fourth season, Irwin Allen promised the cast (in particular Guy Williams) that the scripts would be more well balanced among the performers, featuring stories prominently displaying each main character, such as in the first year.

3.23
THE GREAT
VEGETABLE
REBELLION

Original Airdate: 02.28.68
Earth Year

Ship's Log: *After Dr. Smith is accused of "murder" by a talking carrot, the Robinson expedition engages in jungle warfare on an alien plant world.*

That Does Not Compute

Actually, the entire episode does not compute, but we'll try to be more specific in nitpicking what most fans consider the worst installment of the classic series.

Why is it that sometimes Dr. Smith has no idea how to operate the Space Pod, but on other occasions (such as this episode), he expertly pilots the small craft to a planetary surface?

Since when did the Robot become "programmed" to only answer questions, not ask them?

And where did he suddenly find a knotted rope to throw down into the mulch pit and save Will and Penny's life?

Tybo's human companion, Willoughby, is erroneously listed in the end credits as "Willoughby the Llama." (Note: The character was originally scripted to be played by a purple-dyed Llama, but the animal was unable to perform properly and was cut from the episode.)

Trivia Challenge

1. Whose idea was it to throw the Robot a birthday party?

2. What reason did John give for placing the *Jupiter 2* in orbit around the planet for a few hours?

3. (Fill in the Blank) Dr. Smith descended to the nearby planet in the Space Pod to collect "exotic _____" for the Robot so that the "grateful" mechanical man would act as his "slave forever."

4. Identify the vegetable that the life-saving Tybo used to transplant the spacewrecked Willoughby's heart?
   A. Potato
   B. Lettuce
   C. Celery

5. Who referred to Dr. Smith as "nature boy"?

6. After their spaceship descended to the planet surface, what did the *Jupiter 2* crew use to clear a path through the jungle-like plant life?

7. (True or False) Willoughby offered to free Judy and Will from the entanglement of a mass of vines if they wouldn't tell Tybo, fearing that the vengeful, talking carrot would transmute him into a blue orange.

8. Who commented, "If you've seen one tree, you've seen them all"?

MEMORY BANKS OVERLOAD

What two types of trees did Tybo threaten to transmute Will into?

SPACE AGE FAST FACT

Although most fans despise "The Great Vegetable Rebellion," including Billy Mumy, who has called the episode "the worst television show, not just of *Lost in Space*, but of all time," June Lockhart considers this installment of the series to be her favorite.

3.24
JUNKYARD IN SPACE

Original Airdate: 03.06.68
Earth Year

Ship's Log: *The Jupiter 2 becomes trapped in an intergalactic junkyard, where Dr. Smith convinces a mechanical man to give the crew food in exchange for parts from the Robot.*

That Does Not Compute

The cosmic cloud that the Robot maneuvers the Space Pod through en route to a nearby planet is the same polyethylene wrap so often used by the prop department as planetary radiation belts and force fields throughout the series.

How could the Junkman close the *Jupiter 2*'s hatch to "lock everybody else out" when there is always the "emergency button" right outside the door (which Dr. Smith recently used in "The Time Merchant" to get inside the spaceship only seconds before it was launched from Earth)?

Trivia Challenge

1. What was the title of Dr. Smith's memoirs, which he believed would be "one of the biggest best-sellers in literature"?
   A. *Galactic Castaway: The True Story*

    B. *The True Adventures of a Space Hero*
    C. *Outer Space and I*

2. Which malfunctioning piece of *Jupiter 2* equipment caused a fire in the port fuel cells?
    A. The central stabilizing unit
    B. One of the atomizing fuel tanks
    C. A burnt-out transistor near the oxygen tanks

3. (Fill in the Blank) The entire *Jupiter 2* food supply was completely contaminated by some sort of _____ blight resistant to cold.

4. Which of the Robot's mechanical parts did Dr. Smith exchange for "Beef Stroganoff laced with sour cream, and good wine"?
    A. Stability unit
    B. Memory banks
    C. Transistors

5. Who called the Robot an "unthinking brute"?

6. (Fill in the Blank) Before attempting to melt himself down in the Junkman's blast furnace, the Robot once again said his sentimental farewells to Will: "I cannot remember the past. Only a warm place in my _____ generator tells me we were once close."

MEMORY BANKS OVERLOAD

How many rockets did the Junkman fire from the *Jupiter 2* at Don and the Space Pod?

SPACE AGE FAST FACT

After this episode aired, the cast was officially told that the series had been renewed for a fourth season and they broke for two weeks for the summer hiatus. In reality, though, CBS told Irwin Allen that *Lost in Space* would not be picked up by the network for another year unless he drastically reduced the show's expensive budget. When he refused, CBS canceled the series. Although Allen reportedly tried to sell *Lost in Space* to ABC and NBC, both networks politely declined and the Robinson expedition remained hopelessly lost in space, in syndication and in the hearts and minds of the show's loyal fans.

WARNING! DANGER!

The Mechanics of the Mechanical Man

He was simply known as the Jupiter 2*'s "Robot," "Robot Model B-9," or Dr. Smith's "Bubble-Headed Booby," but to many fans of the series, he was the true cybernetic hero of* Lost in Space.

1. Identify the two episodes in which stuntman Bob May simply blew cigar smoke out through the Robot's plastic collar to produce the "burnout" effect of the automaton.

2. He was known for his creation of Robby the Robot, first seen in the 1956 sci-fi thriller *Forbidden Planet,* and later as the designer and builder of *Lost in Space*'s mechanical man. Name this professional prop maker and art director.

3. Constructed of fiberglass, wood, and plastic, how many pounds did the Robot suit weigh?
   A. 100
   B. 200
   C. 250

4. What was used to electrically power the Robot outfit's neon tubes/voice light, bubble and chest light, and motorized sensors?

5. (True or False) Bob May's blackened face allowed

him to see out between the small slits in the Robot's plastic collar without being seen by viewers.

6. In addition to housing an actor, the Robot was designed to be fully articulate, somewhat expressionable, and mobile. How much did the mechanical man outfit reportedly cost?
    A. $30,000
    B. $50,000
    C. $75,000

7. What did Bob May use in the Robot's left claw to flash the mechanical man's chest light?

8. In scenes requiring the Robot to be filmed traversing across the set in full view, what type of battery was used in the tread section of the costume?
    A. Automobile
    B. Motorcycle
    C. Boat

9. During the first season of the series, movement of the costume was obtained by Bob May actually "walking" in the cumbersome tank treads. To eliminate problems of maneuverability around the set's rather rocky terrain, the "Bermuda shorts" outfit was created, in which the heavy treads were removed and the Robot was filmed only from the legs up. How did Bob May carry the weight of the costume on his back?

10. In which episode was the Robot seen "walking" in the tank treads for the last time.
    A. "Island in the Sky"
    B. "There Were Giants in the Earth"
    C. "Welcome Stranger"

11. (True or False) Special tracks were sometimes installed on the set's floor and the Robot was manually pulled by off-camera workers via a tow cable attached to the tread section.

12. A second Robot outfit, or "long distance" suit was

eventually created with the intention that it would double for the costly "primary" Robot in scenes that required the automaton to be thrown, hit or rendered weightless. Identify the first episode in which this lighter, hollow, "stand-in" mechanical man was first seen.

13. Name the only series segment in which both Robot suits appeared on screen simultaneously.

14. (True or False) Before the construction of the "long distance" suit, steel rods inside the legs of the original "primary" outfit were used to keep the Robot standing upright without Bob May's presence.

15. What did special effects technicians use to suspend the "long distance" Robot from the studio ceiling during the filming of "Condemned in Space," in which the automaton was accidentally released into the vast reaches of deep sea by Dr. Smith?

MEMORY BANKS OVERLOAD #1

Identify the California-based professional model-maker who acquired the stripped down "long distance" Robot suit in the mid-1980s and began a much needed restoration process.

---

16. (True or False) After loops of Bob May's voice tracks were made in each episode, Dick Tufeld, one of the entertainment industry's busiest voice men at the time, would arrive at the recording studio and dub over May's tracks in postproduction, typically sixty to seventy lines of dialogue per episode.

17. During construction of the original Robot suit, who suggested that the mechanical man's head post be allowed to move up and down?
    A. Irwin Allen
    B. Bob May
    C. Robert Kinoshita

18. Identify the short-lived Saturday morning children's show which rented the "primary" Robot suit in 1979 and significantly altered it to fit the needs of the serial.
   A. *The Adventures of the Space Rangers*
   B. *Mystery Island*
   C. *Star Quest 2000*

MEMORY BANKS OVERLOAD #2

He is an executive producer at 20th Century Fox and a devoted fan of *Lost in Space* who obtained the original Robot suit and restored it to its original specifications. What is his name?

TECH SPECS #10

Match the letter to the correct functioning parts and equipment on the Robot.

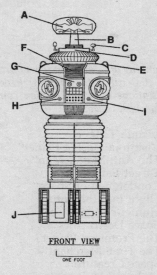

FRONT VIEW

ONE FOOT

Technical drawing by Edwin E. Echols.

1. _____ Programming mike
2. _____ Bubble head bellows
3. _____ Carrying hook
4. _____ Soil sampler door
5. _____ Head assembly
6. _____ Radar section
7. _____ Spinner/sensor
8. _____ Neon tubes/voice light
9. _____ Switch
10. _____ Chest light section

FANDOM EPISODE RANKING:

Season Three

The following ranking of Lost in Space's *third and final season episodes (with 10.0 being the highest) have been posted in various manifestations at science-fiction conventions and in cyberspace on fan-based websites.*

Ranking		Episode Title
1.	10.0	"Visit to a Hostile Planet"
2.	9.74	"The Anti-Matter Man"
3.	7.21	"Target Earth"
4.	7.04	"Condemned of Space"
5.	6.38	"Flight into the Future"
6.	6.15	"Hunter's Moon"
7.	6.09	"Space Destructors"
8.	5.87	"The Promised Planet"
9.	5.79	"The Time Merchant"
10.	5.12	"Space Creature"
11.	4.78	"Junkyard in Space"
12.	4.71	"Princess of Space"
13.	4.38	"Space Beauty"
14.	4.13	"The Flaming Planet"
15.	4.01	"The Haunted Lighthouse"
16.	3.85	"Space Primevals"
17.	3.23	"Fugitives in Space"
18.	3.10	"Kidnapped in Space"
19.	2.79	"A Day at the Zoo"
20.	2.43	"Collision of Planets"
21.	2.22	"Deadliest of the Species"

22. 1.68   "Two Weeks in Space"
23. 1.12   "Castles in Space"
24. 0.00   "The Great Vegetable Rebellion"

ANSWER KEY

(Note: Each correct answer is worth one (1) point. For every MEMORY BANKS OVERLOAD answered correctly, add an additional five (5) points.)

NO PLACE TO HIDE: The Original Unaired Pilot Episode

1. pioneer 2. False (25,000 mph) 3. Will 4. solar 5. B 6. five

MEMORY BANKS OVERLOAD: 1. The University of Stellardynamics 2. International 3. Radioastronomy

MAXIMUM SCORE POTENTIAL: 11

YOUR SCORE: _____

THE RELUCTANT STOWAWAY

1. two 2. False (two) 3. B 4. Five-and-a-half (the duration of the voyage) 5. Upper 6. C 7. False ("Nearly a decade") 8. A 9. To repair the external Navigational Control Guidance System scanner

MEMORY BANKS OVERLOAD: $2 billion

MAXIMUM SCORE POTENTIAL: 14

YOUR SCORE: _____

THE DERELICT

1. A large fire extinguisher 2. Judy 3. ghost 4. Crystalline 5. B 6. True 7. Laser rifle

MEMORY BANKS OVERLOAD: Maureen

MAXIMUM SCORE POTENTIAL: 12

YOUR SCORE: _____

NEVER FEAR, SMITH IS HERE (Part I)

1. I 2. E 3. C 4. G 5. L 6. A 7. B 8. D 9. K 10. F 11. H 12. J

MAXIMUM SCORE POTENTIAL: 12

YOUR SCORE: _____

NEVER FEAR, SMITH IS HERE (Part II)

1. F 2. B 3. M 4. K 5. J 6. L 7. D 8. E 9. N 10. A 11. H 12. I 13. G 14. C

MEMORY BANKS OVERLOAD #1: blundering

MEMORY BANKS OVERLOAD #2: "The Time Merchant"

MEMORY BANKS OVERLOAD #3: "fractious"

MEMORY BANKS OVERLOAD #4: "The Deadly Games of Gamma 6"

MAXIMUM SCORE POTENTIAL: 34

YOUR SCORE: _____

ISLAND IN THE SKY

1. A game of chess 2. Because the Robot only obeyed Dr. Smith's voice 3. B 4. Maureen 5. They ran out of fuel due to Smith's sabotage 6. Judy 7. "Every hour, on the hour" 8. B 9. Will (while imitating Smith's voice)

MEMORY BANKS OVERLOAD: 22 lbs. p.s.i.

MAXIMUM SCORE POTENTIAL: 14

YOUR SCORE: _____

THERE WERE GIANTS IN THE EARTH

1. C 2. A 3. Don 4. richness 5. B 6. Dr. Frankenstein 7. C 8. A parasite requiring another lifeform to reach maturity

MEMORY BANKS OVERLOAD: Potatoes, peas, carrots, tomatoes, squash, and corn

MAXIMUM SCORE POTENTIAL: 13

YOUR SCORE: _____

THE HUNGRY SEA

1. The elimination of "all unnecessary personnel at the earliest opportunity" 2. companionship 3. A 4. B 5. Judy 6. The planet's orbital data 7. C 8. The ready room of a launching pad 9. Don

MEMORY BANKS OVERLOAD: "A matter of life and death"

MAXIMUM SCORE POTENTIAL: 14

YOUR SCORE: _____

GUESTS OF HONOR, Part I

1. B 2. Creech 3. "Deadliest of the Species" 4. Dee Hartford 5. B 6. C 7. True 8. Wally Cox 9. J-5 10. Kurt Russell 11. B 12. A 13. Byron Morrow 14. C 15. Albert Salmi 16. Mercedes McCambridge 17. B 18. Werner Klemperer 19. *The Munsters* 20. Marcel Hillaire 21. "Space Circus" 22. C 3. Effra 24. Arte Johnson 25. B 26. "The Deadly Games of Gamma 6" and "The Dream Monster" 27. True 28. Mrs. Irwin Allen 29. C 30. A 31. False (Francine York) 32. C 33. John Carradine 34. A 35. Aunt Clara 36. A 37. "The Thief from Outer Space" 38. Vitina Marcus 39. A 40. Jim Mills 41. "The Keeper, Parts I and II" 42. Strother Martin 43. "War of the Robots" and "Condemned of Space" 44. *The Odd Couple* 45. John Abbott 46. Strother Martin 47. Parmen

MEMORY BANKS OVERLOAD #1: "Two Weeks in Space"

MEMORY BANKS OVERLOAD #2: Michael Ansara

MEMORY BANKS OVERLOAD #3 Universe

MEMORY BANKS OVERLOAD #4: Joey Russo

MEMORY BANKS OVERLOAD #5: Leonard Stone

MEMORY BANKS OVERLOAD #6: "The Android Machine," "The Toymaker," and "Two Weeks in Space"

MAXIMUM SCORE POTENTIAL: 77

YOUR SCORE: _____

GUESTS OF HONOR, Part II

1. I 2. J 3. B 4. K 5. L 6. D 7. H 8. G 9. C 10. A 11. F 12. E

MEMORY BANKS OVERLOAD: Don Matheson

MAXIMUM SCORE POTENTIAL: 17

YOUR SCORE: _____

WELCOME STRANGER

1. space 2. "Travelin' Man" 3. Saturn 4. Another story of his fantastic adventures 5. B 6. Dr. Smith 7. "HAPGOOD WAS HERE"

MEMORY BANKS OVERLOAD: June 18, 1982

MAXIMUM SCORE POTENTIAL: 12

YOUR SCORE: _____

MY FRIEND, MR. NOBODY

1. A lost explosive capsule 2. True 3. Will 4. tracking 5. Fifty 6. *The Ugly Duckling* 7. John

MEMORY BANKS OVERLOAD: "When a person can't talk anymore. When a person can't move anymore."

MAXIMUM SCORE POTENTIAL: 12

YOUR SCORE: _____

INVADERS FROM THE FIFTH DIMENSION

1. Judy 2. To interface with their ship's guidance computers 3. Smith himself in an attempt to convince the aliens that his brain was substandard material 4. Barbaric 5. A flashlight 6. B

MEMORY BANKS OVERLOAD: 100,000

MAXIMUM SCORE POTENTIAL: 11

YOUR SCORE: _____

THE OASIS

1. "The conservation of water" 2. Maureen 3. The water conversion unit's last good fuel cell 4. His initials, "Z.S." 5. three 6. Pituitary

MEMORY BANKS OVERLOAD: He used suction

MAXIMUM SCORE POTENTIAL: 11

YOUR SCORE: _____

ALPHA CONTROL INTELLIGENCE DOSSIER:
Professor John Robinson

1. C 2. False (January 14, 1957) 3. Lieutenant Colonel 4. quarterback 5. False (he enrolled at the California Institute of Technology) 6. Geological 7. B 8. Astrophysics 9. A 10. Seven 11. Thrust 12. True 13. C

MEMORY BANKS OVERLOAD: Four

MAXIMUM SCORE POTENTIAL: 18

YOUR SCORE: _____

TECH SPECS #1

1. B 2. D 3. F 4. A 5. C 6. H 7. E 8. G 9. I

MAXIMUM SCORE POTENTIAL: 9

YOUR SCORE: _____

THE SKY IS FALLING

1. Penny 2. John 3. Dr. Smith 4. Sneeze 5. B

MEMORY BANKS OVERLOAD: Tauron

MAXIMUM SCORE POTENTIAL: 10

YOUR SCORE: _____

WISH UPON A STAR

1. Dr. Smith neglected to tend to it as he was assigned
2. Two 3. Penny 4. Penny 5. B 6. Will 7. John 8. Six

MEMORY BANKS OVERLOAD: A bicycle and a photographic microscope

MAXIMUM SCORE POTENTIAL: 13

YOUR SCORE: _____

THE RAFT

1. B 2. John 3. The Robot 4. The reactor unit 5. Don 6. A
7. B 8. An open transmitter

MEMORY BANKS OVERLOAD: The Space Theodolite

MAXIMUM SCORE POTENTIAL: 13

YOUR SCORE: _____

ONE OF OUR DOGS IS MISSING

1. B 2. An oxygen release valve 3. Judy 4. To install a series of microwave relay stations 5. mutants 6. spy 7. Maureen

MEMORY BANKS OVERLOAD: An earlier space program test of suspended animation

MAXIMUM SCORE POTENTIAL: 12

YOUR SCORE: _____

A FIRST TIME FOR EVERYTHING

1. In a concealed acceleration couch aboard the *Jupiter 2*
2. B 3. "Wish Upon a Star" 4. False ("The Oasis")
5. "The Derelict" 6. "Return from Outer Space" 7. "Ghost in Space" 8. True 9. C 10. A 11. "The Derelict" 12. True
13. B 14. "Island in the Sky" 15. False ("Blast Off into Space") 16. three 17. "The Derelict" 18. C 19. False ("The Ghost Planet") 20. A 21. "Island in the Sky" 22. C
23. True 24. A 25. C 26. True 27. "Wreck of the Robot"
28. "Island in the Sky" 29. C 30. False ("There Were Giants in the Earth") 31. A 32. "Welcome Stranger" 33. C

34. "Cave of the Wizards" 35. A 36. True 37. B 38. "Condemned of Space" 39. True 40. True 41. B

MEMORY BANKS OVERLOAD #1: "Condemned of Space"

MEMORY BANKS OVERLOAD #2: "Island in the Sky"

MEMORY BANKS OVERLOAD #3: "Wreck of the Robot"

MEMORY BANKS OVERLOAD #4: "The Challenge"

MEMORY BANKS OVERLOAD #5: "Target Earth"

MAXIMUM SCORE POTENTIAL: 66

YOUR SCORE: _____

ATTACK OF THE MONSTER PLANTS

1. A rope 2. Deutronium 3. False (Although Smith did duplicate his watch, it was his shaving kit that first underwent replication) 4. C 5. B

MEMORY BANKS OVERLOAD: superior

MAXIMUM SCORE POTENTIAL: 10

YOUR SCORE: _____

RETURN FROM OUTER SPACE

1. An omelet 2. Hatfield Four Corners 3. instrument 4. B 5. Cape Kennedy, Florida 6. C 7. A bottle of carbon tetrachloride

MEMORY BANKS OVERLOAD: "High noon"

MAXIMUM SCORE POTENTIAL: 12

YOUR SCORE: _____

THE KEEPER, Part I

1. A small reptile of the Iguana family 2. Don 3. C 4. nature 5. B 6. False (200–300 years) 7. B 8. C 9. B 10. A slingshot

MEMORY BANKS OVERLOAD: reason

MAXIMUM SCORE POTENTIAL: 15

YOUR SCORE: _____

THE KEEPER, Part II

1. C 2. Maureen's 3. Maureen 4. John and Maureen 5. A giant spider 6. Dr. Smith

MEMORY BANKS OVERLOAD: Loyalty

MAXIMUM SCORE POTENTIAL: 11

YOUR SCORE: _____

ALPHA CONTROL INTELLIGENCE DOSSIER: Dr. Maureen Robinson

1. False (New York City) 2. C 3. Engineering 4. True 5. A 6. Her older sister, Colleen 7. Colleen 8. B 9. C 10. False (after the birth of her second child, Penny)

MEMORY BANKS OVERLOAD: Biochemistry

MAXIMUM SCORE POTENTIAL: 15

YOUR SCORE: _____

TECH SPECS #2

1. C 2. A 3. D 4. B

MAXIMUM SCORE POTENTIAL: 4

YOUR SCORE: _____

THE SKY PIRATE

1. "Taking human life" 2. B 3. A rock 4. Nick 5. C 6. A starship 7. C 8. B 9. A

MEMORY BANKS OVERLOAD: Tellurians

MAXIMUM SCORE POTENTIAL: 14

YOUR SCORE: _____

GHOST IN SPACE

1. B 2. To make a Ouija board 3. Three 4. A Ouija board and a seance 5. Energy or power 6. True 7. His right boot 8. The early morning light

MEMORY BANKS OVERLOAD: "indecipherable"

MAXIMUM SCORE POTENTIAL: 13

YOUR SCORE: _____

WAR OF THE ROBOTS

1. A Robot was a machine that performed as programmed. A Robotoid was a machine that went beyond programming. It had free choice. 2. Will 3. False (ever since his fusion unit was refined two days earlier) 4. B 5. Checking the weather station 6. pleasure 7. C 8. His protective circuit breakers

MEMORY BANKS OVERLOAD: 100

MAXIMUM SCORE POTENTIAL: 13

YOUR SCORE: _____

THE MAGIC MIRROR

1. Cosmic 2. False (platinum) 3. A banana 4. A cat 5. Cosmic 6. A reflection

MEMORY BANKS OVERLOAD: Five hundred

MAXIMUM SCORE POTENTIAL: 11

YOUR SCORE: _____

COMMUNICATION CHANNELS: Season One

1. Jimmy Hapgood 2. Dr. Smith 3. evidence 4. B 5. The Robot 6. annoying 7. True 8. Don 9. A 10. strangers 11. Judy 12. C 13. citizen 14. A 15. False (John made the statement) 16. history's 17. "The Reluctant Stowaway" 18. Dr. Smith 19. choice 20. The Robot 21. False (Effra in "The Space Croppers") 22. C 23. Dr. Smith 24. bucket 25. True 26. "The Hungry Sea" 27. scope 28. Dr. Smith 29. Misbegotten 30. A 31. energy 32. C 33. container 34. C 35. True 36. Enemy 37. Capt. Tucker 38. Capt. Tucker

39. False (The Keeper made the statement) 40. C 41. A
42. C 43. True 44. hen's 45. Dr. Smith 46. "The Hungry
Sea"

MEMORY BANKS OVERLOAD #1: Will in "His Majesty
Smith"

MEMORY BANKS OVERLOAD #2: "Island in the Sky"

MEMORY BANKS OVERLOAD #3: The Keeper

MEMORY BANKS OVERLOAD #4: "The Keeper, Part
II"

MAXIMUM SCORE POTENTIAL: 66

YOUR SCORE: _____

THE CHALLENGE

1. A 2. His father 3. B 4. An extremely advanced communications system 5. Bravest 6. He threw a spear over his
shoulder into one of the target's bulls-eye 7. C 8. Smith
used the Robot's audio unit as a short-distance receiver

MEMORY BANKS OVERLOAD: 50,000

MAXIMUM SCORE POTENTIAL: 13

YOUR SCORE: _____

THE SPACE TRADER

1. C 2. C 3. The major's laser pistol 4. C 5. A ball and
chain 6. "Quantity and quality"

MEMORY BANKS OVERLOAD: "The inner feelings of
a sensitive man in space"

MAXIMUM SCORE POTENTIAL: 11

YOUR SCORE: _____

HIS MAJESTY SMITH

1. C 2. A 3. False (on his maternal grandmother's side)
4. B 5. King Zachary I 6. Will 7. A 8. essence

MEMORY BANKS OVERLOAD: intelligence/valor/wis-
dom/bearing

MAXIMUM SCORE POTENTIAL: 13

YOUR SCORE: _____

THE SPACE CROPPERS

1. Only once 2. "Our own special blend" 3. For a witch's spell 4. Virus 5. The Robot 6. B 7. C

MEMORY BANKS OVERLOAD: 1) John's portable thruster employed in a rocket belt flight 2) Maureen's flight suit gauntlets 3) An audio tape of Smith's *Meditations of a Galactic Stowaway*

MAXIMUM SCORE POTENTIAL: 11

YOUR SCORE: _____

ALPHA CONTROL INTELLIGENCE DOSSIER:
Major Donald West

1. True 2. B 3. C 4. Eighteen 5. Second lieutenant 6. Three 7. True 8. C 9. A

MEMORY BANKS OVERLOAD: June 2, 1997

MAXIMUM SCORE POTENTIAL: 14

YOUR SCORE: _____

TECH SPECS #3

1. C 2. E 3. G 4. D 5. A 6. F 7. B

MAXIMUM SCORE POTENTIAL: 7

YOUR SCORE: _____

ALL THAT GLITTERS

1. Maureen 2. Searching in the Chariot for a new water supply 3. His watch 4. C 5. False (in over a million miles) 6. B 7. True 8. B

MEMORY BANKS OVERLOAD: wisdom, greed

MAXIMUM SCORE POTENTIAL: 13

YOUR SCORE: _____

THE LOST CIVILIZATION

1. Smith pilfered parts from it for his own air-conditioning unit 2. Will's 3. A 4. He had been programmed with the plots of stories in literature and believed the situation matched *Sleeping Beauty* 5. Princess 6. generations 7. World

MEMORY BANKS OVERLOAD: "Goodbye, Will Robinson. Have fun."

MAXIMUM SCORE POTENTIAL: 12

YOUR SCORE: _____

A CHANGE OF SPACE

1. A cosmic dust pit 2. Will 3. Circumnavigating 4. B 5. John 6. B 7. Mark Twain

MEMORY BANKS OVERLOAD: lord

MAXIMUM SCORE POTENTIAL: 12

YOUR SCORE: _____

FOLLOW THE LEADER

1. A small lizard 2. Dr. Smith was "constantly talking" to him 3. Bugs Bunny 4. strength 5. Dr. Smith 6. C 7. Maureen 8. Love 9. Canto

MEMORY BANKS OVERLOAD: audio

MAXIMUM SCORE POTENTIAL: 14

YOUR SCORE: _____

PICK A NUMBER

(Note: Every correct answer will count as a 5-point MEMORY BANKS OVERLOAD Bonus)

1. eight 2. Five 3. 190 4. Forty 5. 10,000 p.s.i. 6. ten 7. 476 8. Twenty-four 9. Two 10. True 11. 89 cents 12. forty 13. False (175 lbs.) 14. A dime 15. AB 39 62 16. True 17. 1,226,417 18. Alpha 784 19. 80 20. Ten 21. 30 lbs p.s.i. 22. True 23. 756498273 24. Two 25. At 1600 hours 26. True 27. 12,000 28. 007 29. Two 30. At 0600 hours 31. 104 32. Five 33. two 34. False (two weeks) 35. Three 36. 756498274 37. 100 feet (approx. 30 meters) 38. 277-

2211 is actually the phone number for 20th Century Fox studios and IA, of course, stood for Irwin Allen 39. Twenty-two 40. "Welcome Stranger" 41. Fifteen 42. Three

MAXIMUM SCORE POTENTIAL: 210

YOUR SCORE: _____

BLAST OFF INTO SPACE

1. C 2. True 3. quintessence 4. Cosmic 5. The Comstock Lode 6. B 7. B 8. In the magnetic lock

MEMORY BANKS OVERLOAD: At 0600

MAXIMUM SCORE POTENTIAL: 13

YOUR SCORE: _____

WILD ADVENTURE

1. His magnetic ring 2. distance 3. C 4. Intergalactic 5. B 6. C 7. Titanium 8. True

MEMORY BANKS OVERLOAD: Thirty-seven

MAXIMUM SCORE POTENTIAL: 13

YOUR SCORE: _____

THE GHOST PLANET

1. C 2. Andes 3. Will's 4. Believing they were on Earth, he assumed everyone was preparing a "surprise party" for the *Jupiter 2* crew inside the spaceport 5. John 6. A 7. "Hard labor" on an assembly line 8. B-9

MEMORY BANKS OVERLOAD: The landing pad, the spaceport gate, the signs along the corridor, and the assembly chamber

MAXIMUM SCORE POTENTIAL: 13

YOUR SCORE: _____

FORBIDDEN WORLD

1. C 2. The dense fog could possibly be corrosive to metal 3. The Robot 4. B 5. Intelligence 6. C 7. Dr. Smith 8. The

highly explosive drink Dr. Smith ingested, which Tiabo hoped would blow-up the *Jupiter* 2 and its crew

MEMORY BANKS OVERLOAD: 630

MAXIMUM SCORE POTENTIAL: 13

YOUR SCORE: _____

THE ONE AND ONLY

1. "The Challenge" 2. False ("The Space Croppers") 3. C 4. Theodolite 5. True 6. C 7. "Space Circus" 8. Mineral 9. C 10. False ("The Derelict") 11. "Mutiny in Space" 12. False ("The Derelict") 13. "Island in the Sky" 14. "Mutiny in Space" 15. True 16. A 17. "The Hungry Sea" 18. True 19. "Space Primevals" 20. A 21. "The Anti-Matter Man" 22. radar 23. True 24. "The Haunted Lighthouse" 25. False ("Collision of Planets") 26. "Space Creature" 27. activity 28. "Castles in Space" 29. "Target Earth"

MEMORY BANKS OVERLOAD #1: "Rocket to Earth"

MEMORY BANKS OVERLOAD #2: 1) "Deadliest of the Species" 2) "The Flaming Planet" and 3) "Castles in Space"

MAXIMUM SCORE POTENTIAL: 39

YOUR SCORE: _____

SPACE CIRCUS

1. A 2. Nova 3. False ("The Greatest Show in Space") 4. Lesser 5. C 6. B 7. Madame Fenestra 8. "Tiptoe Through the Tulips" 9. B

MEMORY BANKS OVERLOAD: A golden goblet, purple frog, small red ball, and a knife

MAXIMUM SCORE POTENTIAL: 14

YOUR SCORE: _____

PRISONERS OF SPACE

1. C 2. True 3. B 4. Dr. Smith 5. Maureen 6. Two 7. He was found to be mentally incompetent

MEMORY BANKS OVERLOAD: Five years imprisonment on an alien planet

MAXIMUM SCORE POTENTIAL: 12

YOUR SCORE: _____

THE ANDROID MACHINE

1. B 2. A 3. B 4. True 5. She took his teaching pointer away from him 6. B 7. Mr. Zumdish

MEMORY BANKS OVERLOAD: 77B

MAXIMUM SCORE POTENTIAL: 12

YOUR SCORE: _____

THE DEADLY GAMES OF GAMMA 6

1. Fight promoter 2. B 3. Weak 4. One half of "the riches" and passage to Earth 5. C 6. B 7. C 8. His pants belt 9. A

MEMORY BANKS OVERLOAD: The Robot

MAXIMUM SCORE POTENTIAL: 14

YOUR SCORE: _____

ALPHA CONTROL INTELLIGENCE DOSSIER: Judy Robinson

1. B 2. True 3. C 4. C 5. sixteen 6. B 7. She discovered Maj. West was selected to be the *Jupiter 2* pilot

MEMORY BANKS OVERLOAD: At the U.S. Space Corps Training Center in Houston, Texas

MAXIMUM SCORE POTENTIAL: 12

YOUR SCORE: _____

TECH SPECS #4

1. B 2. F 3. E 4. A 5. D 6. C

MAXIMUM SCORE POTENTIAL: 6

YOUR SCORE: _____

THE THIEF FROM OUTER SPACE

1. B 2. A 3. B 4. B 5. A golden arrow 6. Sedan chair

MEMORY BANKS OVERLOAD: "Never trust your best friend, except when you hold a hostage."

MAXIMUM SCORE POTENTIAL: 11

YOUR SCORE: _____

CURSE OF COUSIN SMITH

1. Practicing shaving 2. universe 3. Tauron 4. A 5. A derringer 6. Great Aunt Maude 7. Little Joe

MEMORY BANKS OVERLOAD: Beauregard

MAXIMUM SCORE POTENTIAL: 12

YOUR SCORE: _____

WEST OF MARS

1. Dr. Smith 2. errant 3. B 4. B 5. B 6. Claudius 7. John 8. False (Black Rock Canyon) 9. A

MEMORY BANKS OVERLOAD: Pleiades Pete

MAXIMUM SCORE POTENTIAL: 14

YOUR SCORE: _____

A VISIT TO HADES

1. B 2. Penny's 3. Destroy the harp 4. An alien space-time dimension 5. True 6. interdimensional 7. Crying 8. Judy

MEMORY BANKS OVERLOAD: Lyrae

MAXIMUM SCORE POTENTIAL: 13

YOUR SCORE: _____

LASTING IMPRESSIONS

1. D 2. H 3. G 4. E 5. B 6. A 7. F 8. C

MEMORY BANKS OVERLOAD: "The Great Vegetable Rebellion"

MAXIMUM SCORE POTENTIAL: 13

YOUR SCORE: _____

VOICE ACTIVATED

1. E 2. H 3. F 4. A 5. G 6. C 7. B 8. D 9. I

MEMORY BANKS #1: Joey Tata

MEMORY BANKS #2: Gregory Morton

MAXIMUM SCORE POTENTIAL: 19

YOUR SCORE: _____

WRECK OF THE ROBOT

1. He was an excellent cook 2. The Robot 3. A 4. Crying inside 5. B 6. John

MEMORY BANKS OVERLOAD: Saticon

MAXIMUM SCORE POTENTIAL: 11

YOUR SCORE: _____

THE DREAM MONSTER

1. Maureen 2. For overloading the spaceship's air unit 3. "Little devils" 4. B 5. B 6. C 7. A

MEMORY BANKS OVERLOAD #1: 1. B 2. E 3. F 4. A 5. C 6. D

MEMORY BANKS OVERLOAD #2: A "digitizer"

MAXIMUM SCORE POTENTIAL: 17

YOUR SCORE: _____

THE GOLDEN MAN

1. Judy 2. A bomb 3. The Robot 4. Keema would receive *Jupiter* 2 weapons for his war with the frog-like alien and Dr. Smith would be taken to Earth immediately 5. Dr. Smith 6. The frog-like alien (sarcastically)

MEMORY BANKS OVERLOAD: Turbolaser

MAXIMUM SCORE POTENTIAL: 11

YOUR SCORE: _____

THE GIRL FROM THE GREEN DIMENSION

1. A solar gale 2. A 3. Urso 4. They were too flammable
5. False (index finger on the left hand) 6. Will 7. B

MEMORY BANKS OVERLOAD: Three

MAXIMUM SCORE POTENTIAL: 12

YOUR SCORE: _____

ALPHA CONTROL INTELLIGENCE DOSSIER:
Penny Robinson

1. September 9, 1985 2. False (Roberta) 3. B 4. True 5. A
6. B

MEMORY BANKS OVERLOAD: 147

MAXIMUM SCORE POTENTIAL: 11

YOUR SCORE: _____

TECH SPECS #5

1. D 2. L 3. A 4. H 5. C 6. J 7. B 8. E 9. I 10. F 11. K
12. G

MAXIMUM SCORE POTENTIAL: 12

YOUR SCORE: _____

THE QUESTING BEAST

1. The radioactive atomic regulator 2. The Robot's 3. C
4. B 5. Mice 6. "Enchantment" 7. Every lie he ever told

MEMORY BANKS OVERLOAD: sanity

MAXIMUM SCORE POTENTIAL: 12

YOUR SCORE: _____

THE TOYMAKER

1. A 2. Will, who apologized later 3. "Old Man" 4. fourth
5. A new coat 6. B 7. The children there had "far too
many toys already" 8. He didn't like dark places 9. B

MEMORY BANKS OVERLOAD: Model 512 Deluxe

MAXIMUM SCORE POTENTIAL: 14

YOUR SCORE: _____

MUTINY IN SPACE

1. Quartermaster pro tem 2. A 3. midshipman 4. Penny
5. Dancing 6. B

MEMORY BANKS OVERLOAD: Mr. Kidnoh

MAXIMUM SCORE POTENTIAL: 11

YOUR SCORE: _____

THE SPACE VIKINGS

1. A 2. Brynhilda 3. Frost Giants 4. B 5. "Cunning and
chicanery" 6. Sponges

MEMORY BANKS OVERLOAD: Nefleheim

MAXIMUM SCORE POTENTIAL: 11

YOUR SCORE: _____

THE NAME GAME, Part I

1. "Cave of the Wizards" and "Flight into the Future"
2. "Sloop John B" 3. B 4. "The Lost Civilization" and
"Space Primevals" 5. "The Reluctant Stowaway," "The
Derelict," "Wish Upon a Star" and "The Sky is Falling"
6. SSGT. Joseph L. McWilliams 7. C 8. "Follow the Leader"
and "The Anti-Matter Man" 9. Sean and Chris Penn 10. C
11. "Mutiny in Space" 12. A 13. Mars or Cerberus (he
wasn't sure) 14. B 15. A 16. "Island in the Sky," "Forbidden World," "Hunter's Moon" and "Flight into the
Future" 17. "Blast Off into Space," "Condemned of
Space" and "Collision of Planets" 18. "The Great Vegetable Rebellion" 19. B 20. Puppy 21. True 22. Quano
23. Drun 24. B 25. B 26. Aunt Maude 27. Her cousin, Joan

28. B 29. Johnny Sorenson 30. The Imperial Cassiopean Navy 31. *Candid Camera* 32. "The Reluctant Stowaway," "One of Our Dogs is Missing," "The Thief from Outer Space" and "Target Earth" 33. Sandy Koufax 34. "All That Glitters" and "The Derelict" 35. Geoo ("The Deadly Games of Gamma 6") 36. "Loch Lomond" 37. True

MEMORY BANKS OVERLOAD #1: "The Golden Man"

MEMORY BANKS OVERLOAD #2: "Chapter 13: The Legend of the Shadow World"

MEMORY BANKS OVERLOAD #3: Gog and Magog

MEMORY BANKS OVERLOAD #4: "Frere Jacques"

MEMORY BANKS OVERLOAD #5: "Wreck of the Robot"

MAXIMUM SCORE POTENTIAL: 62

YOUR SCORE: _____

THE NAME GAME, Part II

1. F 2. G 3. A 4. H 5. B 6. L 7. K 8. J 9. E 10. C 11. I 12. D

MEMORY BANKS OVERLOAD: Sobey Martin and Harry Harris, respectively

MAXIMUM SCORE POTENTIAL: 17

YOUR SCORE: _____

ROCKET TO EARTH

1. A baseball 2. The ventriloquist dummy 3. False (frogs) 4. B 5. ten 6. His spaceship 7. False (space sideshows, planet circuses, asteroid county fairs) 8. Neutronic 9. C

MEMORY BANKS OVERLOAD: In the Pacific Ocean

MAXIMUM SCORE POTENTIAL: 14

YOUR SCORE: _____

THE CAVE OF THE WIZARDS

1. The Robot 2. Draconian 3. A million 4. "Golden Boy" 5. Will's stories of their time spent together hiking, playing

chess, etc. touched Smith's heart and moved him emotion-ally

MEMORY BANKS OVERLOAD: 1) Ion 2) The Robot 3) A rock

MAXIMUM SCORE POTENTIAL: 10

YOUR SCORE: _____

TREASURE OF THE LOST PLANET

1. "Good evening" 2. Deek 3. doodlebug 4. Nick, the mechanical parrot 5. Smeek 6. Isruland

MEMORY BANKS OVERLOAD: Beelibones

MAXIMUM SCORE POTENTIAL: 11

YOUR SCORE: _____

ALPHA CONTROL INTELLIGENCE DOSSIER:
William Robinson

1. B 2. B 3. True 4. five 5. Eleventh 6. False (He was only six at the time) 7. Guitar 8. He was able to sneak past the Robot and board the derelict ship, where he encountered large, bubble-shaped aliens

MEMORY BANKS OVERLOAD: 182

MAXIMUM SCORE POTENTIAL: 13

YOUR SCORE: _____

TECH SPECS #6

1. C 2. E 3. B 4. A 5. D

MAXIMUM SCORE POTENTIAL: 5

YOUR SCORE: _____

REVOLT OF THE ANDROIDS

1. B 2. "Crush, kill, destroy" 3. Destroyer 4. A 5. words 6. B 7. False (105)

MEMORY BANKS OVERLOAD: 12, 17

MAXIMUM SCORE POTENTIAL: 12

YOUR SCORE: _____

THE COLONISTS

1. Condor 2. purifying 3. True 4. A 5. B

MEMORY BANKS OVERLOAD: 1. C 2. D 3. B 4. A

MAXIMUM SCORE POTENTIAL: 10

YOUR SCORE: _____

TRIP THROUGH THE ROBOT

1. Don 2. C 3. B 4. house 5. To destroy intrinsic alien bodies 6. C

MEMORY BANKS OVERLOAD: They reversed his ionic processes

MAXIMUM SCORE POTENTIAL: 11

YOUR SCORE: _____

THE PHANTOM FAMILY

1. A 2. lazy 3. B 4. Don and Smith 5. The *Jupiter 2* 6. They would return to cosmic dust "from whence they were formed" 7. friendship

MEMORY BANKS OVERLOAD: Twenty-four hours

MAXIMUM SCORE POTENTIAL: 12

YOUR SCORE: _____

COMMUNICATION CHANNELS: Season Two

1. B 2. "The Space Vikings" 3. A 4. Penny 5. False (Judy) 6. C 7. C 8. "The Golden Man" 9. Enforcer Claudius 10. "Wreck of the Robot" 11. John 12. B 13. "Space Circus" 14. Don 15. A 16. C 17. whoppers 18. "Wreck of the Robot" 19. The Robot 20. B 21. Lemnoc 22. emotions 23. "Revolt of the Androids" 24. Mr. O.M. 25. "The Questing Beast" 26. The Robot 27. The Robot 28. A 29. The Robot 30. Dr. Marvello 31. C 32. Morbus 33. False ("Wreck of the Robot") 34. "The Dream Monster" 35. Don 36. The Robot 37. "The Girl from the Green Dimension" 38. "The Phan-

tom Family" 39. Maureen 40. Will 41. regular 42. wind-up 43. Don

MEMORY BANKS OVERLOAD #1: interpreters

MEMORY BANKS OVERLOAD #2: Charlie

MEMORY BANKS OVERLOAD #3: books

MEMORY BANKS OVERLOAD #4: Verda

MEMORY BANKS OVERLOAD #5: The purple Robot leader in "The Mechanical Men"

MAXIMUM SCORE POTENTIAL: 68

YOUR SCORE: _____

THE MECHANICAL MEN

1. The force field and weather station 2. pygmy 3. ten 4. Don 5. B 6. B 7. Lincoln's Gettysburg Address 8. A blast from John's laser rifle, which deactivated the Robot

MEMORY BANKS OVERLOAD: A fresh power pack, a supply of machine oil, and a picture of the Robinson family

MAXIMUM SCORE POTENTIAL: 13

YOUR SCORE: _____

THE ASTRAL TRAVELER

1. B 2. A 3. James Stuart, King of Scotland 4. B 5. C 6. Bagpipes 7. Hamish's father

MEMORY BANKS OVERLOAD: Ruthven

MAXIMUM SCORE POTENTIAL: 12

YOUR SCORE: _____

THE GALAXY GIFT

1. dead 2. False (high-frequency radio waves) 3. Mr. Arcon's amulet 4. A black rose 5. a hot dog and a Dodgers pennant 6. B 7. central 8. C

MEMORY BANKS OVERLOAD: Royal Imperial Restaurant

MAXIMUM SCORE POTENTIAL: 13

YOUR SCORE: _____

THE WRITE STUFF

1. I 2. D 3. A 4. L 5. H 6. K 7. M 8. C 9. J 10. F 11. H 12. B 13. E

MEMORY BANKS OVERLOAD: S. Bar David and K.C. Alison, respectively

MAXIMUM SCORE POTENTIAL: 18

YOUR SCORE: _____

SPACED OUT TITLES

1. G 2. J 3. L 4. I 5. C 6. A 7. K 8. F 9. H 10. B 11. D 12. E 13. M

MEMORY BANKS OVERLOAD: "The Hitchhiker and the Haunted Lighthouse" and "Alas, Regardless of Their Doom" respectively

MAXIMUM SCORE POTENTIAL: 18

YOUR SCORE: _____

CONDEMNED OF SPACE

1. Seams 2. A 3. B 4. C 5. *Vera Castle* 6. C 7. Two 8. Cat's cradle

MEMORY BANKS OVERLOAD: A39BQ164Z09

MAXIMUM SCORE POTENTIAL: 13

YOUR SCORE: _____

VISIT TO A HOSTILE PLANET

1. impurities 2. October 17 (Saturday) 3. two 4. The Robot 5. C 6. 1970 7. Voltones 8. A cannon from the town square

MEMORY BANKS OVERLOAD: Superior

MAXIMUM SCORE POTENTIAL: 13

YOUR SCORE: _____

KIDNAPPED IN SPACE

1. C 2. Environmental 3. A 4. Institute 5. He was more interested in space exploration 6. A 7. second 8. True

MEMORY BANKS OVERLOAD: Vector Control Tape unit

MAXIMUM SCORE POTENTIAL: 13

YOUR SCORE: _____

HUNTER'S MOON

1. A 2. Radarscope 3. B 4. The retro-rockets 5. laser 6. B 7. "Defective" 8. A

MEMORY BANKS OVERLOAD: Five

MAXIMUM SCORE POTENTIAL: 13

YOUR SCORE: _____

ALPHA CONTROL INTELLIGENCE DOSSIER: Dr. Zachary Smith

1. Colonel 2. November 6, 1945 3. False (his parents were killed in a boating accident) 4. His Aunt Maude and Uncle Thaddeus Smith 5. B 6. three 7. A 8. Air Force 9. C 10. Environmental 11. True 12. His aunt paid a bribe 13. An intelligence operative for a country that considered itself an enemy of the U.S. 14. Aeolus Umbra

MEMORY BANKS OVERLOAD: Marietta, Georgia

MAXIMUM SCORE POTENTIAL: 19

YOUR SCORE: _____

TECH SPECS #7

1. B 2. E 3. H 4. M 5. I 6. D 7. G 8. A 9. J 10. F 11. C 12. L 13. K

MAXIMUM SCORE POTENTIAL: 13

YOUR SCORE: _____

SPACE PRIMEVALS

1. A 2. Their presence as other life-forms contaminated the tribe's evolution 3. B 4. timidity 5. False (the watch belonged to his grandfather) 6. The Great Potinius 7. Zach

MEMORY BANKS OVERLOAD: Because it "refined crude aliens"

MAXIMUM SCORE POTENTIAL: 12

YOUR SCORE: _____

SPACE DESTRUCTORS

1. pinball 2. The Robot 3. B 4. A 5. He fakes being sick

MEMORY BANKS OVERLOAD: Napoleon, leadership, ferocity, Hercules, brain

MAXIMUM SCORE POTENTIAL: 10

YOUR SCORE: _____

THE HAUNTED LIGHTHOUSE

1. Comb and scarf 2. Five 3. Mets and Angels 4. John 5. B 6. True 7. C 8. A lion and a beautiful woman 9. C

MEMORY BANKS OVERLOAD: Three

MAXIMUM SCORE POTENTIAL: 14

YOUR SCORE: _____

FLIGHT INTO THE FUTURE

1. Penny 2. A 3. False (15 minutes) 4. millennium 5. C 6. A

MEMORY BANKS OVERLOAD: ambulatory, cybernetic

MAXIMUM SCORE POTENTIAL: 11

YOUR SCORE: _____

GALACTIC CASTAWAYS

1. Lennier 2. B 3. Marta Kristen 4. True 5. Evita Peron, Argentina's first lady 6. C 7. Angela Cartwright 8. Lucifer 9. B 10. False (*Romper Room*) 11. June Lockhart 12. "Long

Distance Call," "It's a Good Life," and "In Praise of Pip"
13. Altrincham, Cheshire, England 14. Mark Goddard
15. True 16. June Lockhart 17. *Captain Sinbad* 18. Marta
Kristen 19. A 20. *Family Feud* 21. He was listed as "Johnny
Williams" 22. B 23. C 24. C 25. A 26. Story editor Tony
Wilson 27. Marta Kristen 28. True 29. Mark Goddard 30.
He loved "science fiction/space stuff" 31. "Ghost of Moby
Dick" 32. *Zorro* 33. *The Third Man* 34. A 35. Gene (veteran
Vaudeville and stage actor and writer) and actress Kath-
leen Lockhart 36. *All This and Heaven Too* 37. He couldn't
stand "kissy, kissy" host Richard Dawson 38. Billy Mumy
39. Jonathan Harris 40. Jonathan Harris 41. Mark Goddard
42. Mark Goddard 43. B 44. C 45. Guy Williams 46. June
Lockhart 47. Angela Cartwright 48. June Lockhart
49. Angela Cartwright 50. True 51. B 52. Mark Goddard
53. A 54. June Lockhart 55. False (Billy Mumy) 56. Angela
Cartwright 57. Marta Kristen 58. Angela Cartwright
59. Jonathan Harris 60. Angela Cartwright 61. True 62.
Marta Kristen 63. Billy Mumy 64. eight 65. B 66. Guy
Williams 67. June Lockhart 68. False (Jonathan Harris) 69.
Sergeant York 70. B 71. Six 72. Marta Kristen 73. Mark Goddard 74. Jonathan Harris 75. C 76. True 77. Robert Drasnin
78. True 79. *The Sound of Music,* but the young man was
unaware that Angela had a role in the film! 80. *Petticoat
Junction* 81. Jonathan Harris 82. B 83. True 84. Marta Kristen 85. June Lockhart 86. June Lockhart 87. Jonathan Harris 88. B 89. Evil Judge Pyncheon 90. Ming the Merciless
91. Mark Goddard 92. Jonathan Harris 93. True 94. Jonathan Harris 95. Mark Goddard 96. June Lockhart 97. Billy
Mumy's 98. Angela Cartwright 99. Mark Goddard
100. Billy Mumy 101. Marta Kristen, Mark Goddard,
Angela Cartwright, and June Lockhart 102. "The Cave
of the Wizards" 103. Armando Catalano 104. True 105.
Miguel Ferrer 106. Mark Goddard 107. June Lockhart 108.
Mark Goddard 109. *The A-Team* 110. Billy Mumy

MEMORY BANKS OVERLOAD #1: Joseph Anthony

MEMORY BANKS OVERLOAD #2: *Bewitched*

MEMORY BANKS OVERLOAD #3: "Crash"

MEMORY BANKS OVERLOAD #4: *She-Wolf of London*

MEMORY BANKS OVERLOAD #5: Paul Zastupnevich

MEMORY BANKS OVERLOAD #6: *Troll*

MEMORY BANKS OVERLOAD #7: Ruth Martin

MEMORY BANKS OVERLOAD #8: Allen's secretary, Lili Glinski Woodfield

MEMORY BANKS OVERLOAD #9: Gene Polito

MEMORY BANKS OVERLOAD #10: 1. F 2. E 3. J 4. A 5. I 6. B 7. H 8. C 9. D 10. G

MAXIMUM SCORE POTENTIAL: 160

YOUR SCORE: _____

Collision of Planets

1. An irregular orbital path 2. Ilan 3. C 4. obituary 5. Sour apple green 6. B 7. little

MEMORY BANKS OVERLOAD: Universe

MAXIMUM SCORE POTENTIAL: 12

YOUR SCORE: _____

SPACE CREATURE

1. Children first when abandoning ship 2. C 3. methane 4. The sonic washer 5. Will and the alien being 6. Fear and hatred 7. id

MEMORY BANKS OVERLOAD: Rudyard Kipling, although Smith mistakenly believed he was quoting Shakespeare

MAXIMUM SCORE POTENTIAL: 12

YOUR SCORE: _____

DEADLIEST OF THE SPECIES

1. Energizing module 2. "Loneliness" 3. A 4. evaluators 5. The laser-armed women of the spaceship 6. Dr. Smith

MEMORY BANKS OVERLOAD: insensitive, turbo

MAXIMUM SCORE POTENTIAL: 11

YOUR SCORE: _____

A DAY AT THE ZOO

1. Oggo, "the only prehistoric caveboy in captivity" 2. B
3. Cosmos 4. B 5. Forty-five minutes 6. Twenty-five cents

MEMORY BANKS OVERLOAD: His "mommy"

MAXIMUM SCORE POTENTIAL: 11

YOUR SCORE: _____

DIRECTOR'S CUT

1. G 2. L 3. I 4. C 5. F 6. O 7. J 8. D 9. K 10. H 11. A 12.
B 13. N 14. E 15. M

MEMORY BANKS OVERLOAD: Irwin Allen

MAXIMUM SCORE POTENTIAL: 20

YOUR SCORE: _____

TWO WEEKS IN SPACE

1. B 2. C 3. deutronium 4. "Happy Acres" 5. innkeeper
6. A 7. In a lava pit 8. A matter transformer 9. C

MEMORY BANKS OVERLOAD: NON and TAT

MAXIMUM SCORE POTENTIAL: 14

YOUR SCORE: _____

CASTLES IN SPACE

1. Smith fired a rock projectile at the equipment while
teaching young Will to shoot skeet 2. A 3. wind 4. His
reserve computers 5. True 6. bull 7. A folded WANTED
poster of himself

MEMORY BANKS OVERLOAD: Reyka

MAXIMUM SCORE POTENTIAL: 12

YOUR SCORE: _____

THE ANTI-MATTER MAN

1. magnetic 2. B 3. He didn't cast a shadow 4. John 5. The
Robot 6. True 7. The anti-matter John had a hideous scar

that encircled his neck 8. Penny's tape recorder also ran backwards

MEMORY BANKS OVERLOAD: The anti-matter Robot

MAXIMUM SCORE POTENTIAL: 13

YOUR SCORE: _____

TECH SPECS #8

1. D 2. B 3. A 4. C

MAXIMUM SCORE POTENTIAL: 4

YOUR SCORE: _____

TECH SPECS #9

1. I 2. F 3. D 4. H 5. C 6. A 7. E 8. B 9. G

MAXIMUM SCORE POTENTIAL: 9

YOUR SCORE: _____

TARGET EARTH

1. The lower half of the Robot 2. John 3. C 4. awkward 5. A 6. B 7. True 8. Chicago

MEMORY BANKS OVERLOAD: Gilt Proto

MAXIMUM SCORE POTENTIAL: 13

YOUR SCORE: _____

PRINCESS OF SPACE

1. A 2. B 3. Prime Minister 4. Aunt "Gammy" 5. His telescope 6. False (12th class) 7. A new captain's coat 8. computer 9. From Maureen's bureau 10. C

MEMORY BANKS OVERLOAD: Iota, Campa and Sylvia

MAXIMUM SCORE POTENTIAL: 15

YOUR SCORE: _____

THE TIME MERCHANT

1. C 2. False (twenty-seven) 3. A 4. thirty 5. True 6. A 7. 3

MEMORY BANKS OVERLOAD: silver

MAXIMUM SCORE POTENTIAL: 12

YOUR SCORE: _____

OUT OF THIS WORLD FX

1. B 2. daisy, flitters 3. True 4. Two 5. A crane 6. It was always flown on three wires and suspended from a sound boom 7. A two-foot diameter *Jupiter 2* with the mechanical sophistication capable of physically performing the lowering and recovery 8. The shots were accomplished by animation added optically 9. C 10. True 11. four 12. Francine York in "The Colonists" 13. Two 14. A 15. *Gemini* 16. True 17. Robert Kinoshita 18. False (the miniature was 24") 19. C 20. True 21. Affirmative 22. From car dashboards and audio equpment 23. "Wish Upon a Star" 24. "The Magic Mirror" 25. "Flight into the Future" 26. B 27. Eggshell 28. First 29. "Wild Adventure" 30. Dee Hartford 31. "The Golden Man" 32. Creech from "Fugitives in Space" 33. John Chambers 34. Marta Kristen 35. John Chambers 36. "Wild Adventure" 37. Irwin Allen's *The Lost World* 38. A 39. *TV Guide* 40. A regular camera crane 41. True 42. O.J. Simpson 43. Cylindrical cardboard

MEMORY BANKS OVERLOAD #1: *The Day the Earth Stood Still* (Klaatu's ship)

MEMORY BANKS OVERLOAD #2: *City Beneath the Sea*

MEMORY BANKS OVERLOAD #3: Inside a cage

MEMORY BANKS OVERLOAD #4: *Goliath and the Dragon* and Irwin Allen's *Lost World*

MAXIMUM SCORE POTENTIAL: 63

YOUR SCORE: _____

THE PROMISED PLANET

1. A 2. False (three years) 3. B 4. electronic 5. C 6. C 7. Methuselah

MEMORY BANKS OVERLOAD: Penny in Z-8 and Will in Z-7

MAXIMUM SCORE POTENTIAL: 12

YOUR SCORE: _____

FUGITIVES IN SPACE

1. Destruction 2. Control 3. True 4. B 5. B 6. Complete pardons, five silver pieces, and a pair of new boots 7. His mother 8. 282 or 283 (he couldn't remember which was correct)

MEMORY BANKS OVERLOAD: #756498002

MAXIMUM SCORE POTENTIAL: 13

YOUR SCORE: _____

SPACE BEAUTY

1. B 2. Smith 3. Inter-Galaxy Beauty Pageant 4. She sold Farnum's soul 5. True 6. methane 7. A mirror 8. C 9. B

MEMORY BANKS OVERLOAD: Four hundred

MAXIMUM SCORE POTENTIAL: 14

YOUR SCORE: _____

COMMUNICATION CHANNELS: Season Three

1. curiosity 2. "Kidnapped in Space" 3. The Junkman 4. Judy 5. A 6. B 7. "Condemned of Space" 8. Willoughby 9. The Junkman himself 10. B 11. True 12. "The Flaming Planet" 13. "Space Creature" 14. heap 15. C 16. Smith 17. cybernetics 18. "Kidnapped in Space" 19. The Robot 20. Smith 21. A 22. C 23. Chronos 24. springs 25. False ("Space Primevals") 26. "Collision of Planets" 27. The Robot 28. The Robot 29. Dedicated 30. Alien dictator in "Space Beauty"

MEMORY BANKS OVERLOAD: "Space Beauty"

MAXIMUM SCORE POTENTIAL: 35

YOUR SCORE: _____

THE FLAMING PLANET

1. Oranges 2. True 3. Don 4. All of its power was drained 5. fighter 6. Don had a "moral conscience" 7. False (ten) 8. Dr. Smith

MEMORY BANKS OVERLOAD: 10,000 years

MAXIMUM SCORE POTENTIAL: 13

YOUR SCORE: _____

THE GREAT VEGETABLE REBELLION

1. Will's 2. To conserve the fuel supply 3. flora 4. B
5. Don 6. Machetes 7. False (a red banana) 8. Don

MEMORY BANKS OVERLOAD: Willow and silver birch

MAXIMUM SCORE POTENTIAL: 13

YOUR SCORE: _____

JUNKYARD IN SPACE

1. C 2. B 3. rust 4. A 5. He did 6. timing

MEMORY BANKS OVERLOAD: Two

MAXIMUM SCORE POTENTIAL: 11

YOUR SCORE: _____

WARNING! DANGER!

1. "The Challenge" and "A Change of Space" 2. Robert
Kinoshita 3. B 4. A long, thick cable 5. True 6. C 7. A
telegraph key 8. B 9. Via a support harness 10. A 11. True
12. "Condemned of Space" 13. "The Anti-Matter Man"
14. False (wooden support rails) 15. Piano wire 16. True
17. B 18. B

MEMORY BANKS OVERLOAD #1: Greg Jein

MEMORY BANKS OVERLOAD #2: Kevin Burns

MAXIMUM SCORE POTENTIAL: 28

YOUR SCORE: _____

TECH SPECS #10

1. I 2. B 3. E 4. J 5. A 6. D 7. C 8. F 9. H 10. G

MAXIMUM SCORE POTENTIAL: 10

YOUR SCORE: _____

UNITED STATES SPACE CORPS

Scoring Legend

After you have totaled the points from each section to calculate your overall score, determine your United States Space Corps rank as follows:

2264–1915	General
1914–1504	Colonel
1503–1168	Major
1167–839	Captain
838–523	Lieutenant
522–189	Academy Cadet

GENERAL

Congratulations! You've been promoted to General and posted by the Joint Chiefs of Staff to the Pentagon in Washington, D.C. where you will oversee the United States Space Corps of Engineers, the special projects division responsible for the multi-billion dollar construction of Robinson City, the massive metropolis for Earth's two million colonists on the planet Delta in the Alpha Centauri star system.

COLONEL

After reviewing your exceptional career, including the five-year stint you spent as commanding officer of the Corps' Special Operations React Team (developed as a rapid response unit to threats of sabotage to the space program), your U.S. Space Corps Command Orders are as follows: Report immediately to Houston, Texas, where you will supervise the three-year astronaut training program designed for officers chosen to be pilots for future colonization missions.

MAJOR

Spend some quality time with your family during the course of the next seven days. Next Monday at 0600 you are to depart on the shuttle to the Mars Strategic Defense Perimeter, the United States Space Corps defense border designed to protect the inner Solar System. Until recently the boundary was guarded by unmanned pods capable of tracking and destroying enemy space vehicles, but after a Saticon probe easily passed through the perimeter on its way to Earth two days ago, U.S.S.C. Command made the determination to assign you as the Ops Chief in charge of developing a defense initiative against a possible Saticon invasion.

CAPTAIN

"Captain" has a nice ring to it, doesn't it? Now comes the responsibility with the rank. Report to Cape Canaveral by 0700 Monday morning where the *Jupiter 5* is undergoing its final shakedown prior to launch. Henceforth and until further notice, you are the commanding officer of the newest and largest galactic vehicle in the fleet. Watch your back, though. Intelligence reports indicate that traitorous, subversive forces within the ranks of the U.S.S.C. are plotting the destruction of the ship and its crew.

LIEUTENANT

You've still got two years left to complete at the U.S.S.C. Pilot Training Center in Houston and your grades indicate you're on the verge of being dropped from the program in favor of a more career-minded officer. Although you have displayed incredible flying abilities both in simulators and advanced jet trainers at the center, your lack of concentration and poor academic achievement could get you re-posted to Jupiter Outpost SI-7 in the outer part of the solar system.

ACADEMY CADET

You performed above expectations in the Space Scouts, completed ROTC training in high school at the top of your class, but since arriving at the Academy you've acted like an atomic missile with a malfunctioning guidance system. If you want to graduate and have a promising career in the United States Space Corps, you'd better get your head out of the stars and concentrate on the rigorous curriculum.

LOST IN CYBERSPACE

Where do you go online to find the latest news on your favorite television series? Other fans? Collectibles? Fanzines? Episode Guides? Newsletters? Photo archives? Sound bytes? We've compiled a partial list of some of the most frequented outposts in cyberspace, but once you suit up in your silver flightsuit and take the computer keyboard controls, you'll discover more links to your favorite sites as new ones will be coming online every day with the success of the Lost in Space *movie.*

LOST IN SPACE MAILING LIST

The *Lost in Space* Mailing List is an e-mail forum for discussing and exchanging information about our favorite sci-fi show and any related topic. The list has been in operation since 1996 and currently has over 1,000 subscribers from thirty different countries. If it happens in the *Lost in Space* universe more than likely you will hear about it here first.

Subscription to this list is open to all and is free of charge. It's moderated, which means an administrator checks through all the messages and filters off-the-topic messages or e-mail likely to cause offense. On an average day, a subscriber can expect to receive between 15–25.

Joining the list is simple. Just send e-mail to:
majordomo@buffnet.net

In the body of the message write: subscribe lostinspace

THE MUSEUM OF LOST IN SPACE COLLECTIBLES

The ultimate *Lost in Space* website: **http://lostinspace.buffnet.net/index.html**

LOST IN SPACE FANNISH ALLIANCE

Flint Mitchell's LISFAN, the oldest and largest fan club devoted to the TV series: **http://www.as-inc.com/lisfan/lisfan.html**

LOST IN SPACE: THE ULTIMATE UNAUTHORIZED TRIVIA CHALLENGE FOR THE CLASSIC TV SERIES

Visit the authors' website, complete with an in-depth interview and online ordering information for our other sci-fi books: **www.omegapublishing.com**

FRIENDS OF LOST IN SPACE

From the classic TV series to the movie, check out: **http://members.tripod.com/~zammy00/index.html**

LOST IN SPACE TOYS

Shop online for the hottest in collectibles: **http://www.lostintoys.com/**

LOST IN CYBERSPACE

A website dedicated to *Lost in Space* bloopers, behind-the-scenes photos and publicity stills: **http://home.earthlink.net/~kroderick/lics**

THE IRWIN ALLEN NEWS NETWORK

Convention listings, fan clubs, the latest news: **http:ourworld.compuserve.com/homepages/tvnfilm/allenmai.htm**

THE IRREVERENT GUIDE TO LOST IN SPACE

Before *Star Trek: Annoyager*, before *Star Trek* itself, the intrepid space family Robinson . . . **http:web2.airmail.net/pokeys/lis.htm**

LOST IN SPACE EPISODE GUIDE AND INDEX

http://www.concentric.net%7Ewillfs/
LISepguide.html

THE MAGNETIC LOCK

A website devoted to *Lost in Space*'s favorite mechanical
man:
http://members.aol.com/dmd7371067/robot.htm

LOST IN SPACE FAQ LIST

The answers to your frequently asked questions:
http://web2.airmail.net/pokeys/faqlis.htm

LOST IN SPACE IN BRAZIL

Don't worry—it's in English:
http:www.ultranet.com.br/controle.alpha/
index2.html

RALPH'S EPISODE RANKING LIST

http://www.access.digex.net/~ragjr/lostspac.html

PRIPLANUS

Named after the first season planet, this site is proudly
dedicated to the brave pioneers of space, the
Robinsons:
http://members.aol.com/Priplanus/index.html

LOST IN SPACE

Check out:
http:www.geocites.com/Area 51/Vault/9076/
lostinspace.html

PLANET KITSCH

http://www.tvguide.com/tv/allen/

WELCOME TO ALPHA CONTROL

The home of the *Lost in Space* original props:
www.alphacontrol.com/

NEW LINE CINEMA'S CLASSIC LOST IN SPACE TV SITE

www.lostinspacetv.com

BIBLIOGRAPHY

Abbot, Jon. "Fantasy Flashback: Lost in Space." *TV Zone*, July 1997: 42–44.

Airey, Jean and Kim Howard Johnson. "Lost in Babylon." *Starlog*, May 1995, Issue 214.

Alpha Centaurian Newsbrief, Issue #1.

Alpha Centaurian Newsbrief, Issue #2.

Alpha Centaurian Magazine, Spring 1995, Issue #3.

Alpha Centaurian Magazine, Summer 1995, Issue #4.

Alpha Centaurian Magazine, Fall/Winter 1995, Issue #5.

Alpha Centaurian Magazine, Spring 1996, Issue #6.

Alpha Centaurian Magazine, Summer 1996, Issue #7.

Alpha Centaurian Magazine, Fall/Winter 1996, Issue #8.

Alpha Centaurian Magazine, Spring 1997, Issue #9.

Anchors, William E. and Gary Stork. *The Alpha Control Reference Manual.* Alpha Control Press: 1986.

Anchors, William E. (Editor). *The Irwin Allen Scrapbook, Vol. II.* Alpha Control Press: 1992.

Anchors, William E. and Flint Mitchell (Editors). *The Lost in Space Scrapbook, Vol. I.* Alpha Control Press: 1991.

Anchors, William E. and Flint Mitchell (Editors). *The Lost in Space Scrapbook, Vol. II.* Alpha Control Press: 1991.

Anchors, William E. and Flint Mitchell (Editors). *The Lost in Space Scrapbook, Vol. III.* Alpha Control Press: 1991.

Anchors, William E. and Flint Mitchell (Editors). *The Lost in Space 25th Anniversary Celebration.* Alpha Control Press: 1991.

Clark, Mike and Bill Cotter. "Bob Kinoshita: Designing the Robot." *Starlog*, April 1982, Issue 57.